THEOLOGY IN PRACTICE

DENIS FARKASFALVY, O.CIST.
ROCH A. KERESZTY, O.CIST.

Theology in Practice

A Beginner's Guide to the Spiritual Life

IGNATIUS PRESS   SAN FRANCISCO

Unless otherwise noted, Scripture quotations have been taken from the Revised Standard Version of the Holy Bible, Second Catholic Edition, © 2006. The Revised Standard Version of the Holy Bible: the Old Testament, © 1952, 2006; the Apocrypha, © 1957, 2006; the New Testament, © 1946, 2006; the Catholic Edition of the Old Testament, incorporating the Apocrypha, © 1966, 2006, the Catholic Edition of the New Testament, © 1965, 2006 by the Division of Christian Education of the National Council of the Churches of Christ in the United States of America. All rights reserved.

Quotes from foreign-language sources without any translation information have been translated into English by the authors.

Cover art:
Fire
Original acrylic painting on canvas
© istock/nkbimages

Cover design by Roxanne Mei Lum

© 2023 by Ignatius Press, San Francisco
All rights reserved
ISBN 978-1-62164-625-9 (PB)
ISBN 978-1-64229-271-8 (eBook)
Library of Congress Control Number 2022950425
Printed in the United States of America ∞

Contents

Introduction 9

1. The Triune God 15
2. Turning to God 19
    Discovering Oneself 22
    Conversion in the Theological Tradition 25
    From Conversion to Asceticism 29
3. To Follow Christ 35
    The Threefold Way of Love 35
    Union with Christ 41
    The Mystery of the Cross 44
4. Tradition, Community, Communion 53
    Salvation History 53
    The Role of the Ecclesial Community 60
    Mary and the Saints 68
    In the World but Not of the World 75
    Action and Contemplation 79
5. Discerning the Way: Conscience 85
    Conscience as a Transcendent Command 85
    Conscience as Judgment 89
    How Can a Non-Christian Inform His
        Conscience? 91

CONTENTS

How Does a Christian Inform His
   Conscience? 94

6. Virtues in Christian Life 97

   Faith 99
   Hope 107
   Love (Charity) 113
   The Natural Virtues 122

7. The Sacraments 137

   The Sacrament of Baptism 138
   The Sacrament of Confirmation 146
   The Sacrifice of the Holy Eucharist 153
   The Sacrament of Reconciliation 160
   The Sacrament of the Anointing of the
      Sick 174

8. Prayer and Religious Experience 179

   The Dynamics and the Many Forms of
      Prayer 180
   Liturgical Prayer 183
   Meditative Prayer 186
   Prayer of Praise, Thanksgiving, and Petition 190
   The Development of Prayer Life 194
   Different Forms of Devotion 195
   Religious Experience 197
   Religious Experience outside Christianity 205

9. The Unity and Diversity of Vocations 209

   Marriage 215
   Consecrated Life 221
   Priesthood 241

CONTENTS

10. Spiritual Growth through the Stages of Life 261
    Children 262
    Adolescence 264
    Young Men and Women 266
    Parenthood 267
    Old Age 270

Conclusion 273

Introduction

Theology is not some abstract discipline meant for the academic elite. It is quite simply the study of God, which is the task—and the joy—of every single person. Saint Thomas Aquinas insists that "God alone constitutes man's happiness" and that every man and woman has been created to commune with this God not only through the emotions but also through the intellect.[1] Our minds reach after the divine and, in Christ, receive the fullness of the Creator himself. All who pray are, in a sense, theologians.

Yet theology, as taught in universities, might seem to be a field of study like any other, heavy with jargon and split into confusing subfields—systematic theology, fundamental theology, moral theology, ecclesiology. For an untrained believer, especially one without a graduate degree, this could easily trigger the instinct to run away, back toward a God who will judge us on love, not on SAT scores. And indeed, who could be blamed for such a reaction? Our God is personal, not a distant star in a telescope.

But in truth, fleeing from scholarship would not do justice to reality. We know that chemistry and biology *matter* in farming. We know that physics *matters* in building. In the same way, the technicalities of theology *matter* in the Christian life. The planter learns, or at least respects, the science

---

[1] Thomas Aquinas, *Summa theologiae* I-II, q. 2, a. 8 (hereafter cited as *ST*), translated in *The Summa Theologica of St. Thomas Aquinas*, trans. Fathers of the English Dominican Province, 2nd ed. (London: Burns Oates & Washbourne, 1920); *ST* I-II, q. 3, a. 8.

of the wheat seed because he wants it to sprout, grow, and bear fruit. He may not have an advanced degree or keep up with academic literature on biology, but he does care how things work, even on the microscopic level. So, too, the Christian learns, in his own way, from the divine "science" precisely because he is curious about the God he loves and because he wants God's love to sprout, grow, and bear fruit in him, as well as in the world. Theology is about reality, alive and lived in. A Christian who "mastered" theology without walking with the Lord would be, quite plainly, a failed theologian.

Theology meets the Christian life explicitly in the field of *spiritual theology*, or the theology of the spiritual life. What does this mean? Even up to the twentieth century, the term was practically unknown. Literature that dealt with the method for obtaining Christian perfection and describes the extraordinary spiritual gifts accompanying Christian holiness has been labeled instead "ascetical theology" or "mystical theology." There is, however, much more to the spiritual life than ascetical practices and mystical phenomena, as recent theologians have recognized.[2] In a certain respect, all of God's revelation belongs to it, since every word that comes from God is "Spirit and life"[3] and aims at our sanctification.

---

[2] See other important works in this area: Adolphe Tanquerey, *The Spiritual Life: A Treatise on Ascetical and Mystical Theology*, 2nd ed. (Tournai, Belgium: Desclée, 1930); Joseph de Guibert, *The Theology of the Spiritual Life* (New York: Sheed and Ward, 1953); Jordan Aumann, *Christian Spirituality in the Catholic Tradition* (San Francisco: Ignatius Press, 1985). For a modern popular approach, see Andrew M. Greeley, *Life for a Wanderer: A New Look at Christian Spirituality* (New York: Doubleday, 1969). For an excellent summary of biblical and patristic spirituality, see Louis Bouyer, *Introduction to Spirituality* (New York: Desclée, 1961).

[3] Jn 6:63.

How, then, can we identify a single branch of "spiritual" theology? The main difficulty lies in distinguishing spiritual theology from other theological disciplines. The theology of the Trinity, of Scripture, of grace, of redemption, and theological anthropology all deal with questions that are inseparable from the theology of the spiritual life. In fact, the study of every dogmatic truth gathers material that is explored by spiritual theology, which examines the relationship between God and man: the patterns, goals, horizons, and human limitations that color the spiritual life, as well as the means of grace that enable its beginnings and growth. Thus, the theology of the spiritual life is not distinct from other branches of theology in its object—sacraments or history, for example—but in its *subject*, the human believer, in whom all these mysteries of faith become spirit and life. In other words, it studies all the truths of revelation from the perspective of the person whose life they shape and form. It investigates every theological theme with two questions in mind: How does this truth affect the believing person, and how is it related to his ever-growing experience of seeking and possessing God?

This book gives untrained readers an introduction to the world of spiritual theology—the space where theological study meets the interior life. First, in chapter 1, we outline the origin and goal of all Christian spirituality: the Triune God, in whose life we are called to share. In chapter 2, we examine the process of conversion. All have sinned, and repentance is necessary for everyone; the more we turn toward God, the more we must turn away from sin and the more we realize our authentic selves. In chapter 3, we outline the encounter with Jesus and what it means to follow him. At the center of this discussion stands the mystery of the Cross, the means of God's forgiveness and our glorification, as well as a "school of love" for sinful man. In chapter 4, we address the indispensable place of tradition and community in God's kingdom and in the spiritual life. Then, in a more systematic way, we use chapter 5 to outline the role of conscience and chapter 6 to take on Christian virtue: not only the theological virtues of faith, hope, and charity but also humility and the cardinal virtues informed by charity. In chapter 7, we show how the sacraments—except holy orders and matrimony, dealt with later—inform our lives, both within and without. Chapter 8 considers prayer, and chapter 9 considers vocation (sacramental marriage, consecrated life, and priesthood), all as the fruits of the Holy Spirit. In our final chapter, we outline the ways and forms of holiness at every stage of natural human development.

In a book of this size, we cannot aim at completeness. We do not pretend to provide a summary of the rich two-thousand-year history of Christian spirituality. But we cannot ignore history either. Periodically throughout the text, we point out the determining influence of biblical teaching and the Church Fathers on particular theological issues. The reader will find a few explicit quotes from the great Cistercian founder Saint Bernard of Clairvaux scattered throughout, but his four treatises—*De conversione ad clericos*[4] [On conversion, to clerics], *De gradibus humilitatis*[5] [On the steps of humility], *De diligendo Deo*[6] [On the love of God], and *De consideratione* [On meditation]—were our chief sources. These works, with their clear structure and deep biblical and

---

[4] Bernard of Clairvaux, *Sancti Bernardi Opera*, ed. J. Leclercq and H.M. Rochais (Rome: Editiones Cistercienses, 1966), 4:59–116. All quotes from foreign-language sources without any translation information have been translated into English by the authors.
[5] Bernard of Clairvaux, *Sancti Bernardi Opera*, 3:1–60.
[6] Bernard of Clairvaux, *Sancti Bernardi Opera*, 3:109–54.

patristic roots, allowed us to integrate the treatment of the most diverse contemporary issues with traditional teaching. At the same time, we do not present Bernard's theology in any systematic way. Christian and especially Catholic spirituality has always been characterized by a certain pluralism, as evidenced by the colorful multiplicity of its religious orders. Although theological difference has often, throughout history, provoked heated discussions about the borderlines of orthodoxy, the abundant variety of spiritual schools has generally been welcomed as a sign of the Holy Spirit's manifold activity in the Church.

This book does not treat spiritual theology as the way of a chosen few. Yes, the vigor of the spiritual life prompts some in the Church to answer an extraordinary call to pursue the life of a religious or priest, but holiness more often does not entail this. Today's Church is keenly aware that Christian sanctity—in other words, Christian perfection—may be realized in a variety of destinies and in the most diverse paths of life. Never before has the Church believed as strongly as she does today that spirituality must, like leaven, penetrate and transform the ordinary, "average" walks of life. It ought not be limited to those who withdraw from the world.

We attempt to grasp and present the specifically Christian traits of the spiritual life. This task is more important today than ever before, since our ability to evaluate religion from a historical perspective inclines the world to a certain historical relativism. It is true that spiritualities undergo constant changes in history, even within the same culture and society; nevertheless, every genuine Christian spirituality, nourished by the Gospel and remaining faithful to it, displays some common and permanent characteristics. In *Theology in Practice*, we concern ourselves first of all with the vibrancy that springs from the very essence of Christian faith and that—in some way and to some extent—must transform every believing Christian. This vibrancy is rooted in faith and becomes, to varying degrees, a conscious, lived experience in every believer. Unless we hinder its growth or stifle it altogether, it becomes a force that shapes our lives, spurs us to seek God unceasingly, and draws us toward an ever-deepening knowledge and experience of God. This book, colored by the authors' long tenure as Cistercian priests and spiritual directors, sketches out the patterns, laws, characters, and drama of the Christian way, as revealed by the Bible and the Church's immense treasury of experience.

I

The Triune God

What is the goal of the spiritual life? The most obvious answer would be "holiness." But in what does holiness consist? As a matter of fact, Christians can easily define it: holiness is a perfect share in the life of the Triune God—Father, Son, and Holy Spirit. If we are open to him, the Holy Spirit works within us, conforming and uniting us more intimately with Christ, who is one with the Father. Thus, by the Spirit we grow as members of Christ's Mystical Body. He dwells in us, acts through us, suffers within us; his very love reaches others through us. In the words of Saint Paul, we become "one spirit with him" in love.[1] Love, however, not only unites and perfects but also differentiates—that is, the more we are one with Christ in the Spirit, the more we are fulfilled and perfected as *spouses* of Christ, each of us unique and unrepeatable.[2] The Spirit is the source of the wide variety of charisms in the Church, as well as of their harmonious cooperation.[3]

In order to understand better the mystery of our own participation in the Holy Trinity, we need to recall what theology has discovered about the Trinity as it has been from all

---

[1] 1 Cor 6:17.
[2] For further literature, see *The Trinity in Our Spiritual Life: An Anthology of the Writings of Dom Columba Marmion*, ed. Raymond Thibaut (Westminster, Md.: Newman Press, 1953); Dietrich von Hildebrand, *Transformation in Christ: On the Christian Attitude* (San Francisco: Ignatius Press, 2011).
[3] See Rom 12:6; 1 Cor 7:7, 12–14.

eternity—what theologians call the *immanent* Trinity.[4] Our glimpse into the mystery of the life of the eternal Trinity helps us contemplate the unfathomable greatness of our participation in this life. The Father loves the Son, whom he has begotten from all eternity.[5] When praying to God, Jesus calls him "father," or, in Aramaic, *abba*, meaning "dear father," a word that is typically used only in a Jewish family and not in prayer to God. The word on Jesus' lips is no mere metaphor. The God of Jesus is immeasurably greater than any father on earth can be;[6] compared to this fatherhood, every human fatherhood fades away.[7] Paul agrees: the most real and most perfect father is our Father in heaven, "from whom every family in heaven and on earth is named."[8] Therefore, we should approach this mystery through the biblical theme of the Father-Son relationship, understanding it through the threefold way of affirmation, negation, and supereminence: God is a father (affirmation)—not in the sense of an earthly father (negation), but rather in a supereminent sense that, in its perfection, transcends our understanding.[9]

[4] As opposed to the *economic* Trinity—the Trinity as understood through God's self-revelation in human history. See Luis F. Ladaria, *The Living and True God: The Mystery of the Trinity* (Miami: Convivium, 2009).

[5] The Church has always viewed this begetting, or giving birth, as a spiritual activity, but the prevailing psychological interpretation for this begetting or birthing (the Son compared to the "product" of the Father's perfect self-knowledge) cannot be used as a proper analogy for the Divine Father-Son relationship. See Thomas Aquinas, *ST* I, q. 27, a. 1–5.

[6] See Mt 7:11; Lk 11:13; 15:11–32.

[7] See Mt 23:9.

[8] Eph 3:15.

[9] Some Fathers of the Church, including St. Bernard, even spoke of the Son as being born from the womb of the Father. See Bernard of Clairvaux, *Sermones super Cantica canticorum*, sermo 75, in *Sancti Bernardi Opera*, ed. J. Leclercq and H. M. Rochais (Rome: Editiones Cistercienses, 1966), 2:250; *Sermo in Nativitate Virginis Mariae*, in *Sancti Bernardi Opera*, 5:275. This traditional way of speaking about the Father's act of generation as equivalent to

We can gain some further understanding by using the analogy of human love. The logic of love calls for a mutual gift of the self, but on the human level, the gift always remains partial and limited. In the Trinity, the Father gives himself—the fullness of the infinite divine being—to the Son, and the Son returns his own self, identical with the fullness of the same divine being, to the Father in thanksgiving. Since perfect love between two persons cannot be a selfish exclusivity but instead naturally blossoms into a sharing, so, too, does the Father-Son relationship include a third, a *condilecta* ("loved together"), with whom the Father and Son fully share themselves in mutual love: the Holy Spirit.[10]

Naturally, our minds are unable to grasp such an intense communion of love in which each of the three persons possesses one and the same infinite divinity. Nevertheless, this analogy sheds some light on the mystery: if the love between Father and Son is so overflowing that it calls for a *persona condilecta*—the divine person of the Spirit with whom the Father and Son fully share the delight of their love—then it seems appropriate that in this *condilecta*, their love overflows so that their relationship is freely extended to include the creatures created in the image of the Triune God. In the words of Saint Augustine, God is *donabile* ("giveable") only in the Holy Spirit.[11] In God's original plan, the Spirit of God brings life to creation and is breathed into man; he lifts man up and makes him share in the divine life of the

---

giving birth makes clear that heavenly fatherhood transcends the notion of gender. Nonetheless, revelation names the First Person of the Trinity "Father." Because he is the absolute unoriginated origin of the Trinity, this Father also includes the perfection of "mother."

[10] See Richard of Saint Victor, *On the Trinity*, trans. Ruben Angelici (Eugene, Ore.: Cascade Books, 2011).

[11] Augustine, *De Trinitate*, bk. 15, chap. 32.

Son. This process of participation in divine life has been called "divinization" by many of the Fathers.

In our culture, the divinization of man is typically conceived of either as a pantheistic union with the divine All, as taught in Hinduist-Buddhist philosophy, or, sarcastically, as the worship of an absolutist dictator such as Chairman Mao or Joseph Stalin. In the Christian context, however, divinization is the result of God's gratuitous gift of the Holy Spirit, by whom we are made children of the Father and members of the Son's ecclesial Body. Because we are created in God's image, men become their authentic selves, fully and truly human, by this grace of divine filiation. Being lifted into Trinitarian communion, however, always remains an undeserved gift that can be lost by mortal sin in this life, and it calls for unceasing thanksgiving.

The striving for divinization is fundamental to every man and woman. It manifests itself at every point of human history. No thinking man can avoid the choice between striving for a relationship with the true Absolute or creating his own idol, a false absolute such as pleasure, power, or wealth. Mankind, at its beginning, chose the latter, the false way of *self*-divinization, which led to physical and spiritual death. Christ came into the world to heal this wound of original sin and to guide man back to the Father. Yet the process is ongoing, requiring our cooperation. Man must seek to return to God and, in doing so, share in the life and dignity of the Son of God.

2

Turning to God

According to the testimony of the gospels, the first preaching of Jesus was a call to conversion: "Repent, for the kingdom of heaven is at hand."[1] The original Greek word for "repentance," *metanoia*, refers to a radical transformation of the mind and heart, a break with our former mentality and way of life so that we may subject ourselves freely to God as the Lord and guide of our lives. The gospels and Saint Paul's letters alike call us to change our actions: "Let the thief no longer steal, but rather let him labor, doing honest work. . . . Let no evil talk come out of your mouths."[2]

But *metanoia* goes beyond the external and aims at the renewal of our fundamental attitudes: "Be renewed in the spirit of your minds, and put on the new man, created after the likeness of God in true righteousness and holiness."[3] The new man, then, is the one who regains his likeness to God. We find here a clear reference to the first chapter of Genesis, which says that God created man in his own image and likeness.[4] Renewal means return to the original model or archetype according to which God created man at the beginning. Thus, God does not expect us to search for a superhuman or inhuman perfection that would estrange

---

[1] Mt 4:17.
[2] Eph 4:28–29.
[3] Eph 4:23–24.
[4] See Gen 1:27.

us from our own nature. Rather, by unfolding our nature's original potential, we realize the ideal that will fulfill and crown our humanity.[5]

In Christ's teaching we find quite a few allusions to the fact that the original goal for which the first man and woman were created in Eden—communion with God—remains God's purpose, achieved through Christ's redemption. This is implied in Jesus' declaration to the Pharisees on the indissolubility of marriage. When they ask him why Moses permitted divorce, Jesus replies, "For your hardness of heart Moses allowed you to divorce your wives, but from the beginning it was not so."[6] Jesus implies that with the coming of the kingdom in his person, the Mosaic concession to human sinfulness is no longer valid: we are enabled to return to the original law of Creation in paradise. In the same chapter of Matthew's Gospel, we read about the great *paliggenesia*: a new genesis, the restoration of the original order of creation.[7] Luke's Gospel makes clear that the death of Jesus reopens the gate of paradise to all repentant sinners. Christ reassures the criminal who expresses faith in Jesus' kingdom: "Truly, I say to you, today you will be with me in Paradise."[8] Both Gregory the Great and Cyril of Alexandria teach that Jesus' parable of the lost sheep illustrates God's special love for mankind; it was to complete the angelic com-

---

[5] There is no space here to elaborate on the theological distinction between nature and the supernatural. God could have created man without a call to share in his own divine nature. Thus, God's call to become his children does raise us above our pure human potential. But in the actual order of salvation, out of sheer grace, human nature was never just "pure human nature" but always called—and transformed by this call—so that it can find fulfillment only in sharing God's own life.

[6] Mt 19:8.
[7] See Mt 19:28.
[8] Lk 23:43.

munity (represented by the ninety-nine sheep) that God created and redeemed him (the hundredth).[9] Thus, our call to a heavenly communion with God is not an afterthought, tacked onto the original plan of Creation, but rather its original and ultimate purpose.

The oldest Christian commentary on the story of the tax coin offers a similar symbolic meaning. When the Pharisees ask whether they should pay the imperial tax, Jesus notes that Caesar's face is imprinted on the coin and, thus, that the tax rightly belongs to the emperor: "Render to Caesar the things that are Caesar's, and to God the things that are God's."[10] Yet the human soul, symbolized by a coin, bears *God's* image. Although sin has smeared this soul with mud —or covered it with a false image—it has not destroyed the original imprint. To render "to God the things that are God's," then, means to return this "coin" to the one whose stamp it bears after it has been purified.

The figure of the prodigal son is interpreted by the Church Fathers in a similar vein. "I will arise and go to my father"[11] refers to the sinner's return to his own home, to a world that corresponds to his own nature. These topics form a constant current in Christian tradition: the theme of *conversio* as *reversio ad Deum*—the turning to God as a returning to him —is an integral part of patristic and medieval spirituality. The prologue of *The Rule of Saint Benedict*, which has influenced religious life more than any other writing through fifteen centuries, sums up its program in these words: "Listen carefully, my son, to the master's instructions . . . so that, through the labor of obedience, you may return to him from

---

[9] See Lk 15:4–7. See also Thomas Aquinas, *Catena aurea in Lucam*, chap. 15.
[10] Mk 12:17.
[11] Lk 15:18.

whom you had drifted away through the sloth of disobedience."[12] Conversion leads one back not only to the beginnings of Creation and the original ideal of man but also to one's best and most authentic self.

Discovering Oneself

The first step in conversion is the knowledge of one's actual state—good, beautiful, disfigured by sin. In the light of Divine Truth, man becomes aware of himself, of both his dignity and his wretchedness. Paradoxically, though, he cannot realize his misery unless he can compare it to the splendor of his original condition. Only then will he see how far he has fallen. Once he does see it—once he discovers his own greed, his hunger for power, and his sensual shallowness; once he acknowledges with dismay that, estranged from the first harmony between spirit and body, he has been enslaved by a changing, corruptible material world—then he is already on the way home to his deepest nature, to spiritual freedom.

Yet man cannot do this on his own. Nothing would be more opposed to Christian spirituality than to think of conversion merely as an effort to find and transform oneself. Conversion depends not only on the light of the intellect and the right use of the will but also on God's forgiveness and grace. Without this grace, a free gift from above, man would have no awareness of his own poverty. When the converting sinner breaks with his past, it is not for the sake of achieving self-discipline or for the sake of a set of values. He changes course because he has encountered a God who

---

[12] *The Rule of Saint Benedict: Latin and English*, trans. Luke Dysinger (Trabuco Canyon, Calif.: Source Books, 1996), 1–2.

loves him like a son, a God who has overwhelmed him with an abundance of gifts, not only in creating him but also in accepting humiliation and death for his sake. In encountering this generous God, the sinner also sees how far removed he is from him, how unlike him he has become, in both his inward attitude and his external lifestyle. He asks himself how he can regain his likeness to his Creator—and thus regain his true self.

In the process of conversion, man first comes to the shattering realization of original sin in its concrete reality, both within oneself and in others. The convert becomes aware of sin as a milieu, as a given of every human existence. He knows now that sin was an influential factor throughout his normal human growth, as he was establishing himself in the world and developing relationships. It is a world where selfishness seems almost natural: the unlimited craving for possessions, sensual lust, and the instinctive search to dominate others.[13] Practically everything—both outside himself and within himself—subjugates his psychic and physical energies to the service of selfishness, and his relationship to people, things, and self becomes fundamentally corrupted. He senses dissonance and disorder in the fabric of the universe. Without grace, this sensation could throw him into despair, with the conclusion that God is either weak, evil, or nonexistent.

For the convert, the Lord beams light into such an apparently hopeless situation. It may come as a sudden, dramatic intervention or as the result of a long process of maturation. A chance word, a scriptural passage, a sermon, the death of a loved one—all these might be the occasion to shake up a person with such force that a ray of sun finally enters. In

---

[13] See 1 Jn 2:16.

these moments, God appears both as judge and as merciful goodness. Upon hearing a Scripture passage during Mass, Anthony of Egypt rises, leaves the church, sells all he has, and goes out into the desert to begin a new life in search of God. Saint Augustine, in a mood of despair, hears the singsong voice of a child repeating "Tolle, lege" ("Pick up and read")[14] and picks up the Letter of Saint Paul to the Romans, his gaze randomly falling upon a passage that gives him the peace and strength to begin a new life. Paul Claudel, in search of an aesthetic experience, visits the Cathedral of Notre Dame in Paris during Vespers and suddenly discovers in his heart the truth of the Christian faith when the choir begins to sing the Magnificat.

In most cases, conversion takes time. Even in the case of a sudden turn, the converted person realizes in retrospect that a long process of maturation, struggle, and search led him to where he is. Augustine strained after truth for a decade before he heard the voice of the child and read Saint Paul. In all the diverse experiences of actual conversions, however, we find one common trait—radical transformation. The convert reevaluates his whole outlook on life. He sees his role and destiny and his relationship to God, individuals, and society in a new light, and he gives a new direction to his future (at least to the future of his inner life). We will sketch out the contours of this transformation in a later section.

The beginnings of the spiritual life always follow to some extent the pattern we have outlined here. Even someone who grows up in the Christian faith without ever being shaken by serious doubts will come to a point when he is

---

[14] Augustine, *Confessions*, vol. 1, trans. James J. O'Donnell (Oxford: Clarendon, 1991), bk. 8, chap. 12, p. 93.

challenged to experience and appropriate freely what he had accepted as a child—and to commit his life to it.[15] As with the converting sinner, this experience will include the realization of his own fallen state and his infection by original and personal sin, and, in the light of these insights, he, too, will have to rethink and reshape his relationship to God, people, and the world. The beginning, then, is always some kind of personal response to the Good News of Christ: "Repent, for the kingdom of heaven is at hand."[16]

Conversion in the Theological Tradition

This dynamic of returning to oneself in the return to God is implicit already in the Bible, but as a basic principle of spiritual theology, it was consciously formulated beginning in the second century as a Christian response to the heresy of Gnosticism. Influenced by Greek philosophy, the Gnostics wanted to use Christianity as a means to discover and perfect man's inmost being, returning him to the governance of the spirit. There was much of value in this quest. They took seriously the duality in man, which the Bible (and Saint Paul in particular) expresses with the opposing terms of "spirit" and "flesh," *sarx* and *pneuma*—a binary also important for Plato. However, without the light of the incarnate Jesus, who perfectly unites spirit and body, this devolved into *dualism*, the notion that man's metaphysical end is, at least in part, to escape the material world altogether. Gnostics

---
[15] Of course, a baptized child, raised in a family of true personal faith, will experience the reality of this faith by sharing in the faith of his parents. But he is not yet capable of a personal, free appropriation (or rejection) of that faith.
[16] Mt 4:17.

restricted redemption and divine life only to the sphere of the spirit, distorting Christ's Incarnation and disparaging the resurrection of the body. Their doctrine thus posed a grave danger to the authentic teaching of Christ, and the Church confronted Gnosticism on many fronts. In the process, she also learned about her own hidden resources for addressing the same questions about man, bringing about the first great masterpieces of theological literature.

The anti-Gnostic theologians came to understand that the Greek quest for inner enlightenment and happiness actually finds fulfillment within Christianity, rightly interpreted. They were the first to discover that in the process of conversion, man's finding of God is inseparable from man's finding of his true self. Origen and Saint Clement, who both hailed from Alexandria, Egypt, were the most successful in integrating Hellenistic man's quest for personal perfection with the ideal of evangelical perfection, always maintaining —at least in principle—the priority of the Gospel.

Origen and Clement were influenced by two other pioneering Christian authors, Saint Irenaeus of Lyon and Saint Justin Martyr, who attempted to transform the spiritual ideals of Hellenistic philosophers and harmonize them with a Christian worldview. Justin was a philosopher himself, and he found in Christianity what he had been seeking in many different teachings. His theology is characterized by a concern for catholicity, or universality. For one, he treats the problem of salvation from the perspective of all mankind, but he also points out that in Christianity the *whole* man is led to union with God—body, soul, and spirit. According to Justin, Christ as the eternal Logos, the eternal Word, is present not only in the Old Testament prophecies but in all the partial truths the pagan philosophers had uncovered before the Logos' coming in the flesh—a development of

Saint Paul's view of salvation history in the Letter to the Romans.

Continuing the work of Justin, Irenaeus consistently applies this theology of salvation history to all the questions that contemporary heresies, especially Gnosticism, brought to the surface. Irenaeus' own catholicity generates this bold statement: "For the glory of man is God, and the receptacle of God's work and wisdom and power is man."[17] This sentence shows that the response to Gnosticism opened a place in orthodox Christian thought for a theology of man, or a theological anthropology, thereby laying down the foundations for spiritual theology and, with it, a theology of conversion.

In the fourth and fifth centuries, the height of the patristic period, theologians further explored and articulated the dynamics of conversion. Augustine's *Confessions* and the biblical commentaries of the Cappadocian Fathers (Basil, Gregory Nazianzen, and Gregory of Nyssa), among others, irreversibly set the direction of Christian thought on the origins of the spiritual life. For Augustine, *conversio* is first of all a *conversio ad cor*, a "turning to the heart," the astonishing recovery of man's own spiritual identity. The biblical theme of man as God's image and likeness was combined with Plato's formulation that human dignity derives from man's spiritual nature, the *pneuma*. When man returns to the divine likeness, he reasserts his spiritual identity and lets his spirit—charged by God's—take control over his life and actions.

Contemporary exegetes like to emphasize that the Old Testament view of man is very different from a metaphysics

[17] Irenaeus, *Adversus Haereses*, bk. 3, chap. 20, no. 2, translated in *The Scandal of the Incarnation: Irenaeus against the Heresies*, ed. Hans Urs von Balthasar, trans. John Saward (San Francisco: Ignatius Press, 1990), no. 129.

that considers the soul and body as two distinguishable principles of man. In fact, the Hebrew words *basar* (flesh) and *ruah* (spirit) always refer to the whole man under two different aspects. Man is *basar* insofar as he is mortal, frail, and inclined to sin,[18] but he is *ruah* insofar as he is alive and is a personal self. These exegetes also remind us that the Greek *sarx* and *pneuma*, in the New Testament, follow the Hebrew pattern of meaning and should not be misinterpreted in a merely Platonistic sense. Although these cautions are correct, linguistic studies do not render justice to the issue.[19] Human experience and activity is indeed polarized in two directions: on the one hand, knowledge (transcending the level of the senses), freedom (free decisions determining one's life and destiny), and a search for universally valid moral values; on the other, the senses (including the arts) and the needs and functions of bodily existence. If it is true that the sensual instincts often run counter to man's spiritual order, this opposition stems from original sin, which has affected the unity and integrity of man. Declaring himself sovereign master over God's world independently from God, man subverted the order of his own nature. His mortal body began to dominate the spirit that the Lord had breathed into him; pleasure, possessions, and power—with all their attendant anxieties and fears—took the place of free reason. Adam and Eve hid themselves in the bushes because, illogically, they thought the all-seeing God would not find them there.

Liberation and redemption mean, then, to receive a life beyond the dominion of the flesh, but not by escaping ma-

---

[18] See Gen 6:3; Sir 28:5.

[19] Nor is it decisive that some of the books of the Old Testament were already influenced by Hellenistic philosophy (for instance, the book of Wisdom) or that the Palestine of Jesus' age was under strong Hellenistic influence.

terial reality.[20] The new man who walks in the spirit—because God's Spirit now dwells and acts in him, with his free cooperation—gradually restores the original harmony between his body and soul. Scripture and patristic tradition acknowledge the twofold nature in man, but unlike Plato, they do not call into question the unity of man's being, nor do they restrict divine grace to the realm of the spirit. Sin is active in both spheres of human existence; in fact, in its roots, it is a spiritual reality: the rebellion of Satan, a created spirit, against his Creator. Redemption actually aims at the good of the whole person: already in this life it sanctifies the visible, sensible, bodily existence of man and assures the resurrection of his body. Accordingly, in conversion, man encounters not only God's commandments and the evidence of his own sinfulness but, above all, a first glance at his own true, integrated self.

From Conversion to Asceticism

He who has been touched by grace feels as if he has been roused from a slumber. Saint Paul articulates this experience most eloquently: "You know what hour it is, how it is full time now for you to wake from sleep. For salvation is nearer to us now than when we first believed; the night is far gone, the day is at hand. Let us then cast off the works of darkness and put on the armor of light."[21] Conversion is usually followed by a period of grave concern to reverse the direction of one's life. As a rule, this concern gives rise to enthusiastic, even feverish, efforts to change our actions and uproot long-cherished habits and attitudes. At this stage, however,

[20] See Rom 6:6; 8:13.
[21] Rom 13:11–12.

many traps await the inexperienced beginner. He may convince himself that he can change by one great decision of the will. But then, often enough, the mood of enthusiasm yields to a mood of discouragement or even despair. The new convert senses that his feverish activity has achieved nothing; the more he tries, the more he falls back into his old ways. He may come close to giving up the struggle.

If we reach this state, however, our approach is fundamentally mistaken. We deceive ourselves in believing that the transformation of our lives depends on one fundamental act of the will. This belief is false on two accounts. First, just as the beginning of conversion is the work of God's grace, so is its continuation and completion. Second, since man is complex and multilayered, his transformation is also a complex and multilayered process. Turning our whole being to God calls for the renewal of our intellect, emotions, habits, inclinations, desires, and imagination. Moreover, our relationship to our past and our manifold relationships with others all need to be changed. Thus, conversion is only the beginning of a process. Further steps require time and can be taken only at the pace God has determined—and only with his direction and support.

Here enters *asceticism*. Although the word today often has a negative ring, evoking images of whips and hair shirts, asceticism is nothing but man's conscious and consistent cooperation in the Holy Spirit's process of renewal. It has five broad categories: (1) the transformation of the intellect—studying Christian teaching, listening to God's Word, and meditating on the mysteries of the faith; (2) the gradual conformation of the imagination and emotions to the truth assimilated by the intellect; (3) the conformation of one's will to God's will by obeying and accepting God's commands and his plan for our lives, in the light of faith; (4) gaining control over one's passions and instincts and subjecting them to one's will, which in turn subjects itself to God's will; and (5) organizing one's activities and lifestyle in such a way that they serve these new goals. Literature on the spiritual life deals mainly with these five tasks, and over the past two thousand years, the Christian tradition has accumulated resources of immense wealth and depth on asceticism. Today's scholars, with easy online access to libraries across the world, are perhaps the first in centuries to have access to all the vast riches of this storehouse.

From its earliest years, Christian asceticism has worked, in part, against the existential estrangement between spirit and body caused by sin. Belief in the Incarnation and in the sacramental order that derives from it, as well as the anticipation of a universal bodily resurrection in Christ, exclude the view that considers the body and its natural functions as the source or seat of evil.[22] Still, the history of the Church has certainly known many forms of exaggerated bodily mortification and many statements about the lowliness of the body. In some cases, these extremes resulted from erroneous anthropological considerations; at other times, from a lack of medical knowledge on the conditions of physical health. However, discounting extremist positions, there is much room for a pluralism in the realm of ascetic practices within Christianity: styles and forms vary not only from age to age but also according to the needs of individual characters and vocations. All of them, in one way or another, seek to lead the flesh to its supernatural destiny: "The body is . . . for the Lord, and the Lord for the body."[23]

Just as ascetical practices in Christianity are rich and

[22] Cipriano Vagaggini, *The Flesh: Instrument of Salvation* (Staten Island, N.Y.: Alba House, 1969).
[23] 1 Cor 6:13.

varied, so are the strains of spiritual theology that support them. Theologians in every age are called to draw from and further develop the treasures of the spiritual patrimony, as Augustine did with Origen, and Origen with Irenaeus, and Irenaeus with Paul. On the one hand, a theologian must remain in close touch with the primary sources of faith; on the other, he must discover ever anew the concrete requirements of holiness for his own society and culture. This dance between conservation and expansion characterizes the two-thousand-year history of Christian literature on spirituality. Clement of Alexandria's *Paidagogos*, written in the Hellenistic environment of Alexandrian society, differs wildly in form and style from *The Imitation of Christ* by Thomas à Kempis, addressed to the contemplative monks of the late Middle Ages. Again, in modern spiritual literature, there are unmistakable differences among the ascetical works of the American Robert Spitzer, S.J., the German Josef Sudbrack, and the Frenchman Louis Bouyer. The first approaches spiritual life from the perspective of medicine and psychology, the second adopts twentieth-century personalist philosophy, and the third "translates" the biblical-patristic tradition for our age.

Christian spirituality is, in this sense, pluralistic, and it appears even more complex if we include the long traditions and the various schools of spirituality of non-Catholic Christians.[24] In addition, most non-Christian religions also possess their own schools of spirituality and asceticism, which, to varying degrees, display some kinship with the Christian tradition. Many contemporary theologians after World War II, including Henri de Lubac, took up a comparative

[24] Louis Bouyer, Jacques Leclercq, and Francois Vandenbroucke, *Histoire de la spiritualité*, vols. 1–3 (Paris: Aubier, 1960–1965). See volume 3 on the different forms of non-Catholic Christian spirituality.

study of Christianity and oriental religions, which enabled them to describe with greater precision what is *unique* about a spiritual life governed by Christ and his Church.[25]

For all its intellectual and historical richness, spiritual theology—whether ancient or contemporary—is always a response to practical questions: What does it mean to follow Jesus? How are we to live after we are touched by the grace of Christ? How can we cooperate with God's Trinitarian work in us? In the chapters that follow, we will trace the profile of a Christian existence, which derives first and foremost from the person of Jesus Christ.

---

[25] Henri de Lubac, *Aspects of Buddhism* (New York: Sheed and Ward, 1954); *Historia de la espiritualidad*, vols. 1–4 (Barcelona: Flors, 1969). The last volume of this series is entirely dedicated to the study of spirituality in non-Christian religions.

3

To Follow Christ

Visiting a Buddhist monastery, a tourist from the West may find the exercises of prayer, recollection, fasting, and self-discipline strikingly similar to those of a contemplative Christian monastery. He may decide that no essential differences exist between the two institutions, aside from cultural milieus, rituals, and abstract articles of belief. Given the surface of silence and simplicity, many people would even say that a Buddhist monk and a Christian monk have more in common than, say, a Trappist monk and a diocesan priest.

Christian asceticism, as we saw in chapter 2, does not hinge on external practices but rather on the spiritual, intellectual, and physical transformation of the whole person in obedience to the living God—specifically to Jesus, who unites man with the divine. This chapter outlines the unique life, attitude, teaching, and person of Jesus Christ, showing how the truths of Christology radically change the way we experience life and death and unveil the meaning of existence itself.

The Threefold Way of Love

Conversion strips man of his lies and makes him face himself in his naked reality: in contradiction to God, to the world, to his fellowmen, and to his own true self—in short, without love. This recognition calls the new convert to start out on the way of love in order to find harmony, both within himself and without. The unity among love of self, love of neighbor, and love of God is a cornerstone of Christian spirituality. These three loves presuppose, increase, and, upon failure, destroy one another. None of the three loves can truly exist without the other two.

Christian tradition has reflected upon and unfolded the meaning of Jesus' injunction "Love your neighbor as yourself."[1] The love of oneself is presupposed in this command, but it is the love of the true self as Irenaeus and Augustine understood it (see chapter 2), not the ideal, imagined self we wish to project. Faced with his own wretchedness, the convert is seriously tempted to doubt his own worth and even reject himself in disgust. If he yields to this temptation, he can hardly love God. How could he love a Creator who, in spite of his own infinite perfection, created such an abominable monster? How could he open up to such a God who, despite his own eternal happiness, offers man only reproach and despair? As a consequence, he who does not accept himself as a beloved creature of God does not accept his neighbor either. He finds the other as miserable as himself, deserving of scorn and rejection. The more deeply he uncovers in himself the weaknesses of fallen human nature, the more he distrusts his fellow men, doubting the authenticity of their kindness, generosity, and charity. Perhaps he can love the innocent—children and the mentally disabled, who have not had the opportunity to do evil—but he can hardly believe that anyone who lives in the world avoids the hateful human destiny of sin. And of course, he is, in a sense, correct.

Is it possible to have genuine love in spite of sin? The key

---

[1] Mt 22:39.

to Christian love is Christ himself, his Incarnation and his redemptive suffering. When God takes on human nature, he does not become sinful, but he does identify with and make his own the reality of sinful man. After the Council of Trent, which was a sixteenth-century response to the Reformation, Catholic theology often neglected Christ's being "made . . . to be sin"[2] because it was preoccupied with stressing Christ's divinity. According to the Letter to the Romans, God sent "his own Son in the likeness of sinful flesh and for sin."[3] Again, according to the Letter to the Hebrews, "We have not a high priest who is unable to sympathize with our weaknesses, but one who in every respect has been tempted as we are, yet without sinning."[4] God has made our fallen human existence his own and thus rendered it capable of living, expressing, and communicating divine life.

As Paul says, "God shows his love for us in that while we were yet sinners Christ died for us."[5] That God "first loved us"[6] means precisely that God has assumed solidarity with us in full awareness of our sins and worthlessness. He became a citizen of a sinful world and accepted the responsibility to act and work in a society that had fallen into despair. First-century Palestine, in particular, was in steep decline and deeply divided. In his love, God not only accepted the drab, insignificant life of a worker in Nazareth. He not only bore the fatigue from, controversies about, and mounting opposition to his public life. He also suffered failure and rejection. In fact, he experienced the very defeat of

[2] 2 Cor 5:21.
[3] Rom 8:3.
[4] Heb 4:15.
[5] Rom 5:8.
[6] 1 Jn 4:19.

goodness—the malicious execution of God incarnate. He took on himself the destiny of an innocent man persecuted and condemned to death. In the full flower of his young life, he underwent all the horror and torture of a painful crucifixion that crushed both body and soul. The chalice he accepted from his Father while sweating blood—the chalice of his destiny—contained all the consequences of our Fall, all the contradictions and afflictions of a human existence burdened with sin. He drank this cup to the dregs. There is no man—no matter how much he might loathe himself—who would be a stranger to this Christ. There is no one who would remain excluded from this all-embracing divine love.

The universality of God's love manifested in Christ enables a man to love himself and to link this self-love with the love of his neighbor. In the mercy by which he draws me to the Father, Christ includes all others as well. According to the logic of the First Letter of Saint John, if Christ "laid down his life for us; . . . we ought to lay down our lives for the brethren. . . . If God so loved us, we also ought to love one another. . . . If any one says, 'I love God,' and hates his brother, he is a liar; for he who does not love his brother whom he has seen cannot love God whom he has not seen."[7] The inseparable unity of the love of neighbor and love of God is a cardinal principle of Christianity. Christ expressed this inseparability in his teaching on God's forgiveness: he who desires to be forgiven but does not forgive his fellow men remains in his sin and will not avoid punishment.[8] The Lord's Prayer makes very clear that the Father forgives us only if we "forgive those who trespass against us." This

---

[7] 1 Jn 3:16; 4:11, 20.
[8] See Mt 18:23–35.

theme returns as a powerful refrain throughout Christ's ministry. In opposition to the Pharisees' image of God, he announces a kingdom to which the Father invites the beggars and bums from the roadside and from which the sons of the house are thrown out into the "outer darkness."[9] The latter find themselves excluded from the embrace of forgiving love because, considering themselves righteous, they despise and reject sinful mankind.

As scholars like C. H. Dodd and Joachim Jeremias point out, the central message of the parable of the prodigal son is the contrasting attitude of the two sons. The younger son, who squanders his inheritance, finds his way back to the father's love more easily than the elder, who has remained outwardly in his father's house and shared everything his father has except his heart. He cannot identify with his father's forgiving love, and so, sulking and indignant, he chooses to remain outside the house, where the returning son is welcomed by an exultant celebration.[10] The passage on the love of enemy in the Sermon on the Mount eliminates any doubt about whether God has really intended to draw all of us into the embrace of his unbounded love.[11] In fact, he wants us to become as perfect as he, the heavenly Father, is, who bestows the blessings of life on everyone without exception. In loving his enemies, God actually goes much further: he "so loved the world that he gave his only-begotten Son."[12] In this way, he draws the whole world—stuck under the dominion of sin—toward forgiveness and reconciliation. Christ identifies himself so much with every man, in fact, that he interprets the acts or omissions of neighborly love as affecting his

[9] Mt 22:13.
[10] See Lk 15:11–32.
[11] See Mt 5:43–48.
[12] Jn 3:16.

own person. In the Last Judgment, according to the Gospel of Matthew, Christ will reveal, as eternal Judge, that every service done in love was really done to him and that every denial of neighborly love was really a rejection of him.[13]

Christian spirituality, in its most diverse forms, has always been steeped in this truth. Beginning with the first martyr, Stephen, Christians have prayed for their persecutors and executioners, just as their crucified Master did.[14] This ideal of the martyr who loves his murderers and prays for them appears frequently in the writings of the first centuries. Even the hermit who turns his back on the world and moves out into the desert is actually searching for a more radical form of love, dedicating his life to a search for God in union with the community of believers. In the course of Christian history, the search for perfection has brought forth new forms of communities, and even the most secluded of these were meant to be schools of love, not of isolation. Ultimately, Christ's teaching on love is what enables Christianity to undertake the task of shaping society and culture, in mankind's never-ending search for new paths and solutions. In the late Middle Ages, the flourishing Franciscans and Dominicans brought Christ to the poor, lowly masses and, at the same time, found his presence in them: "Truly, I say to you, as you did it to one of the least of these my brethren, you did it to me."[15] The religious of the modern age who care for the sick and the weak, teach the young, and serve in missions are driven by this same basic insight, just as are Christian laypeople who are active in the world. When they seek God, God finds them—and thus their own perfection—in the loving service of their fellow men. These

---

[13] See Mt 25:31–46.
[14] See Acts 7:59–60.
[15] Mt 25:40.

three dimensions of love—God, self, and neighbor—can be lived out and increased only simultaneously.

Union with Christ

For the Christian, the love of Christ is not only a moral standard, an example to follow, or an inspiring historical memory, but it is a reality that affects, transforms, and fills him in the present. Although Christian faith is nourished by the example and teaching of Jesus in his earthly life, it was born in its radical novelty on Easter morning. The experience of the risen and glorified Christ by the first disciples opened a new epoch in human history. Through their encounters with the Risen One, the disciples came to understand Jesus as the ultimate revealing Word of God, the answer to all the questions that the Old Testament had opened up but left unanswered. They began to see the history of salvation in its universality, calling all men to communion with God. They became aware of a new and active presence of Jesus in the world, a presence that transcends the limits of time and space.

The spiritual presence and activity of the risen Christ was first given a powerful written expression by Paul, who had not been a disciple of the earthly Jesus. One of the central themes in the Pauline letters is that "Christ is in us" and that we begin a new life "in Christ." The spiritual life of the Christian is nothing less than an identification with Christ, not merely metaphorically or psychologically but in reality. Jesus Christ is not a mere historical figure from the past; raised up and glorified by the Spirit of God, he lives forever. He remains a man; in fact, he is the perfect man, the second Adam. At the same time, however, Christ the

Lord has a spiritual, divine existence. The risen Christ has become a gift for us in his whole being so that he may lift us up to share in his own divinity.[16] Christian spirituality, then, is a participation in God's own life. The Spirit of God dwelling in us unites us to Christ, "the first-born among many brethren,"[17] and so by the Spirit and through Christ we become sons of the Father.[18] The Spirit's role in our relationship with Christ is twofold: by the power of the Holy Spirit, the personal presence of Christ is realized in us; on the other hand, Christ himself distributes to us the gifts of the Holy Spirit. Transformed by the Spirit, we are conformed to Christ and thereby share in the filial relationship of Christ to his Father.

We find this teaching in the Gospel of John, which had an extraordinary impact on the formation of Christian spirituality. Like the other Gospel writers, John deals fundamentally with the figure of the historical Jesus.[19] In fact, studies from the last three decades[20] have shown that the Fourth Gospel, also called the Theological Gospel, preserved a more detailed and more accurate record than the Synoptics. At the same time, though, John views the deeds and teachings of Christ from a post-Resurrection perspective.[21] All that it

---

[16] See 2 Cor 3:17.

[17] Rom 8:29.

[18] The expression "sons of the Father" applies obviously to both men and women, just as becoming the one bride of Christ, the Church, applies equally to both sexes. Here we cannot elaborate on the anthropological implications of this twofold relationship to Christ.

[19] By "historical Jesus," we understand Jesus as he lived and acted in history rather than by the fragments that historical science can verify about him by means of its own method.

[20] In particular, the works of C. H. Dodd, Raymond Brown, Ignace de la Potterie, Rudolf Schnackenburg, and André Feuillet.

[21] This is, of course, also true—to a lesser degree—for the Synoptic Gospels.

conveys about Jesus is for a purpose: that, through faith in him, we may have life in him.[22] According to John, the word of Jesus becomes intelligible only when it penetrates and transforms us as "Spirit and life."[23] To understand Jesus' deeds and words, his signs and teachings, we need the gift of the Spirit, whom we can receive only from Christ's crucified and risen body.[24] The earthly activity of Jesus reaches its true purpose and effect only when—through the presence of the Holy Spirit, the Paraclete—he begins to dwell in those who have been reborn in baptism and united with his Flesh and Blood in the Eucharist. The Lord's long discourses in John unfold this paradox: through Christ, God has really broken into the milieu of human experience, the sphere of the "flesh,"[25] yet he truly communicates himself to us only when, as a fruit of his passion and Resurrection, he "[gives] up his Spirit" and breathes the Holy Spirit upon us.[26] "It is the Spirit that gives life, the flesh is of no avail."[27]

The Gospel of John delineates for the first time the theological structure of the relationship of Christian spirituality to Christ—a structure repeated by Paul. We can sketch this with four key points: (1) belief in the man Jesus, who truly lived in history, truly performed miracles, truly suffered and died for us, and truly rose from the dead; (2) recognition through these facts that Jesus is the Messiah, the Son of God; (3) trust in Jesus' teaching about his own divinity and his unity with the Father; and (4) union with Christ in the Spirit, mediated by faith and sacramental signs (primarily

---

[22] See Jn 20:31.
[23] Jn 6:63.
[24] See Jn 7:38–39; 19:30; 20:22.
[25] Jn 1:14.
[26] Jn 19:31; see 20:22.
[27] Jn 6:63.

baptism and Eucharist), and union with the Father through Christ. The Pauline and Johannine understanding of union with Christ is the foundation of any kind of Christian spirituality. The Pauline corpus and the Fourth Gospel became the common treasure of Christianity toward the end of the second century. We find no significant Christian theologian or school of spirituality that has not drawn extensively upon these sources. It is no exaggeration to assert that the chief theologians of Christian spirituality have always remained Saint John and Saint Paul; consequently, Christian spiritual life has always meant primarily a life with Christ and in Christ.

The Mystery of the Cross

Christ calls those united with him to follow him, and following Christ includes carrying his Cross. No one can enter the glory of Christ except through the path to Calvary. "If any man would come after me, let him deny himself and take up his cross and follow me."[28]

Christian spirituality, then, not only accepts the necessity of suffering as a matter of fact but also places it at the center of our redemption. For philosophers, suffering is the chief scandal of human existence. As a conscious and free spiritual being, man feels that he was born to obtain happiness. In his intellectual and spiritual abilities, he transcends the limits of mere material existence, and he yearns to go beyond the limits of the life of an animal. His quest for truth, freedom, justice, and love spurs him to break through all barriers. Yet in this striving for infinity, he becomes aware of the unbreakable boundaries of his finite, physical existence. All his personal efforts and struggles, he recognizes,

[28] Mk 8:34.

are ultimately doomed to the certain failure of death. The awareness of mortality calls into question the worth of all human endeavors: no one can hope for a lasting home, or even for an immortal monument to himself, here on earth. The impenetrable darkness of death can make the disintegration of one's physical existence—every man's fate—bitter and painful.

This confrontation with death haunts all mankind, and the starting point for all major religious philosophies is the awareness of human mortality. In one way or another, each attempts to explain (or explain away) the absurdity of death. Popular Hinduism offers mankind the consolation of many reincarnations. The Stoics and the religion of the Upanishads exhort us to look forward to the individual's dissolution into and fusion with some Divine Spirit. Original Buddhism teaches us to extinguish all desires, including the desire for our own existence, and thereby obtain the ultimate peace of Nirvana. Christianity, too, proceeds from an awareness of man's end, seeing a link between sin and death in the history of salvation. This link is manifest already in the Old Testament, but its full meaning becomes accessible only in the light of Christ's redemption. God did not include either physical or moral evil in his original plan of Creation. Suffering and death are the result of sin. Man abused his freedom, wanted to be a law unto himself, and did not accept his own reality as a creature who depends on God. Claiming independence from the Eternal, he lost eternity.

The doctrine of original sin regards pain, frailty, and mortality as the necessary product of the common sinful condition of mankind. When man seeks happiness by asserting his absolute autonomy, he makes himself, his own finite reality, into the only absolute, his only horizon and law. In doing so, he rejects God's offer of communion. Had man's spirit been united to God's Holy Spirit, he would have been able to fulfill his vocation, to unite in himself the worlds of spirit and matter. Left to his own resources, however, the human spirit cannot rise above the tyranny of the laws of a mere animal existence but becomes subjected to the inexorable laws of his physical and biological being. Thus, man receives what he has freely chosen in sin: his own finite existence in a state of distortion, separated from the source of his own being. He who was destined to be the crown of creation now experiences himself as the scandal of creation. He cannot possess the harmony in which soul and body would have mutually increased each other's delight. Instead, he experiences himself as an absurd duality: a mortal immortality, a search for happiness doomed to unhappiness, a desire for infinity imprisoned in a finite existence. This recognition surfaces first in the Letter to the Romans (chapters 5 to 7), in a characteristically Pauline manner: an unsystematic piling up of one thought upon the other, combined with a powerful surge of emotion: "Wretched man that I am! Who will deliver me from this body of death?"[29]

God answers Paul's impossible question—not with verbal explanation but with the scandal of the Cross. God the Son, who is absolute spirit, shares our suffering in his own person: "Jews demand signs and Greeks seek wisdom, but we preach Christ crucified, a stumbling block to Jews and folly to Gentiles, but to those who are called, both Jews and Greeks, Christ the power of God and the wisdom of God."[30] God takes upon himself our suffering as the result of his sovereignly free decision. We can appreciate its benefits and show the "fitting reasons" for it (*rationes conveni-*

---

[29] Rom 7:24.
[30] 1 Cor 1:22–24.

entiae, to use the Scholastic term), but we cannot hope to comprehend it. Already in the earthly life of Jesus, the Cross appears as an unacceptable stumbling block. Peter takes the liberty of reprimanding Jesus for announcing his imminent suffering. Jesus replies with a passionate rebuke: "Get behind me, Satan! For you are not on the side of God, but of men."[31] The disciples begin to understand the place of the Cross only after Jesus' Resurrection—not as a philosophical necessity but as part of God's plan of salvation, which was already anticipated in the writings of the Old Testament: "Thus it is written, that the Christ should suffer."[32] Jesus explains his Cross to the two disciples traveling to Emmaus as not only "necessary" but also the way to "enter into his glory."[33]

a. The Fulfillment of Old Testament Prophecies

When explaining where it was "written, that the Christ should suffer,"[34] exegetes often point to a handful of distinct prophecies about the destiny of Jesus—a few psalms (especially Psalm 22) and the "Suffering Servant" songs of Isaiah.[35] However, almost every document of the Old Testament confronts the reader with the sufferings of the chosen people, the figure of the innocent victim, and the apparent nonfulfillment of God's promises of salvation—a dilemma that, without Christ, remains unsolvable. Isaiah, Jeremiah, Ezekiel, Job, and the Psalms together present us with the question of suffering in its real dimensions. The historical

[31] Mk 8:33.
[32] Lk 24:46.
[33] Lk 24:26.
[34] Lk 24:46.
[35] C. H. Dodd, *According to the Scriptures: The Substructure of New Testament Theology* (London: Nisbet, 1952).

period between the destruction of the first Temple and the time of Jesus was filled with a growing tension. Every new beginning was followed by a greater destruction; every liberation brought only a more bitter disappointment. For many in Israel, the aspirations of Davidic messianism melted into thin air; for others, they degenerated into an irrational fanaticism. From a human perspective, the writings of the Old Testament would seem to reflect a turbulent whirlpool of contradictory views, trends, and desires. At the threshold of the New Testament, no one could see how all of God's promises could in truth be fulfilled.

Like a flash of lightning, the Resurrection illumines the darkness of these frustrated expectations. Christ's victory reveals that only at the price of the Cross and by means of the Cross could the reign of the Messiah begin. He has become king of Israel—indeed, of the universe—through his complete defeat. As the Risen One, he has conquered death, and he rules already now in the hearts of his followers. But only those who are ready to share in his Cross will reach the fullness of the kingdom. As Peter declared on the day of Pentecost, "God has made him both Lord and Christ, this Jesus whom you crucified."[36] The Cross of Jesus provides the key to understanding both the whole of Old Testament history and the apparent absurdity of individual suffering.

b. The Way of Purification

In order to escape the sins of conceit and the passions of the flesh, all must enter the path of obedience and self-denial—an insight by no means unique to Christianity. The Cross and Resurrection, however, bring something utterly new to

---

[36] Acts 2:36.

asceticism. The suffering Christ helps everyone who goes through the agony of conversion by taking these pains upon himself. He not only accepted the burden of our mortal nature but also became the target of human sinfulness. A sign of contradiction, he exposed the corruption in many hearts[37] and concentrated sinful man's hatred of God upon his own person.[38] By enduring all this in patient obedience to his Father—even though he was innocent and in no need of conversion—he showed us the beauty of embracing all that is necessary for the purification of our own fallen nature.

This perspective is clearly expressed already in the First Letter of Peter: "Since therefore Christ suffered in the flesh, arm yourselves with the same thought, for whoever has suffered in the flesh has ceased from sin, so as to live for the rest of the time in the flesh no longer by human passions but by the will of God."[39] We, too, can embrace the attitude of Christ in everyday life, even when the stakes do not seem high. Christian spiritual writers connect all the smaller sufferings and renunciations in the life of Jesus (misunderstanding, disappointment, poverty) with his final sacrifice; to follow Jesus is always to share in his Cross. Death, the final and definitive experience of our human limits, is truly anticipated in every act in which we accept our own finitude. Humility, the fundamental attitude of a follower of Christ, is, according to Paul, the same disposition that led Christ to become "obedient unto death, even death on a cross."[40]

[37] See Lk 2:35.
[38] Raymund Schwager, *Must There Be Scapegoats? Violence and Redemption in the Bible* (San Francisco: Harper & Row, 1987).
[39] 1 Pet 4:1–2.
[40] Phil 2:8.

c. Giving Up Our Lives for Others

Christ accepted death out of obedience to his Father and out of love for us. His suffering reveals the greatest of love, for he gave his life for his friends[41]—in fact, for his enemies, as Paul says.[42] In Christian spirituality, the death Jesus accepted in love has always remained the prime example and source of self-sacrificial love. Such love entails giving up one's own goods in order to benefit others, but it is much more than this. Sharing in the Cross of Christ joins us to our fellow men in a new way. Sin is more than just personal; it is collective, communal. Our sins are bound to those of others. We teach one another how to sin, confirm one another in evil by our tacit or explicit approval, and lower the standards of public morality and virtue. But if sin has a collective dimension, our share in the Cross of Christ joins us together all the more in God's work of redemption. When we freely accept suffering for the sake of others, we can contribute to atoning for their sins. When, in our pain and loss, we acknowledge the common debt and our own complicity in others' sins, we help loosen bonds of evil not only for ourselves but also for all sinful mankind. The suffering person, united with Jesus through grace and faith, unites with him also his sufferings and thus truly participates in the redemption of his fellow men.

Participation in the Cross takes on a special intensity if we accept the injustices and sufferings inflicted upon us deliberately by our fellow men—that is, if we do this with the attitude of Christ, seeking the good of the ones who hurt us, with love and forgiveness in our hearts. "Father, forgive

---

[41] See Jn 15:13.
[42] See Rom 5:10. Saint John's statement in 1 Jn 4:10 comes close to Paul's formulation in Rom 5:10.

them," cried Jesus, "for they know not what they do."[43] In such situations, we follow the example of the Father, who "makes his sun rise on the evil and on the good."[44] The Christian martyrs of the first centuries knew that it was through pardoning their executioners, and even offering their sufferings for them, that they would most authentically become disciples of Christ, sharing explicitly in his Cross.

Thus, the doctrine of the Cross is welded to the doctrine of love. To love, one must accept the Cross. The Cross is the means of redemption insofar as it is the triumph of love over hatred. Sin, as the expression of egotism, undermines human community. Instead of joining the individual to his fellow men, it creates competition and opposition. When man craves the belongings of his neighbor and envies his achievements, egotism fragments and divides the world into a collective of hostile individuals. The power of the Cross contradicts this dynamic of sin that permeates society. The Christian forgives in spite of the injury suffered and does not "insist on [his] own way" even when everyone around him is pushing, shoving, and hoarding; he "bears all things, believes all things, hopes all things, endures all things."[45] In the generous love of Christ, good conquers evil.[46]

---

[43] Lk 23:34.
[44] Mt 5:45.
[45] 1 Cor 13:5, 7.
[46] See Rom 12:21.

4

Tradition, Community, Communion

When the Christian accepts Jesus in faith, he calls him Christ, which means "Messiah: the Anointed of God." To acknowledge Jesus as the Messiah is to become part of a several-thousand-year-old tradition that begins with Abraham and leads through the winding path of Old Testament history to Jesus. It is to join the whole community of believers, from the first century to the present day. Christ's presence in this community, ever since the descent of the Holy Spirit at Pentecost, is mediated by his disciples. "Where two or three are gathered in my name," he promises, "there am I in the midst of them."[1] Following Jesus is more than an individual personal commitment; it is a total immersion in a living tradition—a people, a family, a body. In this chapter, we will focus on the theological dimensions of community and history in the spiritual life.

Salvation History

Christianity sprang from Judaism, with all its cultural complexity and historical layers. The early Christian evangelists turned first to the Jewish communities, for they were proclaiming Christ above all as the fulfillment of God's promises to Israel. Even in preaching to the Gentiles, they

[1] Mt 18:20.

always told the extraordinary story of God's choosing for himself a people through which salvation would be prepared for all mankind. The Christian preachers of the Gospel acknowledged and proclaimed the truth of the Old Testament writings to the converting pagans as well as to the Jews, for they were convinced that these writings contained the "prehistory" of Christ. No one can understand Christ without understanding the Old Testament, for the ultimate meaning of the Old Testament Scriptures is fulfilled by Christ. The most ancient Christian writings testify to the apostolic Church's Christocentric interpretation of the Old Testament, whose origin in the encounter with the risen Christ is admirably expressed in the last chapter of Luke's Gospel: "'These are my words which I spoke to you, while I was still with you'"—says the risen Christ to the eleven apostles —"'that everything written about me in the law of Moses and the prophets and the psalms must be fulfilled.' Then he opened their minds to understand the Scriptures."[2] According to John, the risen Jesus communicates to his disciples the Holy Spirit; according to Luke, he communicates to them the understanding of the Scriptures. Soon, the Christian tradition will express its conviction that the two gifts are ultimately one and the same, terming this christological interpretation of the Old Testament "spiritual interpretation" (*sensus spiritualis*): it is in the Holy Spirit that the christological meaning of the Old Testament is disclosed.

By finding its center in Christ and uniting us to the Father through Christ, Christian spirituality is deeply rooted in the salvation history of the Old Testament. In the Gospel of John, Christ says, "You search the Scriptures, . . . and

---

[2] Lk 24:44–45. In Judaism the above threefold title (the Law of Moses, the prophets, and the Psalms) designated the whole of Scripture.

it is they that bear witness to me."[3] This is not an isolated statement. The whole of apostolic teaching strove to unveil this testimony by pointing out the presence of Christ in all the major events and figures of the Old Testament. But even the first Christian generation did not restrict the use of the Old Testament to mere apologetics—that is, when they examined the christological meaning of an Old Testament text, the apostolic writers did not merely try to demonstrate that Jesus was indeed the promised Messiah; they were searching for a deeper understanding of Christ himself, in whom God's plan of salvation found its center and fulfillment.

In the first twelve centuries of Christian history, the literary genres of theology, biblical exegesis (interpretation and commentary), and spiritual literature were so tightly interwoven that they can hardly be divided into three different categories. Theological reflection and prayerful meditation on the mysteries of faith (with the purpose of transforming one's life) preserved their organic unity and mutual interdependence. Since the most important source for both types of reflection was the Bible, biblical interpretation, theology, and spirituality remained inseparably linked in this age. It is worth quoting the most influential works to shed light on this threefold relationship. Origen, the great exegete and theologian of the third century, exerted one of the deepest influences on Christian spirituality, and the majority of his extant works are Scripture commentaries or homilies. We are in possession of 574 such works, mostly on the books of the Old Testament. His commentary on the Song of Songs was one of the most widespread spiritual texts up to the end of the Middle Ages; directly or indirectly, it influenced the theological understanding of spiritual union with God. Saint

---

[3] Jn 5:39.

Augustine, the great theologian at the end of the fourth century, transmitted most of his spiritual teachings to posterity in the form of Scripture commentaries. His two best-known works are his commentaries on the Psalms (*Enarrationes in Psalmos*) and on the Gospel of John, which have both served as main sources of Christian spiritual literature for about a thousand years.

Toward the end of the sixth century, a deacon of the Church of Rome, the later pope Saint Gregory the Great, spent several years in the imperial court of Constantinople as the pope's personal legate. There he gave a series of conferences to a monastic community. The work resulting from this series of talks is, again, a biblical commentary on the book of Job, known as *Moralia in Job*, a verse-by-verse interpretation. Here Gregory concentrates on the moral meaning of Scripture—that is, on the way the teaching, life, passion, and Resurrection of Christ should shape one's life and actions. It became one of the most popular books on Christian spirituality in the Middle Ages. The patristic tradition of providing spiritual teaching in the form of biblical interpretation was continued in the monastic literature of the Middle Ages. Saint Bernard's commentary on the Song of Songs, comprised of eighty-six sermons and composed over the course of almost twenty years (from 1135 up to his death in 1153), is the most famous example of such medieval spiritual biblical commentary. Although the work is unfinished, it is the richest depository of Bernard's spiritual doctrine.

Only after the sixteenth century did the literary forms of biblical exegesis and spiritual literature become differentiated and begin developing in different directions. However, this process of specialization, which yielded various clearly distinguishable theological disciplines, was actually a mixed blessing for the spiritual and intellectual life of Christianity for the next four hundred years. By driving a wedge between the authentic sources of faith and the specialized theological disciplines, it impoverished the theology of spiritual life. During the biblical and liturgical renewal of the twentieth century, in the decades preceding Vatican II, many exegetes became aware of the urgent need for restoring the organic link between faith, spiritual life, and biblical exegesis. They worked on this new synthesis by fully exploiting the fruits of the historical-critical and literary analysis techniques of the modern age.

However, as a result of Pope Pius' encyclical *Divino Afflante Spiritu* (1943), and especially in the wake of Vatican II, Catholic biblical exegesis slipped into a paradoxical situation. On the one hand, it received all the necessary freedom and encouragement to use the results of contemporary historical and literary criticism to promote a better understanding of the Bible. On the other hand, the abundant (and at times overabundant) use of this method only led in most cases to the accumulation of literary and historical data. Instead of promoting the disclosure of the full meaning of a biblical text—centered on Christ and cultivating faith and the spiritual life of the Church—these quantities of complex data mostly served to increase the number of unsolved (and, by means of literary and historical criticism, unsolvable) problems. In this way, the new techniques hindered rather than promoted the exegetes' efforts to disclose the full meaning of a biblical text.

Those who perceived this danger took refuge in the study of the exegesis of the Fathers and saw great promise in modernizing their method of exegesis. The most important products of this trend are the works of Henri de Lubac on the exegetical method of Origen and medieval theologians,[4] a brilliant rediscovery of ancient spiritual exegesis and a rich depository of its best examples. Yet this return to the Fathers also has its own dangers. First, like the trends it seeks to remedy, it may stop at merely accumulating historical and literary data. Also, contemporary biblical science may not accept the results of ancient spiritual exegesis, which is ignorant of the literary and historical methods that today's exegetes consider. For the time being, the relatively best solution is provided by some works of "biblical theology," a special theological discipline that summarizes the results of scholarly exegesis and makes them available for systematic or dogmatic theology. It is mostly from these works that we may receive direction and inspiration to shape our lives and deepen our faith by biblical teachings. Of course, biblical literature that is aimed directly at the cultivation of faith and spirituality, such as spiritual biblical commentaries, biblical meditations, and homilies,[5] is also important.

Because it is centered on Christ, Christian spirituality is inconceivable without the study and spiritual appropriation of salvation history—and the written record of salvation history given and guaranteed by God is the Bible: the abiding presence of God's works among us in the form of human words. Saint Paul's statement remains true for all time: "For whatever was written in former days was writ-

---

[4] Henri de Lubac, *History and Spirit: The Understanding of Scripture according to Origen* (San Francisco: Ignatius Press, 2007); Henri de Lubac, *Medieval Exegesis*, 4 vols. (Grand Rapids, Mich.: Eerdmans, 1998).

[5] In particular, the biblical works of André Feuillet, Ignace de la Potterie, and Albert Vanhoye are all enriching to the spiritual life. The monumental work of Erasmo Leiva-Merikakis, *Fire of Mercy, Heart of the Word: Meditations on the Gospel according to St. Matthew*, 4 volumes, is a felicitous synthesis of exegesis and meditation (San Francisco: Ignatius Press, 1996–2021).

ten for our instruction, that by steadfastness and by the encouragement of the Scriptures we might have hope."[6] The Church has always understood the works of God in salvation history as paradigms of his works in the lives of his children. They are enduring models of how he treats, educates, admonishes, and leads us, and how, after testing us, he fulfills his promises. This teaching echoes through the whole patristic age: whatever God has done for his people in the history of salvation, he does daily for us in a spiritual sense. The same God who called Abraham, revealed himself to Moses, led his people through the desert, gave them a law, introduced them into their own land, and taught and warned them through catastrophes concerns himself also with our salvation. Christ's saving, forgiving, and condemning word, which explains and fulfills the words and deeds of God in the Old Testament, also interprets God's work in our lives.

This spiritual reading of the Bible—the personal appropriation of its meaning for our own lives—cannot take place unless we believe in the reality of divine providence, displayed so vividly in the Old Testament. As Saint Bernard taught his monks, the God who numbers the hairs on our heads has not left even the smallest detail without significance in the inspired text of the Bible.[7] This means that whatever refers to salvation history in the Bible also has meaning and importance for the personal history of our own salvation.

---

[6] Rom 15:4.

[7] Bernard of Clairvaux, *Homiliae in Laudibus Virginis Matris*, homilia 1, chap. 1, in *Sancti Bernardi Opera*, ed. J. Leclercq and H. M. Rochais (Rome: Editiones Cistercienses, 1966), 4:14.

The Role of the Ecclesial Community

To find and apply this meaning of salvation history to our own lives is both a personal and a communitarian task. The beginnings of faith, as a rule, derive from a personal experience. The converting person feels that he was singled out as a unique individual: God addressed him as if he had been the sole object of all his concern and providence. But because conversion leads the individual to Christ, it therefore also leads him to the Church, the universal community of salvation. Throughout salvation history, God always shows himself as the one who calls every single person to salvation, but he offers his plan of salvation to the entire human community. The phrase "people of God" became a popular slogan after Vatican II, but the expression, more than just a fad, brings to light a general pattern of salvation history. Not only did God create man as a communitarian being, and not only is it a psychological fact that our intellectual and emotional development is arrested unless we enter into personal relationships with our fellow men, but, taking into account this basic law of human nature, God has also determined for us a communitarian way of salvation: from age to age he gathers a people to himself.[8] We cannot find the way to salvation by striking out on a solitary path.

In the Old Testament every revelation takes the form of a dialogue between God and his people; God's spokesmen receive the privilege of direct divine communication not for their own personal use or spiritual enrichment but for the good of the people of God. Even when Jesus calls individuals, his purpose is not simply the spiritual development of

---

[8] See Eucharistic Prayer III of the Mass.

these select few. He appoints his apostles "fishers of men" to proclaim the imminent reign of God.[9] That he chooses twelve shows continuity with the people of the Old Testament: Israel's twelve tribes derive their existence and their privilege of being God's chosen people from being the descendants of the twelve sons of Israel. However, the choice of twelve also establishes something new: on the basis of a new revelation, the Twelve become the patriarchs, or fathers, of the new people of God by way of a new spiritual generation. This people calls itself *ekklesia* (church) or *ekklesia tou theou* (an assembly called together by God).[10]

The preachers of the Good News of Jesus are at the same time community organizers and community leaders. They do not merely sow the seed of the Word and leave the seed's growth to the Holy Spirit alone; they do not merely preach the Word and then entrust the further development of the converted individuals' relationship to God only to the inner working of grace. From its very beginnings, Christianity emerges as the coherent unity of organized local communities. The earliest work that describes the origins of the Church, the Acts of the Apostles, provides ample evidence for this view. The community of Jerusalem is extending itself in ever-widening circles to embrace the whole world.[11] The apostles and the Christian missionaries around them return again and again to the communities that sent them

---

[9] Mk 1:17.

[10] Even the phrase *ekklesia tou theou* shows the continuity between Israel and the Church. This Greek expression is used in the Septuagint to translate the Hebrew *qehal* Yahweh, which designates Israel as an assembly called together to worship Yahweh and listen to his Word.

[11] Acts, however, ends with the arrival of Paul in Rome and his proclaiming in Rome the kingdom of God for two years without hindrance (see 28:30–31). This signals that, at least in Luke's mind, the center of the Church's unity has been transferred from Jerusalem to Rome.

out on a missionary journey, but they also visit from time to time the churches they have founded. They do this not only to continue the work of preaching and instruction but also to strengthen their community structures, to appoint presbyter-bishops and deacons as their representatives, and to settle controversies, conflicts, and crises.[12]

This emphasis on community can be seen in the way most of the letters of Saint Paul, the first documents of the New Testament, respond to the concrete needs of the local churches. The apostle aims at extending his personal presence through these letters to the churches he has founded in order to assure their unity in doctrine and Christian life as well as their union with him and one another. His greatest concern—and the endeavor that causes the greatest suffering of his life—is to maintain and foster unity among Christians of Jewish and Gentile origin. When the mother church in Jerusalem suffers from famine, Paul organizes a collection among his churches. He is carrying this fund with him at the end of his third missionary journey to Jerusalem when, at the instigation of his enemies, he is arrested and jailed by the Roman authorities. No one has ever struggled with as many difficulties and suffered as much for the visible unity of Christians as Paul did. No one has thought about the theological foundations of the Church's unity more deeply than he. For him, the Church is the Body of Christ, and by being united to the crucified and risen body of Christ through faith, baptism, and especially the Eucharist, Christians extend Christ visibly into the world, in the sense that

---

[12] We cannot delineate here the history of the development of church offices. Suffice it to say that the terms for the various church offices—*episkopos*, *presbyteros*, and *diakonos*—were not clearly distinguished until the beginning of the third century. Before a clear differentiation of meaning, the terms *presbyteros* and *episkopos* were used synonymously for a long time.

they allow Christ's life and love to be present and active through them. Christians are members of one another because they are members of Christ—that is, their union with one another is based on their union with Christ. The gift of grace a Christian receives is a gift not simply for himself. Everyone, according to his own gift and calling, has to offer his own service for the good of the community. The one Christ who rules over us—the one Spirit who dwells in each of us—enlivens, empowers, and guides this one Body. The members complete one another's functions and work for one another's good; no member could live without the others, and no one could realize his own growth and perfection without serving the others.

The formulation of Pauline ecclesiology and the organizational structure of the primitive Church were only the first steps (though decisive and constitutive for the rest of Church history) on the long road of constant change and development. The further consolidation of the Church's structures took place especially in the second and third centuries, but she truly became a "world church" only after Constantine the Great. Throughout her two-thousand-year history, her unity has always been threatened by schism and heresy, and her claim to be the visible presence of Christ in the world has been constantly called into question by the sins of her members. Nevertheless, she has always managed to reassert and reinforce her unity in Christ by new means and ways and to radiate the love of Christ in every age through her repentant and saintly members.

The communitarian nature of Christian spirituality can be clearly seen in the way that all the different schools of spirituality, established at various stages of the Church's history, display the common characteristic of preparing people for the service of the Church. This distinctive mark of

Catholic spirituality cannot be explained away as merely the result of the hierarchy's efforts to assure its own power or the achievement of political goals at the expense of the personal interests of individual members. Rather, it derives from the very essence of Christian teaching. If the redemptive work of Christ consists in giving life to those he loves by giving away his own life;[13] and if, therefore, the love that serves others is at the center of Christian spirituality; and if God's goal is to join a people to himself rather than individuals separately, then Christian spirituality must necessarily be communitarian.

However, it is not only the fruit of salvation—the love of Christ in which we share—that is community oriented by its very nature: so also are the means of salvation. We listen to the Word of God in community, and by obeying his Word, we build up the church community. The sacramental signs belong to the Church, are administered by the Church, and integrate us in some new or deeper way into the Church. The sacrament of baptism not only cleanses the individual from sin but, at the same time, signifies and causes his entrance into the church community. It accomplishes this not only in an external, juridical fashion but also by inserting us through grace into the Body of Christ. Similarly, the Holy Eucharist, the sacrament of the Body and Blood of Christ, can be celebrated only as the sacrifice of the Church and for the Church.[14] We always celebrate it together with all the angels and the saints, in union with the whole heavenly Jerusalem, as well as in communion with

---

[13] See Jn 15:13.

[14] This should not be misunderstood in such a way as to imply that a private celebration of the Eucharist is meaningless. Certainly, whenever possible, a communitarian celebration is to be preferred, but even a private celebration is ecclesial in its intention and fruits.

all the local churches and, particularly, with the bishop of Rome.

Yet this communion with the whole Church does not remain merely on the level of ritual commemorations; the ritual expresses and effects a real communion. The Body of Christ that becomes present in the celebration of the Eucharist is the whole Body: head and members. As Saint Augustine points out time and again: "Your own mystery is on the altar." When we receive the Body of Christ, through Christ we enter into communion with all members of the Church. This communitarian aspect, however, is inseparable from the aspect of Eucharistic worship and sacrifice: I cannot give myself to God in worship and adoration unless I am inserted into the Body of Christ. And at the same time, the more I give myself to God in sacrifice, the more I become a living member of his Body. Thus, Saint Augustine could define the sacrifice of Christians as "the many making up one body in Christ."

Along with baptism and the Eucharist, the sacrament of reconciliation (or penance) also expresses the ecclesial dimension of the Church, which is already present in its very name. Just as sin separates one from both God and the Church, the reconciliation of the sinner with the Church through the Church's representative signifies and causes our reconciliation with God. The sacrament of the anointing of the sick also effects our union with the whole Body: when we receive this sacrament, by uniting ourselves to the suffering Christ, we are also joined to all the suffering members of the Church. In fact, the whole Church offers her prayers, united to the prayer of Christ through the priest, which obtain from God the fruit of this sacrament: we share in the victory of the risen Christ over suffering and death.

The foundation of the communitarian structure of Christian spiritual life is twofold: first, God adjusts his way of dealing with us to the communitarian nature of man. But second, because God has created man in his own image and likeness, the ultimate ground for man's communitarian nature is to be found in God himself. God is not a solitary person in the splendid isolation of his infinite majesty, but rather the most perfect communion of Father and Son in the Holy Spirit. God is the perfection of love in such a complete sharing and self-giving that the Father does not retain anything for himself but gives all that he has and is to the Son; the Son receives and returns all that he has and is to the Father. This perfect sharing takes place in the Holy Spirit, in whom Father and Son are one. If, then, man is created in the image of God—or more precisely, as many Fathers like to point out, in the image of the Son—then Christian perfection cannot be found in solitary isolation from one's fellow men. On the contrary, it is inseparable from communion with others and results in the building of a community by a common participation in God's gifts. Founding, building, and extending the Church, then, is ultimately an extension to all mankind of the Trinitarian communion. We can be saved only if in the one Spirit we become brothers and sisters of the firstborn Son and enrich one another by sharing and exchanging the gifts we have received from our common Father.

All this should not be misconstrued to mean that in God's eyes the individual person is merely an anonymous, faceless member of the huge collective mass of mankind. The person in his unique individuality, his prayer, his virtues, and his services cannot be dissolved into the activities of the community. Every person is unique in God's eyes, not only insofar as he is personally responsible for his good and evil acts but also because, through a unique gift of God, he receives a unique share in the mission of Christ. Hans Urs von Balthasar makes explicit an ancient element of Christian tradition in asserting that the individual human subject becomes "person" in the full theological sense of the word when he accepts his unique mission in the kingdom of God.

In spite of the communitarian nature of the Church, then, in God's kingdom, no one is expendable or exchangeable; no one can be substituted for anyone else. The parable of the lost sheep would be unintelligible if God did not care about the individual as an individual. Christ's command to "follow me" is not the slogan of a mass movement but a personal call: Christ encounters each one of us in a unique situation, which is established both by Christ's unique act of free initiative and by our unique, free response to it. Christ's love not only embraces my human nature in general but also addresses the "I" that makes me the person I am. The book of Revelation promises the victor "a new name . . . which no one knows except him who receives it."[15] Paul also emphasizes that Christ gave up his life not simply for "us" but for him and for every person both personally and individually. For this reason, he says, we need to be considerate of the scrupulous brother, "for whom Christ died."[16]

Thus, our communitarian destiny does not swallow up our personal worth. But we should put our unique personality, with our gifts of nature and grace, in the service of the community of the Church. Just as the Son "did not count equality with God a thing to be grasped, but emptied himself, taking the form of a servant,"[17] we are also called not to retain ourselves for ourselves but to place our lives and talents at the service of the community. "Whoever loses his

---

[15] Rev 2:17.
[16] 1 Cor 8:11; cf. Gal 2:20.
[17] Phil 2:6–7.

life... will save it."[18] This principle of the Gospel provides the key to understanding the relationship between individual and community. At the same time, it leads us to reflect on the mystery of the Cross.

Mary and the Saints

Christians know that the communitarian nature of the Church is not restricted to this world. The Church also includes Christ as her head; his mother, Mary; all the saints in heaven; and the souls in the state of purification in purgatory. The heavenly Church is fully involved with the purification of souls and the struggles of the Church here on earth. The heavenly Church rejoices with us, feels compassion for us, and is waiting to meet us in heaven. Of course, everything comes from Christ, but Mary and the saints are not passive spectators. They are active on our behalf because of their union with Christ, whose priestly and royal dignity they share. Their presence in our lives gives this stage in the history of salvation its special interim character: the final eschatological reality is already coming—in fact, constantly coming—into this world because the Son of Man has been coming since his passion and Resurrection. The heavenly liturgy is being celebrated in full splendor in heaven and in humble signs on earth, but Satan is still not fully vanquished. His rage is immense since he knows his time is short. Yet all this is still hidden, perceptible only to the eyes of faith.

a. Mary, the Mother of the
Totus Christus, Head and Members

In chapter 12 of Revelation, the correspondence of the Church, Mary, and the people of the Old Testament is sym-

[18] Mk 8:35.

bolically presented in the woman who is about to give birth. With the twelve stars on her crown for the twelve tribes of Israel, she represents the people of the Old Testament, and the child who is born in painful travail is the royal Messiah of Israel (who will "rule all the nations with a rod of iron"[19]). But she is also the Church, since she has other offspring: those who "keep the commandments of God and bear testimony to Jesus."[20] If the woman represents the Old Testament people insofar as she gives birth to the Messiah, then she must also signify Mary, who through Israel has fully realized her vocation to become the mother of the Messiah.

However, the image of her giving birth in wailing and pain does not represent the joyful birth in Bethlehem. Because of the parallel text in John 16:2, the French biblical scholar André Feuillet believes that these birth pangs point to the Messiah's suffering and death, which completed his birth in Bethlehem. Through his death, he becomes the glorious king of Israel and of the whole world. Like Jesus' Messianic enthronement, so, too, Mary's motherhood is completed at the hour of Jesus' death. By accepting the final consequences of her Yes to Gabriel's message, she becomes, in the full sense of the word, the mother of the Messiah at the foot of the Cross. Within this same process, God opens up her motherhood so expansively as to embrace all believers, the brothers and sisters of Jesus, as her own children. "Woman, behold, your son!"[21] Jesus says to Mary, and he says, "Behold, your mother!"[22] to the beloved disciple, who represents the disciples throughout all time. Thus, when Mary becomes the mother of the Messiah in the full sense of the word at the foot of the Cross, she assents to

[19] Rev 12:5.
[20] Rev 12:17.
[21] Jn 19:26.
[22] Jn 19:27.

becoming the mother of the Messiah's brothers and sisters: that is, the Church. From the point of view of her motherly attachment, however, she had to fully give up her Son so that she could stretch out her love to embrace all believers.[23]

As Mary accompanied Jesus to the Cross and shared in his self-offering to the Father, so, too, does she accompany all of her children through their lives until they safely reach eternity. Just as her motherhood of Jesus reached its fulfilment at his death, her motherly role in our lives is completed for us at the hour when we are born to eternal life: we say in the Hail Mary, "pray for us sinners, now and at the hour of our death."

Common sense throughout the ages knows what qualities a mature woman possesses. She is not only intuitive, sensitive, affectionate, and empathetic—the usual feminine qualities we appreciate—but also strong, objective, and courageous, possessing a spine of steel—the qualities we instinctively attribute to men. At the same time, the mature man is not simply the cool, detached, and valiant warrior but also someone who is affectionate, compassionate, warm, and personable. Full humanity requires the integration of both masculine and feminine virtues into one's personality. This does not mean, however, the development of an androgynous personality. The male in this process becomes a mature man, the female a mature woman, each with his or her own fully developed psychological identity.[24]

A healthy Marian piety helps both sexes in the maturation to full humanity. The man who receives Mary into his life and heart will allow Jesus to be born in him and will help

---

[23] For the foundation of this view in the Gospel text itself, see Andre Feuillet, "L'heure de la femme (Jn 16,21) et l'heure de la Mère de Jésus (Jn 19,25–27)," *Biblica* 47 (1966): 169–84, 361–80, 557–73.

[24] See Carl Jung, *Psychology of the Unconscious* (Tel Aviv: Dvir Co., 1973 [originally 1916]).

others give birth to Jesus in their hearts. The awareness of such a motherly task will help him integrate this feminine spiritual role in a complementary way into his manhood. The woman who receives Mary into her life and heart will also give birth to Jesus and help others do the same. But by growing to the extent of the full stature of Christ, she will also attain "mature manhood"[25] in the sense of integrating the masculine virtues into her female personality. This process of men and women actualizing their full humanity is part of that "hundredfold," the earthly reward for following Christ with Mary.

This deeper theological understanding of Mary should inform our spiritual lives. The concrete ways in which we can express our love for her and ask for her help are many indeed, but I would like to mention a few.

The Rosary is a favorite of Catholics in the Roman rite —and also, we know, of the Blessed Mother herself, since she promoted it at Lourdes and Fátima. It is important that we pray the Rosary in the presence of Mary and not just for the purpose of performing a duty, doing a good work, or fulfilling a promise. These are not bad motives, but they miss what is essential. The Rosary is a personal greeting to Mary. When we say "Hail, Mary, full of grace, the Lord is with thee. Blessed art thou among women and blessed is the fruit of thy womb," we make the greetings of the archangel Gabriel and Elizabeth our own. We may meditate on the mysteries, but if we cannot, we should try to greet her each time we say a Rosary in a better, more personal, more reverential, and more trusting way. We need to greet her over and over, time and again, so that our prayer moves from a rote recitation to a sincere greeting. She responds in one way or another, at times sharing with us the joy she

---

[25] Eph 4:13.

felt when she heard those greetings for the first time. When we meditate on the Rosary, Hans Urs von Balthasar tells us, "We should look at the mysteries of Jesus' life—and thereby at the mysteries of the trinitarian embodiment of salvation—from her point of view, according to her memory."[26]

Mary can also be a great help for us when we receive Holy Communion. According to Hans Urs von Balthasar, she is the only one who could fully participate (as much as any human can) in the Eucharist because her gift of self to Jesus and through Jesus to the Father was perfect, without any trace of selfishness.[27] We may often feel totally unfit to receive Christ, even though we are not aware of any mortal sin—we are simply unable to love and praise him as he deserves. We can ask Mary to complete what we are unable to do and help us join her in her thanksgiving.

b. The Saints

It is not only the apostles sitting in judgment on twelve thrones[28] who carry out God's plan for the world and for individuals; every saint[29] shares in this task. Each one of us can find a saint whose psychological makeup and personality are similar to ours and can develop a close friendship with him. Our favorite saints can make Christ more real and more imitable for us. Contact with the saints in heaven diminishes our anxiety about the world beyond and makes heaven more humanly attractive. Their victorious striving for holiness encourages us to become saints by carrying out

---

[26] Hans Urs von Balthasar, *Mary for Today*, trans. Robert Nowell (San Francisco: Ignatius Press, 2022), 56.

[27] Hans Urs von Balthasar, *Theo-Drama: Theological Dramatic Theory*, vol. 4, *The Action* (San Francisco: Ignatius Press, 1994), 389–406.

[28] See Mt 19:28.

[29] See Rev 3:21.

God's plan for our own lives. Here are a few character traits we can learn from them.[30]

The saints do not compromise regarding God's will. Beyond just obeying his commands, they also listen to God's gentle requests. For example, at Mass, Saint Anthony hears the words of the Gospel that tell us to "sell all you have and come follow me," and he sells his land and retires to pray and work in the desert. Saint Francis hears the same Gospel, gives up all his possessions, and becomes destitute with the destitute to bring them the love of Christ. Saint John de Brebeuf gives thanks to God for allowing him to become a martyr among his beloved Indians.

The saints will passionately and with their whole hearts. When they say "yes," they mean yes, and when they say "no," they mean no. They know that half-heartness is from the Evil One. In their passionate fervor many saints exaggerate their mortifications at the beginning and ruin their bodies—what Saint Francis called "brother ass"—which they come to regret. At a later stage, however, their bodies become most helpful cooperators in carrying out their masters' will so that many saints astound the world with their energy and accomplishments. Even with chronically bleeding ulcers, Saint Bernard worked for the Church more than anyone else at his time. Pius XII, so frail in his adolescence that he could not attend public school, worked every day until 2 A.M. during most of his pontificate.

The saints make the supernatural a natural part of their lives. Saint Thérèse of Lisieux, for example, said that if you are serving someone whom you intensely dislike, you should treat this person as if you dearly loved him. When she was assigned to an old cantankerous nun who repelled everyone

---

[30] For a more detailed study on the phenomenology of the saints, see Louis Lavelle, *Four Saints: The Meaning of Holiness* (Notre Dame, Ind.: Notre Dame University Press, 1963).

else, she served her so lovingly that the woman asked her, "Sister Thérèse, could you tell me what attracts you so much to me?" Thérèse, stunned, thought to herself, "Jesus, who is in you." Obviously, to make such supernatural kindness natural took much prayer and struggle. We can also think of Saint Teresa of Calcutta, who endured forty years without spiritual consolation. Finally she told Jesus, "All right, if you don't smile at me, I will smile at you." And she kept smiling all her life. Nobody knew—except her confessor—what it cost her.

The saints do not find the created world with its material realities, such as plants and animals, to be indifferent or hostile, but they feel at home in God's world. All things are friends—brothers and sisters—to them. The legends about friendship between saints and animals—such as the wolf of Gubbio, whom Francis tamed, or the swallows who flapped their wings enthusiastically as Francis preached to them, or the morose old Jerome carefully removing a thorn from a lion's paw—all point to something quite real: around the saint, something of the peace of paradise is restored.

The saints "know that in everything God works for good with those who love him,"[31] so they are grateful for success and failure, for praise and criticism, for life and death. Saint Cyprian, bishop of Carthage, said only two words as the Roman magistrate declared the sentence of his decapitation: *Deo gratias*—"Thanks be to God!"[32] A Cistercian monk, dying from painful bone cancer, wrote to a young woman, "Hold out in being good. We never regret what we do for him."

---

[31] Rom 8:28.
[32] *The Treatises of S. Cæcilius Cyprian*, trans. John Henry Newman (Oxford, 1839), xxii.

But it is not only the heroic acts and virtues of saints that make them endearing to us. It is also their weaknesses, as they wage the strenuous fight to accept God's will, and their witness to the gentle mercy of God, who saves them from a humanly certain fall. We gain confidence and courage from their examples and help from their intercession.

In the World but Not of the World

We have spoken so far in this chapter about our membership in the community that is the Church. But for now, we also live in the world. What should our relationship be to the world and the earthly communities we live in? How should our membership in the community of the Church inform how we see and act in the world?

The title of this section is a reference to a well-known text of John, where Christ says, "And now I am no more in the world, but they are in the world. . . . I do not pray that you should take them out of the world but that you should keep them from the evil one."[33] In the Johannine writings, "the world" often refers to the sphere of Satan's influence that keeps mankind subjugated under the power of sin. In this sense of "the world," those who come to Christ through faith no longer belong to the world but have joined the original group of Christ's disciples. In this community they share in the Holy Spirit, whom the first disciples received from the risen Christ, and form a community of love, peace, and forgiveness in the midst of a sinful world that lies in the grip of the Evil One.[34] Thus, Saint John's warning is understandable: "Do not love the world or the things in

[33] Jn 17:11, 15.
[34] See Jn 20:19–23; 1 Jn 5:19.

the world. If any one loves the world, love for the Father is not in him."[35]

However, in a seemingly complete contradiction to this text, Jesus declares in the Gospel of John, "For God so loved the world that he gave his only-begotten Son. . . . For God sent the Son into the world, not to condemn the world, but that the world might be saved through him."[36] Jesus also gives his flesh "for the life of the world."[37] This apparent contradiction points to two interrelated but different meanings of the "world" in Johannine literature. Insofar as the world embodies Satan's influence and is the means of his power, Jesus does not pray for the world.[38] But insofar as the world has been created by God and consists of sinful human beings, it is the object of the love of the Father, who gives his Son for the world, and the object of the love of the Son, who offers his own life for it.

We see a similar dialectical relationship of God, Christ, and the Christian to the world in Saint Paul's letters. On the one hand, the world is the object of God's judgment in its present form, and it will pass away.[39] On the other hand, God, who had created the world, reconciled it to himself in Christ and entrusted the message of reconciliation to the apostles; the temporary rejection of the Jews also serves to bring about the reconciliation of the world.[40] In one text, Paul warns the Corinthians, "Do not be mismated with unbelievers. For what partnership have righteousness and iniquity? Or what fellowship has light with darkness? What

[35] 1 Jn 2:15.
[36] Jn 3:16–17.
[37] Jn 6:51.
[38] See Jn 17:9.
[39] See Rom 3:6; 1 Cor 7:31.
[40] See 2 Cor 5:19; Rom 11:15.

accord has Christ with Belial? Or what has a believer in common with an unbeliever?"[41] But he also writes to the same community in a different vein: "I wrote to you in my letter not to associate with immoral men; not at all meaning the immoral of this world, or the greedy and robbers, or idolaters, since then you would need to go out of the world. But rather I wrote to you not to associate with any one who bears the name of brother if he is guilty of immorality or greed."[42] In his Letter to the Romans, Paul says that every power (even the power of a pagan emperor!) is derived from God, and he therefore encourages Christians to live in peace with all men.[43]

Thus, already the first Christians became aware of their paradoxical situation: faith in Christ both separates them from the world and sends them into the world with a mission and a task. The more the Church spread into the world and acquired truly worldwide dimensions, the more difficult this balancing act became for the Church as a community and for the Christian as an individual.

Insofar as the world is the collective embodiment and means of sin, the Christian must renounce the world. The medieval phrase *fuga mundi* (escape from the world) expresses this attitude dramatically. Medieval Christianity created a whole lexicon of expressions that articulate this attitude: the one who seeks God abandons the world, detaches himself from the vanities of the world, and enters a monastery or cloister as a new milieu that will be conducive to his growth in spiritual life. Yet, the same monastic movement that withdrew from the world also converted Europe. The great missionaries of Christianity in European

---

[41] 2 Cor 6:14–15.
[42] 1 Cor 5:9–11.
[43] See Rom 13:1; 12:18.

countries were mostly monks: Saint Patrick in Ireland, Saint Augustine in England, Saint Boniface in Germany, Saints Cyril and Methodius among the Slavs, Saint Gerard among the Hungarians. While Christianizing these people, the same monks also transmitted to them the worldly cultural values of antiquity, and in this way, they transformed and saved many elements of the ancient pagan cultures of these nations. They enriched the world with a great number of literary works and produced invaluable works of art in sculpture, architecture, painting, and illuminated manuscripts. In sum, they were committed to building a society and culture inspired and transformed by Christian values. So even these monks who had renounced the world knew the term also has a positive meaning: "the world" was the object of their love and apostolic endeavors.

As Christians, we follow their example, even though the ways we escape from and involve ourselves in the world have varied and will always vary according to the circumstances of historical situations and the differences in individual vocations. Like the saints, Christians must never give up either pole of this antinomy and must endure the tension that accompanies the task of reconciling two seemingly contradictory attitudes. They must oppose collective and institutionalized forms of inhumanity, immorality, and unbelief and avoid their contagious influence. But both their missionary vocation stemming from their Christian faith and their love for mankind and human values will involve them in the world. They will participate—each according to the measure of his own talents and vocation—in those activities of the world that work to save and ennoble human lives, eliminate or at least mitigate injustice, and alleviate physical and emotional suffering.

If we fail to retain both poles of our vocation—renouncing the world and working to transform it—we abandon the ground of Christian faith and action by taking one of two extreme positions: we despise the world and give up responsibility for it (which means giving up responsibility for our neighbor); or we dedicate ourselves to the improvement of mankind's lot on earth to the point that, instead of preparing for and expecting God's kingdom, we focus all our energies on building the "Secular City," an attempted utopia of temporary, biological happiness.[44]

Action and Contemplation

The polarity between being in the world but not of the world is also seen in the tension between action and contemplation. Human life includes both the inward—the realm of the spirit—and the outward—the material realm of human activity. When ancient Christian writers apply this understanding of human experience to the spiritual life, "action" (*actio*) usually refers to the practices of asceticism (self-denial, physical work, deeds of charity for one's neighbor), while "contemplation" (*contemplatio*) refers to inner acts of faith, prayer, and love. Even in this sense, both action and contemplation are inseparably present at every stage of Christian life, although there is development in spiritual experience: at the beginning there is often a preponderance of hard work accompanied by the fear of God and sheer faith in his goodness and mercy (*zoe praktike*, *vita practica* or *activa*); gradually, however, the exercise of Christian virtues becomes easier

[44] Harvey Cox, *The Secular City: Secularization and Urbanization in Theological Perspective* (New York: McMillan, 1966).

through an experience of God's goodness and love (*zoe theoretike* or *vita contemplativa*).

Since asceticism is required only because of the conditions of this earthly existence, whereas the inner experiences of faith and love anticipate eternal life, the Fathers often point out the superiority of contemplation—for the contemplative life will be perfected and last for all eternity, while external activity is necessary only for our life on earth and thus reflects the not-yet-perfected state of man's redemption. Patristic exegesis often uses biblical symbols to explain this polarity. The most widely known is the contrast between the figures of Martha and Mary.[45] Since Mary is praised for choosing "the better part"[46] (or "the best part") by sitting at the Lord's feet and listening to his word, the text is used by many of the Fathers to explain and extol the excellence of contemplation.

The modern age shifted the emphasis from the terms "contemplation" and "action" to instead describe external institutional frameworks intended to concentrate on either action or contemplation. Thus, religious orders were divided into "active" and "contemplative." This shift of perspective from the anthropological to the institutional viewpoint brought about a confusing change in the meaning of the terms. From the new perspective, the physical work of a contemplative religious—originally considered as an ascetical exercise and thus belonging to the realm of active life—is now viewed as part of the contemplative life. At the same time, the intellectual and spiritual activities of a religious who belongs to an active order—his studies, research,

---

[45] See Lk 10:38–42.
[46] Lk 10:42 (NABRE).

teaching, and preaching—are now counted as part of the active life. The concepts are still not fully clarified: the mixed use of the terms in various texts that belong to different ages does not make distinguishing them easier. However, to consider "contemplative life" superior to an "active, apostolic life" (in the modern, institutionalized sense of the terms) is certainly a false assumption that has no basis either in Scripture or in tradition.

In today's spiritual climate there appears to be a growing consensus on complementary unity of action and contemplation (in an anthropological sense). Now they can be seen as two aspects of any human activity, rather than two separate categories of activities. This insight derives from the philosophical conviction—stronger today than ever before—that one cannot separate inward intellectual/spiritual activities from outward sense experience, or volitional/affective acts from outward physical activities. These two aspects of human activities are mutually and rigorously interdependent. The intellectual/spiritual insights of man, the free decisions of his will, and his affective experiences are nourished by contact with the physical world and expressed in tangible, bodily signs. At the same time, as a union of spirit and matter, man collects and systematizes his sense impressions, appropriates them intellectually and spiritually, understands their causes and meaning, and, by his will and emotions, takes a personal stand on the basis of this understanding. Briefly put, by intellectualizing and spiritualizing the sense impressions of his bodily existence, man realizes himself as a spiritual being. His vocation is to unfold this spiritual existence in the knowledge, love, and service of God. In this sense, contemplation and action belong to every human vocation. The human character of every action, and thereby its moral and spiritual value, results from contemplation, whereas both the nourishing source and expression of contemplation is (some form of) action.

The unity of action and contemplation is also required by the very nature of love. Our love for God and our love for neighbor are inseparable: he who loves God must also love his neighbor. Moreover, a love of neighbor that consists only in internal acts and does not pay attention to his basic needs or care to help him is a lie or, at best, a delusion. As Saint John says, "If any one has the world's goods and sees his brother in need, yet closes his heart against him, how does God's love abide in him? Little children, let us not love in word or speech but in deed and in truth."[47] Throughout the history of the Church, it was always the dynamic force of Christian love that broke through the limits of traditions and institutions, and—often in spite of inadequate theoretical foundations—realized in practice the unity of contemplation and action. The ideal of Saint Ignatius of Loyola, *actione contemplativus* (contemplative in action), was achieved in different ways by every great figure of Christianity. Pope Saint Gregory the Great, while overburdened by cares and anxieties for the Church and building the walls of Rome to ward off the attacks of barbarian hordes, returns again and again to the relief of contemplation. Saint Bernard is constantly snatched away from the leisure of contemplation by the pressing needs of his own monks and of the Church and society at large. Don Bosco learns to pray and be united with God in the midst of watching over and playing with the children he had rescued from the streets and slums of nineteenth-century Italy. Saint Thérèse offers her cloistered life for the missionary Church, while, even in the supposed

---

[47] 1 Jn 3:17–18.

peace of the cloister, she has to build her prayer life in the midst of petty intrigues and the constant interruptions of her novices. The tension between the two poles is inevitable, a consequence of our present human existence: we live after the Fall and redemption, but before our glorification. Sometimes this duality feels like being torn to pieces. Saint Bernard writes to his friend, the prior of a Carthusian monastery, in a tone of despair: "My monstrous life cries to you. . . . I became a chimaera of my age."[48] Yet he finds peace knowing that in accepting the turmoil of worries and activities, he is seeking to do God's will. He writes of David, who faithfully carried out all the commands of the king, holding him up as a model:

"My heart is ready," he says, "my heart is ready,"[49] not only once but twice, that is, "I am ready to spend time with you and ready to serve my neighbors." This is indeed the best part which will not be taken away; this is the best attitude which will not change wherever you call him. He who serves well, obtains a good degree of perfection. He who spends time with God, obtains perhaps a better one; but he who is perfect in both has obtained the best.[50]

If the soul's eye is simple—that is, if his intention is pure, not seeking his own will but the will of his Lord—then interruptions to spiritual studies will not harm him. Whenever he interrupts his contemplation for the sake of "one of

---

[48] Bernard of Clairvaux, *Epistolae*, epistola 250, chap., in *Sancti Bernardi Opera*, 8:147. A chimaera is an imaginary monster portrayed by ornamental sculptures in Gothic cathedrals; its different members resemble various animals: a lion, a she-goat, and a serpent.
[49] See Ps 57:7.
[50] Bernard of Clairvaux, *Sermo in Assumptione Beatae Mariae Virginis*, in *Sancti Bernardi Opera*, 3:3.

the least,"[51] he experiences the act as one of laying down his life spiritually for him.[52] In this way, he integrates the active and the contemplative—being in the world but not of the world—into one radical act of love.

---

[51] Mt 25:40.
[52] Bernard of Clairvaux, *Sermo in Assumptione Beatae Mariae Virginis*.

5

Discerning the Way: Conscience

After sketching out different aspects of the dynamics of the spiritual life, we will look in a more systematic way at the virtues the Christian needs on his way to holiness. First, however, we need to examine conscience, the spiritual organ in the human being that distinguishes a virtuous act from an evil one—that distinguishes moral good from moral evil.[1] Where does the voice of conscience come from? How can we integrate it fully into our spiritual lives, and how can we inform and develop it?

Conscience as a Transcendent Command

There are people who always watch the tastes and opinions of those on whom they are economically or socially dependent—a government, a party, an institution, or just popular individuals—so that they may adjust their own way of thinking, speaking, and acting accordingly. They are loyal and even servile to those on whom they depend until their interests advise them otherwise.

We find, however, another type of people, at times influential, such as Saint Thomas More, but also often unknown —ordinary people whose behavior distinguishes them from

---

[1] Philippe Delhaye, *The Christian Conscience* (New York: Desclée, 1968); Joseph Ratzinger, "Conscience and Truth," *Communio* 37, no. 3 (Fall 2010): 530–38; J. Budziszewski, *What We Can't Not Know: A Guide* (San Francisco: Ignatius Press, 2011).

the previous type. At times they obey their government; at other times they critique it. At times they follow a party leader, but in other cases they stand alone, opposing the "politically correct" views of the majority. They are not immobilists, but when they change their position, they have good reason. If asked why they acted in a way that is so different from how important people would have counseled them, their reply might be very simple: "I did what I thought was right." This choice has cost some of them their wealth, their power, or their very lives.

When we say, "I did what I thought was right," or, more concisely, "I followed my conscience," what do we mean? What is this voice that we are obeying, and where does it come from? First, conscience is a voice that expresses obligation: when we speak this way, we are recognizing our obligation to do the right thing. Second, it is a voice that appeals to our freedom: no one is pressuring us; no external or internal force is overcoming us. Third, the command to act in a certain way comes not only from ourselves but, at the same time, from somewhere very much above us. Fourth, it is a voice that has inescapable authority over us, such that if we do not obey it, our own judgment will condemn us. If we act against this command, we introduce a deep split into our own person. According to Saint Bernard, we are dragged before the tribunal of our own selves, and our best self condemns our sinful self.[2] Obeying the command of our conscience is therefore inseparable from our own sense of self-worth: if we disobey its voice, our self-esteem is diminished; we cannot help condemning ourselves. If we obey its command, however, our sense of dignity and inner peace increases.

---

[2] Bernard of Clairvaux, *De conversione ad clericos*, chap. 3, in *Sancti Bernardi Opera*, ed. J. Leclercq and H. M. Rochais (Rome: Editiones Cistercienses, 1966), 4:73–74.

Many people agree in general that we must do what is right, but they quickly add that what is right or wrong depends on the personal decision of each person: "What is right for me may not be right for you." This subjectivist stance is only partly true. On the one hand, some standards do vary from person to person. Saint Paul counseled the Roman Christians, who had split into rival schools of liturgical practice and dietary asceticism, "One believes he may eat anything, while the weak man eats only vegetables. Let not him who eats despise him who abstains, and let not him who abstains pass judgment on him who eats; for God has welcomed him. . . . Let every one be fully convinced in his own mind."[3] On the other hand, man has absolute limits. In his Letter to the Galatians, Paul lists the "works of the flesh" with trenchant objectivity: "immorality, impurity, licentiousness, idolatry, sorcery, enmity, strife, jealousy, anger, selfishness, dissension, party spirit, envy, drunkenness, carousing."[4] By denying that the command of conscience comes not only from within us but also from above us, subjectivists create a split within the person that cannot be reconciled. If what is right is *only* a personal decision, and how I act is also only a personal decision, then there are no grounds for asserting the authority of one personal decision over another. Self-condemnation becomes meaningless, and the concept of conscience dissolves into nothing. But we do suffer self-condemnation when we go against our conscience. This is why Paul, who warns against judgment of others, orders everyone to be "fully convinced in his own mind." This conviction is an earnest belief in a truth that lies outside oneself. We experience the conscience that issues commands as the highest and deepest voice within us.

[3] Rom 14:2–3, 5.
[4] Gal 5:19–21.

It is an "antenna" capable of identifying with an unconditional imperative: you must do what is right.

Such an absolute command can ultimately come only from an absolute person: God. The Judeo-Christian tradition bases its moral judgment on revelation, such as the Ten Commandments, and on the natural law, which God reveals to us through the workings of the created world. A morally good act is one that protects the rights and the dignity of human nature, individually and in community; a morally evil act is one that goes against these values. The absolute obligation of upholding human dignity derives from the divine image that every person represents. For this reason, offending man is offending God.

But our conscience does not always speak clearly to us. Its sensitivity is obscured by both original sin and personal sinfulness, so that human reason is not always able to recognize the principles of natural law. We are able to perceive general moral rules, such as "always act justly," but when it comes to applying these rules to individual actions, much confusion reigns. God's revelation, preserved and unfolded in the Church, confirms and enlightens our understanding of the implications of the natural law.

If we obey our conscience, its sensitivity will develop so that it will register not only the commands of God that apply a general moral principle to a concrete situation but also his gentle intimations. God leads everyone in a uniquely personal way. At times his plan for a person will become manifest simply by the individual's desires, abilities, and concrete situations. But we are likely to perceive God's gentle personal calls only if we have developed a sensitive conscience. Saint Teresa of Calcutta, for example, felt a gentle call for a long time: "My children are dying on the streets of the cities. Would you take care of them for me?" Eventually she obeyed, and the congregation of the Missionaries of Charity was born.

Conscience as Judgment

We have spoken of the conscience as a "voice" or "command" that transcends the person who hears it. But this is not to say that it originates in some kind of impersonal vacuum, coming to a person out of the blue. It takes shape in, and is expressed by, the individual person's judgment. It evolves from a reasoning process in which one's basic approach to values plays a part.

When we are faced with a choice, we examine our possible courses of action. We ponder the values involved in the various alternatives and, eventually, arrive at a judgment about which course of action is the right or best one to take. Since conscience has a crucial role to play in this process, we should consider two practical rules concerning the judgment of conscience:

1. You must always follow the certain judgment of your conscience, provided that you have honestly tried to inform it. Just as apprehending sounds requires a person to use his sense of hearing, discerning and appreciating moral values requires the use of one's conscience. But acknowledging what your conscience has perceived requires truthfulness. If, in order to please an influential person, you were to claim you heard beautiful music when you actually heard the sound of fingernails on a chalkboard, you would be dishonest. Likewise, it would be wrong for you to seek favor with a powerful person by pretending that a request he has made is morally right, when in fact your conscience has advised you against it.[5]

---

[5] This is different from a complex situation in which your best choice is

Continuing with this analogy, we know that the sounds we hear do not originate in our sense of hearing; that sense simply registers and transmits the sounds to the brain. In a similar way, our conscience is not a creative function. It does not invent moral values; it mediates them to us from a source outside ourselves. Just as we ought to develop and refine our sense of hearing so that we can distinguish, for example, an off-key musical instrument from a well-tuned one, we need to take particular care in preparing to deal with moral issues so as to avoid making bad judgments. Arming ourselves with solid principles and carefully applying them to the choices presented will satisfy this rule: that we honestly try to inform our conscience.

However, we are not infallible, and in spite of our honest efforts, it is possible that we may come to a conclusion about a matter that is objectively wrong. For example, a judge convicts a man who is actually innocent after conscientiously weighing all the evidence available to him. The judge is in a state of what is called "invincible ignorance": he holds his erroneous conviction in good faith, without any evil intent and without neglecting his duty to discover the truth of the matter by looking more deeply.

Even when your conscience is in a state of invincible ignorance, you must comply with its judgment. This principle follows from the transcendent authority that conscience must be afforded. Even for someone mistaken, disobeying one's conscience means, for that person, disobeying God.[6]

---

unclear to you: in such a case, your conscience might well prompt you to seek the advice of a more competent authority.

[6] Note that we are speaking of the duty to obey one's own conscience. It does not follow that we always have a duty to uphold the decisions of another person's sincere conscience. Sometimes a sincerely held but objectively false

2. *As long as you remain in a state of vincible ignorance, you must not act.* Not all cases of ignorance are invincible, however. When someone is aware of his ignorance concerning a moral issue on which he must act and he is able to do something about this ignorance, he is in a state of vincible ignorance: ignorance that can be overcome—and that must be overcome before he can responsibly act. Vincible ignorance is bad-faith neglect of one's duty to overcome it. Suppose, for example, that after a long period of tranquil unbelief, an atheist discovers he has some serious doubts about his views. He neglects, however, to study the problem further, either from sheer indolence or a fear that he might be radically changed by belief. This decision—his refusal to pursue the problem—becomes sinful.

How Can a Non-Christian Inform His Conscience?

We have seen that the judgment of our conscience mediates something transcendent, which the theist knows to be the will of God. Of course, God's command is often distorted by the human process of mediation. Yet even an invincibly erroneous conscience expresses something divine: the unconditional and unassailable command to do good and avoid evil. Even when someone knows nothing of God's revelation in history (in contrast to Jews, Muslims, and Christians), his willingness to obey his conscience will reveal to him not just this general imperative to do good but also more

---

conviction poses a serious threat to other people. Suppose, for example, that a child's life is at risk unless he receives an immediate blood transfusion, but the child's parents refuse on religious grounds to allow the procedure. In this case, the state ought to intervene and, in order to save the child's life, overrule the parents' will.

concrete and specific details about God's will. This happens for two reasons.

First, God created all people for loving communion with himself and with one another. He never ceases to inspire them with his Holy Spirit and to call them to this communion. This call reaches man in the "heart," or conscience. The difficulty is that even though we hear this call inwardly, the ignorance caused by the original Fall and by our personal sins clouds our moral and spiritual sensitivity. Thus, it comes as no surprise that in this state, and without God's revelation, even the most virtuous pagans fail to understand the full implications of God's call. Nevertheless, we cannot deny that some of them have shown remarkable insight. The Chinese philosopher Confucius, for example, taught that the highest virtue is goodwill toward one's neighbor and community, and the author of the Hindu Bhagavad Gita presents loving devotion to God as the highest perfection of man.

Second, everyone may know God through his creation. Looking reflectively upon the world around him, every man of goodwill can grasp his own moral obligation to preserve this beauty. Specifically, by reflecting on his own nature and that of his fellow men, he discovers the dignity within the human person, and this discovery leads to the conclusion that a human being has certain inalienable rights, such as the right to life, freedom, justice, and respect. Many other moral values, along with their corresponding obligations, follow from this discovery. As we mentioned earlier, the sum total of the obligations that can be derived from reflecting on human nature is designated the *natural moral law*.

Each of the two adjectives here deserves some comment. "Natural" in this context does not refer to those laws that govern only the body of man, such as physical, biological, and chemical laws. Instead, the word signifies that the law we are talking about is derived ultimately from the essential nature of man. The natural moral law is concerned with the total person. For instance, a command to be truthful speaks to the entire person, not merely the body, except insofar as the body helps fulfill the command through speech, written language, and gestures.[7] In addition, the natural moral law does not just describe how things act, as the laws of physics do. "Moral" indicates that free obedience is involved, as opposed to necessity—it is prescriptive, not descriptive. Obeying the laws of nature—say, the law of gravity—is hardly a matter of choice. By contrast, the moral law confronts a person with a "should" or "ought."

The natural moral law is perhaps the Christian's strongest link with those who know nothing of God's revelation in history. Saint Paul, for example, points out that the pagans have the basic demands of the Law of Moses engraved upon their hearts. On the Day of Judgment, they will be judged according to their fulfillment of this law.[8] In similar fashion, the natural moral law offers a common "language," or medium of discussion, for Christians and non-Christians on such critical moral issues as war, abortion, racial discrimination, and social injustice.

---

[7] Regrettably for the clarity with which we might want this law to speak to us, man's nature is fallen; that is, it has grown sick or distorted through sin. The result is that by simply looking at human history and society, we might have difficulty identifying what man's essential nature would require him to do. For example, could we deduce from the nature of man that he ought always to be truthful? We could, but not many people would be convinced by our argument. So there *is* a natural moral law, but without the revelation of Christ, we would find it extremely difficult to spell out concretely what it means to be a good person.

[8] See Rom 2:14–16.

How Does a Christian Inform His Conscience?

A Christian obeys the natural moral law because he knows that God wants him to be fully human without any moral distortion. In this striving, however, he is helped by the teachings and the ongoing life of the Church, recognizing in them the example and teaching of Christ.

The Christian conscience is ultimately influenced by two "mentors" working together: the Holy Spirit "inside" and the Church "outside." The Holy Spirit present in the individual Christian leads him to discern and accept, in the teachings of the Church, not just the words of men but the very word of Christ. The Holy Spirit present in the magisterium, the teaching office of the Church, enables the pope and the bishops to interpret correctly the teachings of Christ and apply them again and again to new situations—for example, bioethical dilemmas, sexual issues, economic disparities, or other social problems.[9] Without the Holy Spirit, the individual Christian would remain closed to the teachings of the Church, and the official Church could not authentically interpret the teachings of Christ. Without the magisterium of the Church, however, there would be no human agency to articulate in human words, for contemporary situations, the teaching and example of Christ.[10]

---

[9] Of course, the assistance of the Holy Spirit does not dispense the Church's leaders from struggling with the new moral issues that arise all the time. As a result, not all Church teachings have the same degree of certainty. The teachings held with an infallible certainty are called dogmas.

[10] What if we had access only to the Holy Spirit's inner guidance, without the external teachings of the Church? The lives and teachings of great moral philosophers, such as Confucius and Socrates, probably offer us our best guess about the result. These people appear to have been unusually responsive to God's internal guidance, yet they lacked the additional insight offered by the

Christ's moral teaching and his living example of what it means to be fully human clarify the tenets of the natural moral law. But they do more than that. By merely contemplating human nature, we never could have imagined that we are meant to be not mere creatures and servants of the Creator but the very children of God the Father, who are called to share the life and love of the Holy Trinity. Far more convincingly than rational speculation could have done, Christ has shown us how to live and die as children of God. Recognizing his life, teaching, and death as the ultimate standard of human behavior, we may designate this standard *the law of Christ*. It includes but surpasses the natural moral law.

---

teachings of Christ. For that reason, they developed some admirable concepts, but their teachings fall short of the ethical ideal of Christ.

6

Virtues in Christian Life

The last chapter showed how the Holy Spirit himself becomes the Christian person's "educator," helping him to assimilate the teachings of Christ and to share in his life. In this chapter, we will investigate what this sharing in Christ's life really means. This sharing is the positive side of the healing of man's alienation from himself, from God, and from his fellow men. In turning to Christ, the person becomes a child of God again, which means being called to live and act in accordance with his divine dignity. To live as a child of God does not divest him of his humanity but rather perfects it. God deepens and stirs up our desire to find fulfillment only in him.

When we discussed conscience, we were speaking of the application of the moral law to individual actions. Now we will look at the Christian life more broadly and explore not just goodness in specific acts and decisions but the general habit of choosing good actions simply because of their goodness so that we live a life consistent with human and divine dignity. God infuses us with new abilities or powers to act in a way that shares in the life of Christ.

We will discuss the Christian virtues according to their two traditional categories. First, we will consider the theological virtues of faith, hope, and charity. Faith enables us to share in Christ's knowledge of the Father; hope allows us to share in Christ's trust of the Father; and charity, or love, gives us the ability to love God and neighbor with the very love of Christ.[1] Second, we will look at the natural virtues, such as prudence, justice, temperance, and fortitude, which receive a new, infused quality in the life of the Christian.[2]

Although we will discuss them one by one, the three theological virtues of faith, hope, and charity are always interwoven in this earthly life, relying on one another. To have divine love—in technical terms, Christian "charity"— means that one must necessarily have both faith and hope as well. Someone cannot love God unless he *believes* that God's Word is true and *hopes* that God, in his goodness, cares for him. Thus, love cannot exist without faith and hope. By contrast, one may have some faith in God's revelation and hope in God's goodness without truly loving him. A sinner may believe and hope in God and yet still be too weak to abandon his sinful ways and unite his will to that of God, which is the essence of true love. Saint Paul instructs us to acknowledge that love is the greatest of all virtues.[3] At the end of our life on earth, our faith will be replaced by our seeing God face-to-face, and our hope will be replaced by our actually possessing him; but love will come to fulfillment and remain forever.

---

[1] Josef Pieper, *Faith, Hope, Love* (San Francisco: Ignatius Press, 1997); Joseph Ratzinger, *To Look on Christ: Exercises in Faith, Hope, and Love*, trans. Robert Nowell (New York: Crossroad, 1991); Christopher Kaczor, *Thomas Aquinas on Faith, Hope, and Love: Edited and Explained for Everyone* (Ave Maria, Fla.: Sapientia, 2008).

[2] Josef Pieper, *The Four Cardinal Virtues* (Notre Dame, Ind.: University of Notre Dame Press, 1965); Christopher Kaczor and Thomas Sherman, *Thomas Aquinas on the Cardinal Virtues: Edited and Explained for Everyone* (Ave Maria, Fla.: Sapientia, 2009); Bill Donohue, *Why Catholicism Matters: How Catholic Virtues Can Reshape Society in the Twenty-First Century* (New York: Image, 2012).

[3] See 1 Cor 13:13.

Faith

The word "faith" is used in many ways. Saint Paul, following Jesus, speaks about faith as the surrender of the whole person to God by believing, trusting, and loving him. We shall return to this comprehensive biblical notion of faith when discussing prayer. In this chapter, however, we treat faith in a narrower sense, distinguishing it from love and trust. In this sense, "faith" means *accepting God's Word as true and holding fast to that Word because I believe that God is truth and truthful.*

Faith is more than simply believing that a fact is true when we lack empirical or rational evidence for it. This kind of belief yields a weaker relationship to the truth than rational knowledge does. When we believe not just a fact, but a person, we are basing our belief on the person's self-revelation. Belief in a person's self-revelation is, from a certain viewpoint, higher than even empirical or rational knowledge since the inner life of a person is impenetrable to the empirical or rational and can be reached only by faith. If we accept that the human person is the highest reality on earth, then knowledge of this through faith must rank higher than scientific evidence. Faith is a necessary condition of personal communication among people, for without mutual personal self-disclosure, people would remain strangers. If faith in this sense is necessary for establishing and cultivating relationships among people, how much more is faith necessary in responding to God's self-revelation?

As Saint Thomas Aquinas teaches, accepting God's self-revelation means accepting his Word, his eternal Son made flesh, Jesus Christ.[4] In his life, death, and Resurrection he

---

[4] *ST* II-II, q. 11, a. 1.

manifested and communicated to us his divine life, as well as the way and the means to return to him and be united with him: conformed to the Son by the Holy Spirit, we become children of the Father. Every doctrine of Christian faith can be thought of as a further unveiling of this basic mystery.

The first step, then, is to believe that all that Christ is —all that he did, suffered, and taught—is true. The absolute truthfulness of God's Word is the determining reason Christians believe in him. Our faith rests on a foundation that is much more solid than any human knowledge can be. To accept Christian teachings simply as useful human opinions—that is, to believe in them in the weaker sense— but not on God's authority is to lack the supernatural gift of Christian faith.

How do we know that Jesus Christ is truly the fullness of God's revelation and that all he taught is true? First, we have reasonable grounds for believing. We have a chain of witnesses, beginning with the writings of eyewitness apostles and their disciples (the New Testament), from whom we know that Christ has promised his effective presence in his Church and that the gates of hell will not prevail against her. Moreover, throughout the centuries, the Church has educated a great multitude of saints who have shown in their lives the truth and power of his teaching and who in some real sense have made Christ present for their contemporaries. However, a detailed investigation into why it makes sense for us to believe in the truth of our Catholic Christian faith does not belong to a theology of spirituality, for such an inquiry simply shows that it is reasonable to believe; it does not compel us to do so. As we have seen, faith is more than merely rational grounds for belief; it is a divinely infused virtue—a freely given grace that raises us up to share in God's knowledge.

a. The Development and Cultivation of Faith

Although faith is a divine gift, we should not just wait passively for this grace but pray for it and make the decision to believe. In retrospect, we will see that this free decision to believe was itself a gift of grace, and in the act of believing, we will have an intuitive, overwhelming awareness of its truth. To understand how faith can be cultivated and what dangers the Christian encounters along the way, it is helpful to look at the typical development of the faith of a child born into a Christian family.

Children learn about the world from their parents, and through their parents' faith, they learn about God and his kingdom. If their parents' faith is real—something more than social façade or mere habit—then the children will instinctively understand that they share in something authentic and valuable. As if by osmosis, their faith may also become real and develop an intuition of its truth. Those who teach religion to little children are often amazed at the sincerity and depth of their experience of God and supernatural things. They have not yet sinned seriously, so they feel very certain about God's love and heaven and are capable of developing a genuine personal relationship with Jesus.[5] The Church testified to the holiness of the children who witnessed the revelations of Mary at Fatima by beatifying them.

On the other hand, if the parents only pay lip service to Christianity and there is no one else near the child to take

---

[5] Robert Coles, *The Spiritual Life of Children* (Boston: Houghton Mifflin, 1990).

interest in and nurture his faith, he may be spiritually deprived, "undernourished" in matters of the soul. Children can sense a lie behind their parents' words, a void behind their actions. When such children reach adolescence, they may very likely face a serious crisis of faith.

Even children whose parents have true faith may experience a crisis of faith, a period of doubt and confusion about things they once took for granted, in their teenage years. Typically, the crisis comes when adolescents begin to scrutinize the way of life they have been exposed to by their parents and other important people in their lives. The parents' and teachers' beliefs seem suspect. Adolescents are no longer willing to accept certain things simply because someone tells them to. They reject their earlier reasons for believing, which they associate with immaturity and dependence, yet they have not found any substitutes for those reasons. They must now struggle toward a personal decision by which they can freely and independently accept the faith of the Church.

Anyone at any age may encounter a crisis of this kind. There are two great dangers at this stage. The person experiencing such a crisis may panic, fearing that he may lose his faith completely. Rejecting all rational inquiry, he may decide that faith should be mere emotion, a blind commitment of the heart alone. Those inclined in this direction easily fall victim to cults, which in return for the security of belonging to a close (and close-minded) group demand unthinking allegiance. At the other extreme, a person at this stage may throw himself into complete rationalism, deciding to accept only what he can understand. A person who chooses this way erroneously closes himself off to a rich experience of God's revelation: while God's mysteries are not alien to the human mind, they are infinitely above human comprehension. With the insight afforded by faith, however, the human mind can always pursue such mysteries further, forever discovering new reasons for admiring and loving God.

For anyone who is having a crisis of faith, the following practices are recommended:

1. Ask God for faith, in imitation of the prayer of the father who brought his sick boy to Jesus, saying, "I believe; help my unbelief!"[6]

2. Dig deeper into what the Church really believes rather than running in fear from the rational objections to faith. Many times, such spiritual difficulties, especially for adolescents, relate directly to lack of information. More knowledge leads to a more firmly grounded faith, even though faith requires us to go beyond mere human knowledge by relying on the truth of God's Word.

3. Continue practicing the faith, in spite of doubts, because one cannot really learn the truth of the Christian faith unless he practices it. For example, if someone believes he should obey Jesus' instruction to return good for evil—and believes it sufficiently to put it into practice—then he will learn on his own that he was right. Anytime someone obeys God's Word, he will have more peace in his soul and more goodness in himself, which will give him practical evidence that his faith is correct. Conversely, disobedience to God's Word proves the same thing in a negative way: inner peace and goodness begin to crumble as soon as one disobeys the Word of God.

In these ways, a person may pass through this crisis of faith and come to see that only the infinite God is totally transparent or intelligible to himself; he is *the Truth*. As God reveals himself and his plan, the person participates in God's self-understanding. But, to the person's finite intellect, God

---

[6] Mk 9:24.

in his inner life and plans appears as impenetrable mystery.[7] Yet as he adheres to God not only by faith but also by love, God begins to dwell in him, enlightening his mind and transforming his being. His soul regains its likeness to God and achieves a connaturality with the truths of faith. The dogmatic formulas he had been questioning now become signposts that direct his soul beyond itself to encounter the living Christ in his personal reality. The darkness of faith remains, and there may be no emotional reassurance; yet he now trusts that Christ lives in him. The mysteries of faith reveal their beauty, the infinite riches of God's love. Everything coheres, and what the soul had accepted beforehand out of obedience to the Church now begins to make sense. As he practices his faith, he becomes increasingly aware that doing God's will is a source of peace and contentment that nothing can take away from him.[8]

b. Sins against Faith

To better understand how faith develops, let us look at the consequences of failing to cultivate faith. Lack of faith, however, is not always caused by the failure to cultivate faith. Someone may have been open to the truth and investigated the ultimate questions of human life and yet, through no fault of his own, have failed to arrive at an explicit faith in God. "Explicit" is a necessary modifier here since a person who obeys his conscience and acknowledges that he must

[7] Jean Mouroux, *I Believe: The Personal Structure of Faith* (New York: Sheed and Ward, 1959); David Ruel Foster and Joseph W. Koterski, *The Two Wings of Catholic Thought: Essays on* Fides et Ratio (Washington, D.C.: Catholic University of America Press, 2003); Pope Francis, encyclical letter *Lumen Fidei* (June 29, 2013).

[8] In patristic and medieval tradition, these gifts are called understanding, knowledge, and wisdom.

do what is right, regardless of personal gain or loss, is already obeying God—even though he lacks explicit knowledge of him. One frequently encounters such nonbelievers who are closer to God than some Christians who only pay lip service to him.

On the other hand, lack of faith may indeed be the result of personal sins. Take, for example, the person who has never discovered God or Jesus Christ simply because he has not bothered to investigate. Perhaps he felt it was more important for him to assure his own material well-being or to further his career than to pursue the meaning of life. Such negligence occurs in varying degrees, the gravest form being a *total indifference to the truth*. How can the Holy Spirit lead someone to the truth who claims to have no interest in it? In our affluent society, where many people seem to have no time or energy to pursue any interest beyond the limits of their immediate lives, this sin is widespread.

Total indifference differs only slightly from the sin of *bad-faith unbelief*. The person who recognizes God, or Jesus Christ as coming from God, and nevertheless opposes this recognition commits the sin of bad-faith unbelief. For Saint John, this is the single greatest sin of which the world is guilty: the world refuses to acknowledge the Son of God and therefore remains in death.[9] This is the sin against the Holy Spirit referred to in the Synoptic Gospels as the sin for which there is no forgiveness; for the Holy Spirit alone can forgive the sinner, yet the sinner refuses to acknowledge him.[10]

Denial of one's faith is another sin against faith. A Christian is obligated to profess his faith openly, whenever and

---

[9] See 1 Jn 5:16.
[10] See Mt 12:30–32; Mk 3:28–30; Heb 6:4–6.

wherever God's glory and people's good require it. Under no circumstances is he permitted to deny his faith. Where there is a risk of persecution, the Christian need not affirmatively come forward, but when questioned by public authorities, he must acknowledge his faith, even if torture and death are the foreseeable results. Christ instructs us quite explicitly on this point: "Every one who acknowledges me before men, I also will acknowledge before my Father who is in heaven."[11] From its earliest days, the Church has never lacked the devoted participation of martyrs, who chose to die rather than deny their faith. To paraphrase a third-century theologian, the blood of martyrs has in many eras and in many countries proved to be the seed of Christians: that is, in demonstrating that the truth of the Gospel is more valuable to him than his very life, the martyr calls attention to the Gospel. He accepts his sufferings in peace and, forgiving his persecutors, helps to point their awareness to the presence of Christ's power in him.

A Christian commits the sin of *heresy* if he rejects in bad faith a truth revealed by God and taught as such by the Church (in theological language, this kind of truth is known as *dogma*). Bad faith is at work when, knowing the Church is the infallible teacher of God's revelation, he nevertheless rejects part of her dogma. *Hairesis*, from which we get the word "heresy," means "selection." The heretic's sin is his attempt to set himself up as a judge over God's Word. He tries to exercise dominion over that Word, choosing what to accept or reject, instead of allowing God's Word to rule over him.[12] Instead of hunting out heresy in other people,

---

[11] Mt 10:32.

[12] From the foregoing definition of "heresy," it should be clear why the Church does not think of modern Protestants as heretics. A person raised in a Protestant congregation will hardly be aware that, in rejecting various

we ought to be vigilant first and foremost of the danger of heresy in ourselves. We should be aware of how easy it is to approach God's Word like students choosing elective courses, abandoning whatever truth strikes us as too difficult and walking away from any doctrine that might demand a change of heart on our part. Each of us learns to be conveniently forgetful of certain parts of the Gospel. We can learn sober lessons from those so-called conservative Catholics, who like to forget about the obligations of the rich toward the poor, or from those so-called liberals, who appear to have forgotten about the sanctity of unborn life.

Hope

The second theological virtue, the virtue of hope, is well illustrated for us in salvation history. With the call of Abraham, Isaac, and Jacob, God begins a long and patient education course—a training in hope, whose goal is to prepare them and their descendants, the people of Israel, for the gift of his Son, in and by whom they are to share in God's own life and to proclaim and extend this gift to "all the families of the earth."[13]

a. The Hope of Israel

The lessons in hope that Israel learned in her history are of enormous value to every Christian. If we want to understand God's purpose in our lives and what he expects from

---

Catholic teachings, his church actually rejects part of God's revelation. Indeed, many Protestants actually believe, in good faith, the opposite: that they have preserved God's Word in its original purity, while Catholics have distorted it or added to it man-made doctrines.

[13] Gen 12:3.

us, we must attend the same "school" where Israel learned so much.

Over and over again, God allowed Israel to fall into humanly hopeless crises: Pharaoh enslaved and cruelly treated her; his army pursued her to the brink of the sea; the Israelites found themselves wandering in the desert, where there was neither food nor water. Having finally reached the Promised Land, they soon realized that it was a dangerous buffer zone between themselves and the competing powers that sought to destroy them. Throughout all this, God insisted upon complete trust from Israel. He showed his people that he alone could save them from Pharaoh's army; that he would provide them food and drink in the desert; that he would give them the land he had promised; and that he would preserve them from Assyria, Egypt, and Babylon if they would only trust in him instead of engaging in political maneuvering. Even when God punished the sins of Israel by sending her into exile, the punishment served to purify the remnant of her people. This traumatic history left Israel in suspense: After so much infidelity from his people, would God still fulfill his promises? In Christ, it became clear that God had given to Israel—and through Israel to the world—more than he had promised through the prophets. He himself became the inheritance of his people and, through his people, of the world.

b. The Hope of Jesus

Jesus relives, in his own life, the history of Israel, and his life perfects Israel's hope. The Gospel of Matthew, for example, recounts his baptism in the Jordan and his temptations in the desert. Jesus demonstrates complete trust in God under circumstances in which Israel refused to trust. As the storm clouds of opposition begin to gather around him, Jesus announces God's kingdom: God's forgiving, healing presence for all those who deliver themselves up to God in repentance. In the midst of increasing threats, Jesus knows that "not a hair of [their] head will perish,"[14] that his Father will see to their every need. Even when, in the Garden of Gethsemane, he confronts complete failure—his own people reject him, and his disciples fall asleep in fear and lack of understanding—Jesus continues to address God as "Abba, Father."[15] On the Cross, he prays the words of Psalm 22, which begins with a cry of anguish: "My God, my God, why have you forsaken me?"[16] but ends on a note of trust that the suffering of the Just One will bring about the kingdom:

> All the ends of the earth shall remember
>   and turn to the LORD;
> and all the families of the nations
>   shall worship before him.
> For dominion belongs to the LORD,
>   and he rules over the nations. . . .
>
> Posterity shall serve him;
>   men shall tell of the Lord to the coming generation,
> and proclaim his deliverance to a people yet unborn,
>   that he has wrought it.[17]

c. The Hope of the Christian

The hope of the Christian follows the hope offered to Israel and perfected in the life of Christ. A Christian's hope is not merely his own anticipation of reaching heaven; its object

---
[14] Lk 21:18.
[15] Mk 14:36.
[16] Ps 22:1; Mk 15:34.
[17] Ps 22:27–28, 30–31.

is the coming of God's kingdom, in which we will enjoy perfect communion through Jesus with the Father.

This hope is expressed when the Christian says in his everyday prayer, the Our Father, "Thy kingdom come," which means, "God, come into my heart and into the hearts of all people today through your Holy Spirit. Rule over us so completely that we want only what you want and that we carry out your will in all we do. May you also come in glory at the end of time to wipe away all tears. Destroy all evil so that your light may shine in a renewed universe, not just in me, but in everyone you have created and redeemed." All the petitions in the Our Father are powerful articulations of hope. For example, when we say, "Give us this day our daily bread," we express our hope that God will give us all that we need today—that he will take care of both the material and spiritual needs that must be met if we are to partake in his kingdom today and at the end of our lives.

In fact, we hold to the hope that "in everything God works for good"[18]—that everything that happens to us throughout the day, pleasant or unpleasant, joyful or painful, will serve to increase our ability to love God and other people. We should not limit this hope to ourselves but should extend it to all people and pray with the Church for them as well. The object of every Christian's hope for himself and for everyone may thus be defined this way: *to share in God's kingdom both now and, in its fullness, at the end of one's life.*[19]

The Christian must never lose sight of the paradoxical truth that one's true life begins at death and that everyone's

---

[18] Rom 8:28.
[19] Pope Benedict XVI, encyclical letter *Spe salvi* (November 30, 2007); Gabriel Marcel, *Homo Viator: Introduction to the Metaphysic of Hope*, trans. Emma Craufurd (London: Gollancz, 1951); Charles Péguy, *The Portal of the Mystery of Hope* (Grand Rapids, Mich.: Eerdmans, 1996).

day of death must therefore be thought of as his birthday. With this in mind, the Christian cannot fail to see how important every day of his earthly life now is. With God's grace, and through personal struggle in everyday situations and relationships, he aspires to develop the loving communion with God and other people that will definitively unfold its power only upon his death. Every one of his secular tasks—building his business, doing research, teaching, or whatever his work entails—will be vitally important to him, for the Christian knows that unless he is found faithful in small things, God will not entrust to him greater tasks in heaven.[20]

Like faith, hope is a virtue that develops throughout a Christian's life. Especially at the beginning of his spiritual journey, his hope tends to waver between confidence and fear. When we think about God's infinite love and faithfulness, we are inclined to be confident in our own salvation and that of others; but when we start to dwell on our capacity for unfaithfulness and evil, we find ourselves plummeting toward despair. However, as time passes, the many signs of God's mercy will convince us that he will use even the sins we repent of to bring us closer to him. For example, the memory of a confessed sin can humble us, making us more watchful for future temptations and more merciful toward others who may be struggling with the same sin.

As our hope develops and strengthens, it becomes clear that the ground of Christian hope is God himself—his absolute goodness and fidelity—and not anything that comes from us. The virtue of hope has been aptly summarized in the Latin phrase *sperare Deum per Deum a Deo*: "to hope for God from God through God." God is both the object and

---

[20] See Lk 16:10–12.

the source of our hope. Some Protestant churches believe that once someone has accepted Jesus Christ as his Savior, he is saved and cannot be lost. The Catholic Church, on the other hand, teaches that no one can be absolutely certain about his salvation. The outcome of everyone's earthly perseverance remains a matter of doubt unless and until God chooses to reveal it to him. Saint Paul urges the Philippians, "Work out your own salvation with fear and trembling."[21] Likewise, he warns the Corinthians against complacency: "Let any one who thinks that he stands take heed lest he fall."[22] Paul even admits his own concern about being rejected: "I do not run aimlessly, I do not box as one beating the air; but I pommel my body and subdue it, lest after preaching to others I myself should be disqualified."[23] Where do we feel safer, in God's hand or in ours? In hope the Catholic relies on God's mercy, not on his own affirmations of faith.

d. Sins against Hope

Sins against the virtue of hope fall into three categories. The first is indifference—either toward God's promises or toward spiritual values in general. This is a widespread sin, although it is hardly recognized by those who are guilty of it. We must beware of becoming the sort of Christian who worships God and works for his Church only to assure himself of material well-being or social standing. By not taking God's promises seriously, such a person shows that he does not consider God's goodness to be worthy of any real desire or effort on his part.

The second sin against hope is presumption: the Christian

[21] Phil 2:12.
[22] 1 Cor 10:12.
[23] 1 Cor 9:26–27.

continues to sin, taking it for granted that God will eventually forgive him. This, too, demonstrates a lack of appreciation for God's goodness, as if to say, "God is infinitely merciful, so he will forgive me. I already fell into sin, so let me then continue sinning until my next confession."

Finally, there is the opposite sin of despair, which is the Christian's conviction that he is so worthless that God either cannot or chooses not to forgive him. He thinks his sins are too great for God's mercy. Notice that here again, the root attitude is one of discounting the reality of God's goodness. To be distinguished from sinful despair are the mere feelings of despair or despondency. Feeling despair is not the same as committing the sin of despair—even Jesus and the saints felt despair, but it became for them a catalyst toward richer and deeper trust in God, a means of affirming that trust even more strongly. Clinical depression must also not be confused with the sin of despair. It is an illness, a psychiatric disorder that requires trained professional treatment.

Love (Charity)

As with the virtues of faith and hope, God is both the source and the goal of the virtue of love. Love is at the same time the beginning and the end of God's plan: it is his motive for creating man and his motive for entering into human history after man's fall. Likewise, it is the final goal of his plan: that all creation be taken up into the Trinitarian life of God.[24] Because God's love for us is both our source and

---

[24] Pope Benedict XVI, encyclical letter *Deus caritas est* (December 25, 2005); Francis de Sales, *The Art of Loving God: Simple Virtues for the Christian Life* (Manchester, N.H.: Sophia Institute Press, 1998); *The Conferences of St. Vincent de Paul to the Sisters of Charity*, 4 vols. (Westminster, Md.: Newman Press, 1952).

our end, the best way to understand the virtue of love in the life of the Christian is first to examine God's love for us.

a. Love as the Motive of Creation and Redemption

To approach the biblical notion of God, we have to move away from the popular misconception of him as an all-perfect but totally solitary Supreme Being. Instead, we should try to conceive of a *community*, one so perfect that its members share with one another all that they have and all that they are. This analogy is quite helpful, since Scripture and history show God to be a perfect communion of Father, Son, and Holy Spirit; in fact, the communion between these persons in their knowledge, their love, and their being is so complete that God is one nature, one being.

Since God is a perfect community, it should be clear that he did not need creation to enhance his own perfection and happiness. After all, how could love add anything to Love itself? What could joy add to Joy itself, or being to Being itself? In creating man and deciding to redeem him from sin, God aimed not at his own fulfillment but at the fulfillment of man. He created and redeemed man in order to share his own life and joy with him. The Father wanted to see his Son's beauty and goodness reflected in an innumerable multitude of children; the Son wanted to have many brothers and sisters; the Holy Spirit wanted to love the Father and the Son in many hearts. The analogy of a large, happy family helps us understand this mystery of God's generosity. When such a family decides to adopt a baby, it will not be because they need that child to make their family complete; rather, it will be because they want to share with him the love and happiness they already enjoy with one another.

The Christian view, then, should be clear: No person is

an accident. No person is unwanted. God wants us *to be* and *to grow* until we reach the fullness of life and love in him.[25]

With these considerations in mind, we are now prepared to look at God's love for mankind as it has been expressed historically in his spousal love for Israel and the Church. Scripture compares God's love for Israel to the jealous love of a husband for his bride. But Yahweh's love is at the same time very different from a husband's, for no husband creates his wife, whereas Yahweh, in sheer mercy, does create Israel and fashions her into a beautiful bride. Also, unlike any earthly husband, Yahweh has no need for Israel. In fact, his love transcends any human need. Taking all these qualifiers into account, we can nevertheless say that the metaphor of spousal love is indeed appropriate.

Since God longs for us, he chases us as a jealous husband goes after his unfaithful wife, and our turning back to him gives him great joy. Scripture also shows that when Israel becomes unfaithful and allows herself to be distracted by foreign gods, Yahweh punishes her with unrelenting wrath. Still, he remains faithful to her, and in "the fullness of time" he will forgive her all her iniquities. After purifying Israel, he will espouse her to himself forever in love, fidelity, and holiness.[26]

At the time of Jesus, those who were familiar with this Old Testament background would have understood the following exchange well: "'Why do John's disciples and the disciples of the Pharisees fast, but your disciples do not fast?' And Jesus said to them, 'Can the wedding guests fast while

---

[25] On the underlying philosophical issues see D. C. Schindler, *Love and the Postmodern Predicament: Rediscovering the Real in Beauty, Goodness, and Truth* (Eugene, Ore.: Cascade Books, 2018).

[26] See Ezek 16; Hos 2–3.

the bridegroom is with them?' "[27] The Messianic wedding feast proclaimed by Ezekiel and Hosea has been realized in the person of Jesus. And it is on the Cross that this bridegroom at last acquires his bride, the Church: "Christ . . . gave himself up for her, that he might sanctify her, having cleansed her by the washing of water with the word, that he might present the Church to himself in splendor, without spot or wrinkle or any such thing."[28] Ultimately, as the end of the New Testament foretells, the new Jerusalem shall be seen "coming down out of heaven from God, prepared as a bride adorned for her husband."[29]

So although God does not need us, he passionately pursues us, more ardently than the most jealous husband would. While we live, his love is offered to us in the sacraments: in reconciliation, his forgiveness; and in the Eucharist, the Body and Blood of his Son. The Church as a whole will be God's faithful bride for all eternity, but the individual children of God remain free to reject, in a definitive way, God's offer of spousal love.

A true lover is not content with partial gifts: he wants to give his whole self and invites his beloved to do the same; their goal is perfect exchange, perfect communion. And so in his desire to unite himself with us, God took upon himself a full human nature and a full human destiny, including the burden of our sins.[30] In his turn, God, in his Son, shares with us the fullness of his divine life. Through the Son, we are "filled with all the fulness of God."[31] This, then, is the perfect exchange about which the Fathers of the Church

---

[27] Mk 2:18–19.
[28] Eph 5:25–27.
[29] Rev 21:2.
[30] See, e.g., Is 53:4–5, 10; 2 Cor 5:21; Gal 3:13.
[31] Eph 3:19.

wrote so much: God makes his own all that is human and gives us all that is his by taking us up into his divine life.

By the mercy of God, we attain a certain mutuality, in love, with God himself. In Saint Bernard's words,

> Among all the movements, feelings, and emotions of the soul, love is the only one by which the creature can—even though not on an equal plane—respond to God or react to him in a way similar to his own. For instance, if God is angry with me, should I also become angry with him? Of course not. Rather, I fear and tremble and ask for pardon. Similarly, if he scolds me, I do not scold him in return, but rather acknowledge that he is right. If he judges me, I do not judge him, but rather worship him.
>
> When saving me, he does not at the same time seek to be saved by me; nor does God, who frees everyone, seek to be set free by anyone. If he rules, I must serve him; if he commands, I must obey him rather than give him orders or tasks.

Now you begin to see how different it is with love. When God loves, all he wants is to be loved. He loves for no other purpose than to be loved in turn. He knows that those who love him are made happy by this very love.[32]

b. The Development of God's Love in the Christian

The love of God, though, is much more than just a model for us: *the Christian is enabled to love with the very love of God*. God takes us up into his divine Trinitarian life by pouring into our hearts his Holy Spirit, the bond of love between Father and Son. Thus, in the Spirit we are enabled to love

---

[32] *Sermones super Cantica canticorum*, sermo 83, chap. 4, in *Sancti Bernardi Opera*, ed. J. Leclercq and H.M. Rochais (Rome: Editiones Cistercienses, 1966), 2:301.

Christ and our fellow men with the love with which the Father loves them. We share in the same love that causes the Father to wait for all his prodigal sons and forgive all his enemies—all those who have contributed in some way to the murder of his only Son. We also share in the love with which the Son loves his Father and carries out the Father's plan to save fallen mankind—the love by which he gave his life for all sinners, his enemies. These are the reasons a Christian's love must not be selfish, cliquish, or exclusive. The Christian extends forgiveness to his enemies just as he himself has been forgiven by the Father and redeemed by the Son, who died on account of his sins.

As it reaches into and transforms the person, God's love acts as the source of a threefold love: self-love, love for God, and love for one's neighbor. Only God's love is powerful enough to create a good person and then to re-create that goodness in him after he has fallen. Only God's love is powerful enough to convince a person that he is valuable, not just for a while, but for eternity. So once God has forgiven us and renewed us by his forgiveness, we have a solid basis for self-esteem.[33] Having learned to accept and value ourselves, we can extend our acceptance and appreciation to others. We feel motivated, then, to love God, whose love has made us valuable. On the other hand, without self-esteem, we cannot love our neighbor, who may appear so much like

---

[33] Lack of self-esteem or self-love is quite common. It manifests itself in a variety of ways, including (a) envy of others: the person who lacks self-esteem wants to be someone other than himself; (b) compulsive talk about himself: he tries to prove, with words, his importance; (c) self-effacing silence: he does not risk saying anything, for fear his incompetence may be exposed; (d) obnoxiousness: subconsciously believing he deserves rejection, he acts in ways that assure he will, in fact, be rejected: "No matter what I do, they despise me, so I must be worthless"; or (e) hatred of others: "No matter what I do, they despise me, so they must be truly evil."

ourselves that he deserves scorn or so much better than we are that we envy his comparative greatness. We also find ourselves hating the Creator, who did not make us better than we are.

As creatures blessed with the love of God, we are responsible for communicating this love to one another, thereby helping in one another's growth. Consider, for example, how important the role is that parents play during the first years of their child's life. Before he can even express it in words, the baby feels and learns true love. If he feels loved and accepted for his own sake, rather than as a mere extension of his parents' egos, then as time passes, the child will be convinced of his own worth and of the reality of love in the world. He will find it easy to believe in a loving God whose love his parents have mediated to him. In a similar way, spouses and friends, priests and teachers are called upon to mediate God's love. Every human relationship, in fact, must in its own way be transformed by this love.

c. Love for One's Enemies

If a Christian shares in the love God has for him, he cannot avoid loving his enemies, since God loves those who are his enemies: "God shows his love for us in that while we were yet sinners Christ died for us. . . . While we were enemies, we were reconciled to God by the death of his Son."[34] Since Christ died for his enemies, his instruction is credible: "You have heard that it was said, 'You shall love your neighbor and hate your enemy.' But I say to you, Love your enemies and pray for those who persecute you, so that you may be sons of your Father who is in heaven; for he makes his sun

---

[34] Rom 5:8, 10.

rise on the evil and on the good, and sends rain on the just and on the unjust."[35]

Many times, enmity is the result of a misunderstanding or an offense for which I am just as responsible as my supposed "enemy." Taking the initiative in apologizing and trying to clear up the misunderstanding may well settle the issue; by showing respect and appreciation for the other person, I am likely to open up the way to a friendlier relationship. But suppose my enemy is genuinely bent on harming me. What if, even when I give him the benefit of the doubt with regard to his motives, those motives still look unambiguously evil to me? To love even such people as these becomes psychologically possible when we consider the following: we are not commanded to *like* our enemies but to *love* them—that is, to accept and appreciate them as persons and to do good to them if they are in need and we can help them.

We ought to hate not the evil person himself but the evil within him. This distinction rests on the truth that he was created in God's image and redeemed by the blood of God's Son. As long as he is here on earth, he retains the potential for good.[36] We want this potential to increase and develop. This is love. But again, making this distinction in our enemies is possible only if we are able to make it in ourselves: just as we identify and condemn the evil in ourselves and yet love ourselves and desire to improve, we do the same for those we are tempted to despise. In fact, the very act of perceiving

---

[35] Mt 5:43-45.

[36] We cannot make this distinction in the case of a person in hell. The damned person has definitively identified himself with evil. He has so hardened his opposition to God that there is no more potential for good in him, and thus he cannot convert. So it would no longer make sense at this point to "hate the evil but love the person." *The person himself has become evil*; this is why he is in hell. See Bernard of Clairvaux, *Sermones super Cantica canticorum*, sermo 50, chap. 7, in *Sancti Bernardi Opera*, 2:82.

and condemning the evil in my enemy places me in a kind of solidarity with him. If I am repelled by the evil I can see only on the surface of his soul, how much more repugnant must God find the evil he can see in the depths of my heart! Yet God forgives me again and again. As contemptible as my actions and thoughts have been, he surrounds me with his love. Knowing this, how can I reject my enemy?

d. Sins against Love

As unpleasant as it is to hear someone blurt out "I hate his guts!" the real sin of hatred is not simply an unthinking expression of intense dislike. The sin of hatred comes in two forms. The first is refusing to accept another person, wishing evil on him or doing evil to him, or enjoying the evil done to him by a third person. The second kind of sin against love—a sin that is even more serious than hatred—is *indifference*. A hater can be more easily transformed into a loving person than one who simply doesn't care. And unfortunately, falling into an attitude of indifference is much easier than actively hating someone. For example, a wealthy employer may not feel any hatred toward an employee who has been hit with some terrible misfortune and has nowhere else to turn, but if the boss simply walks away in indifference, that would be a serious sin. Similarly, if a leading politician of a prosperous country could help a country starving from famine but refuses to do so, this also would be a sin against love, for "love your neighbor as yourself"[37] applies to relationships between countries as well as to relationships between individuals.

Many times, the sin of indifference masquerades as an all-permissive kindness. Parents or teachers who simply close

---

[37] Lev 19:18.

their eyes to the faults of those entrusted to their care do not really love them. By allowing everything, they show that they are indifferent; they cannot pretend to want the children's good if they are unwilling to oppose whatever threatens this good.

The Natural Virtues

In addition to the theological virtues of faith, hope, and love, there are natural virtues. Here, we will discuss humility, temperance, asceticism and self-denial, courage, justice, and prudence and wisdom. The virtues are best understood as ways in which the theological virtue of love is expressed. The perfection of love of God and love of neighbor is the goal and aspiration of Christian moral life, which is never fully attained on this earth. But in order to be perfect, love must have some definite characteristics: these are the natural virtues. They are called "natural" because people in a state of mortal sin who do not possess the theological virtues of faith, hope, and love may still possess to some extent these natural virtues by their own powers. In contrast, the theological virtues of faith, hope, and love are gifts of undeserved grace freely bestowed by God. For those who receive them, the natural virtues will also receive a new finality and new perfection. They will become the concrete expression and modality of love.

a. Humility

What have I not received from God? I owe him not only the origin of my entire being but the whole of my being at every moment of my life; he has given me the ability to accept the Holy Spirit freely and to decide to cooperate with his grace freely. All this good in me is pure, undeserved gift. Put simply, humility is the recognition of that fact. *It is accepting the reality of my relationship with God and other people.* It acknowledges the almighty power of God at work in creating free creatures and giving them the power to actualize their freedom. Saint Paul is quite clear on this point: "What have you that you did not receive? If then you received it, why do you boast as if it were not a gift?"[38]

A simple question like this will prevent me from comparing myself with somebody and thinking, "I'm better than he is." How can I know, for starters, how much that other person has received from God? Perhaps I have received much more than he has and yet have cooperated with God's grace much less than he has. Moreover, how can I foresee either his or my ultimate end? Perhaps he will change for the better while I will fall further and further from God. And how do I know which is dearer in God's sight: a decent life with a streak of hidden conceit or a "bad life" that ends in sincere sorrow?

These considerations will help us understand the truth of Jesus' words: "Whoever exalts himself will be humbled, and whoever humbles himself will be exalted."[39] From a superficial reading, we may interpret these words as a clever trick to assure promotion, but the true meaning expresses the fundamental law of Christian holiness. If I think I am great by myself, I don't allow any place in me for God's gifts to enter. Thus, I am, in reality, nothing. To the extent, however, that I acknowledge that I am nothing by myself, I allow God's ennobling—indeed, divinizing—love to lift me up. Thus, Christian humility is the way to attain a very high, but also correct, self-esteem, knowing ourselves to be children

---

[38] 1 Cor 4:7.
[39] Mt 23:12; see also Lk 14:11.

of God.[40] There are, of course, obvious variations among natural talents, abilities, and achievements. The essence of humility is to acknowledge the truth; thus, to deny our talents or achievements could only be called false humility. Instead, each of us should rejoice in our talents and achievements but give the credit for them to God.

But Christian humility incorporates more than just this acknowledgment of the truth. It is also solidarity with the poor and lowly, in love and in imitation of the humility of the Son of God. If all that the Son of God had wanted was to live according to the truth of his being, he could have clung to his equality in dignity and glory with his Father. And yet he "did not count equality with God a thing to be grasped, but emptied himself, taking the form of a servant, being born in the likeness of men. And being found in human form he humbled himself and became obedient unto death, even death on a cross."[41] That is, the Son renounced his glory, his divine way of life, and lowered himself to the extent of becoming not only a man but a slave, the least of all men—and then carried the burden of our sins and suffered our death.

Humility in itself is a natural virtue. But Christian humility is more than that—it is a share in the humility of Christ. It is a readiness to give up even well-deserved high status or legitimate privilege and to take up solidarity with the poorest and lowliest. To use the popular phrase coined by the bishops of Latin America, humility is a "preferential option for the poor." Church history is full of ingenious ex-

---

[40] Bernard Bonowitz, *Saint Bernard's Three-Course Banquet: Humility, Charity, and Contemplation in the* De Gradibus (Collegeville, Minn.: Liturgical Press, 2013); J. Augustine Wetta, *Humility Rules: Saint Benedict's Twelve Step Guide to Genuine Self-Esteem* (San Francisco: Ignatius Press, 2013).

[41] Phil 2:6–8.

amples of saints who lived in solidarity with society's downtrodden. They did this not because misery and suffering are values in themselves but because a loving person naturally wants to bridge the gap between himself and his loved ones. In this way, they combined humility with Christian love, which recognizes the image of God even in an unwashed face or crippled mind.

b. Temperance

A Christian psychologist has said,

> When we hear the word temperance, we are likely to conjure up an image of a dull, self-righteous, moralizing old maid who has channeled all the goodness urges into hypocrisy and vindictiveness. We think of her going around trying to prevent others from enjoying food or drink or card playing or dancing or sex. She is a distant cousin of the Irish monsignor who used his thorn stick to break up crossroad dances. Her nose is blue, her brow is furrowed, her body is lean and haggard, and she is *against*.[42]

Such distortions of the ideal of temperance have occurred repeatedly during the Church's history. It is easy to understand why. Since the Fall, man has been inclined to abuse pleasure, especially those pleasures associated with the instincts of self-preservation and of preserving the species. The problem is that these pleasures of the flesh have the tendency to take over a man's entire life.

To counter this threat, we often seek an immediately appealing, albeit false, solution in the opposite extreme: "Let us diligently suppress all pleasure and live as if we had no

[42] Andrew M. Greeley, *Life for a Wanderer: A New Look at Christian Spirituality* (New York: Doubleday, 1969), 57.

body." But to ignore our bodies is to risk losing our humanity. If one fails to find delight in eating a good meal or in seeing a beautiful person of the opposite sex, he becomes a less sensitive person. Trying to force these powerful instincts out of existence, instead of channeling them in the right direction, is like damming up a strong-running river. Admittedly, the river needs strong walls to guide it, but any attempt to block it completely can only lead to disaster: sooner or later, it will overwhelm the dam that has been built. Thus, it is no accident that wherever Puritanism has ruled supreme, sexual licentiousness has inevitably followed.

Pleasure and joy normally indicate the presence of a value. Every value, in turn, is linked to some pleasure or joy. While these two words are often used interchangeably, there is an important difference between them: "pleasure" connotes some gratifying physical reaction, while "joy" refers to a pleasant emotional reaction. In what follows, we shall use the words in accordance with these two distinct yet connected meanings.

A material good or value (for instance, tasty food or a beautiful body) will normally cause some pleasure; an aesthetic, intellectual, or spiritual good or value (such as solving a difficult math problem, reading a good novel, meeting a friend, or becoming absorbed in prayer) may cause joy. But man is, after all, the unity of soul and body; therefore, we cannot entirely separate the realm of pleasure from that of joy. My savoring of a wonderfully prepared meal—a bodily pleasure—may blend with my intellectual enjoyment of the dinner conversation or with the emotional comfort I take in my friends' having included me in the event itself. Likewise, a spiritual value like prayer will sometimes be accompanied by an actual sensation of pleasure in the body. The point is that *both pleasure and joy are meant to transport us outside ourselves, to open us up to the world, to other people, and to God.* Pleasure and joy should bring home to us with wordless authority the knowledge that everything God has created is very good: our lives, our bodies, lush meadows and calming sunsets, other people, and, above all, God.

Tragically, though, as a result of original sin, the sins of our ancestors, and our own personal sins, pleasure and joy are no longer entirely reliable indicators of value. A person may let the pleasures of the senses, such as eating and drinking and engaging in sexual pleasure, or the emotional craving for wealth or power dominate his life and blind him to higher values. If a person allows himself to be swept away by blind indulgence, he will begin to close in upon himself. His indulgence will make him selfish and withdrawn. Every time he looks at the world or other people, this preoccupation will express itself with the questions, How can I use this or that thing or person? In what way can I get pleasure from this object?

The virtue of temperance does not mean we must detest or deny pleasure or joy. That would imply a denial of the goodness of God's creatures. And lest we imagine that food, drink, sex, possessions, and power are the only values accompanied by pleasure or joy, we should recognize the power and attraction of intellectual and spiritual values: there is a joy to be felt in the contemplation of beauty, in finding truth, and in achieving moral goodness in oneself or admiring it in others. But the most uplifting joys lie in unselfish love of people and, even more, in love of God. If we have never experienced such joys in our lives, the reason may be that we have allowed ourselves to be overwhelmed by these lower passions. Rather than avoiding pleasure and joy, then, temperance seeks order in one's approach to pleasures and joys so that they may help rather than hinder one's growth in the love of God's creation and especially of other people and God himself.[43]

c. Asceticism and Self-Denial

Original sin has resulted in a disorder of our desires for pleasure and joy. This distortion makes asceticism and self-denial necessary. Christian asceticism, from the Greek *askeo* (to struggle), involves exertion to create order in our lives: we discipline our desires so that we may become balanced, mature people who are in communion with God and others and who enjoy the goodness and beauty of creation.

One of the biggest roadblocks to happiness in Western culture is our ready access to instant gratification. We are accustomed to having whatever we want, whenever we want it: we can study, watch TV, listen to music, and chew gum, all at the same time. Yet, *paradoxically, if there is no restriction on our pleasures, life feels boring and empty.* Fascinated by endless possibilities, we find it impossible to choose some and give up others. As a result, many people remain in an adolescent mentality of just "exploring life" and may not find any worthwhile goal before their midthirties or beyond.

To counteract this tendency toward boredom and restlessness, we need to impose order on our lives. We need to choose some goals and discover the pleasures offered by them; at the same time, we need to realize that this will entail cutting out other possibilities that are incompatible. One cannot simultaneously be a park ranger and a business executive or be married and celibate. Rather, in choosing and then devoting ourselves to a goal—a vocation—we focus our energies and intensify our joy in living. Picture a

---

[43] Josef Pieper, *Fortitude and Temperance* (New York: Pantheon, 1954).

stream running between solid banks: it will have far greater energy and power than if the same water were allowed to spread out in all directions over the plain.

Having acknowledged all this, we must nevertheless recognize the need to deny ourselves even legitimate pleasures on occasion. We must at times go without even those things that we could enjoy without jeopardizing our life's project. Doing so offers invaluable training for the inevitable moments when our life project or our love for people and for God will require giving up some intense and apparently indispensable pleasures. For example, a person might discipline himself by restricting or even avoiding on certain days the pleasures of eating and drinking (fasting) or by getting up earlier than normal in the morning; married people might agree to abstain for a while from sexual intercourse. These acts of self-denial offer a greater freedom from the pleasures of the flesh and also a greater desire for other values, such as prayer, study, and helping others.

There can be no doubt that God has created us for joy and happiness. In the end, he will give us back our bodies, raised to a new and immortal life in the Spirit. When that time comes, we will be able to enjoy everything according to its true value. Until then, however, we struggle to appreciate everything according to its true value because the pleasures and joys we feel sometimes confuse us.

As long as our highest value remains love of God and love of people, some pure joy—holding in itself the promise of mysterious fulfillment—will always remain with us here on earth. This has proven to be true, no matter how terrible the circumstances. Imagine, for example, being locked away in a concentration camp, sick, starving, and without any access to loving family or friends. Yet people who lived through such situations in World War II have testified that those in the camps who had a deep love of God were able to survive enormous afflictions with peace and dignity.

d. Courage

Temperance, as we have seen, serves love by creating order among the various pleasures, helping us choose those pleasures that conform with true love and reject those that do not. Courage, or fortitude, is a virtue that also serves love by helping us do what it requires, even in the face of shame or terror.

Sometimes, in order to do the good required of us, we must accept great risks. As we have already seen, one must accept death rather than deny one's faith. In most places today, at least in the West, professing one's Christianity almost never subjects a person to physical danger, yet there are other, more insidious pressures: the sting of being teased, the loss of a job or image, the loss of friends. A person may jeopardize election to a prestigious post if he holds certain "politically incorrect" positions. Health-care workers, especially, are in danger of losing their jobs if they refuse to cooperate in procedures that violate the natural moral law. Other situations arise in which death may be a very real possibility if one is to save another human being. For example, a doctor or priest who risks contracting a deadly disease is still obligated to care for the sick and dying.

But it often takes more courage to live than to die. One needs courage, for example, to accept and care for an intellectually or physically disabled child. Indeed, simply being willing to raise children in today's world requires courage. Often we need courage just to be ourselves, to think and say what we believe, instead of parroting safe clichés or voicing opinions that endear us to people with power. We cannot commit our entire lives to a cause or to a person without this virtue; how do we know now that we will feel the same way twenty years from now? A lack of courage may be one reason that so many people are afraid to get married, preferring just to live together, or that so few have dared to commit themselves to the priesthood. A courageous person does not know any better than a coward does how he will feel twenty years from now, but he remains confident in his own strength and God's grace that he will stay faithful to his commitment.

e. Justice

Justice is the virtue that steadfastly gives to all people, all communities, and all institutions what is due to them. In upholding personal justice, a person pays his debts; avoids cheating on his income tax; pays appropriate wages to his employees; gives enough time, attention, and material comfort to his family; and provides for his children a good education both at home and at school. A just legislator pushes for just laws. A just member of the executive branch sees to just enforcement of the law. A just judge does everything possible to impose just punishment on the guilty and to acquit the innocent. In everyday terms, the virtue of justice simply means fulfilling one's measurable obligations, whether as payment, work, or teaching. It does not necessarily directly involve love.

Conversely, however, true love presupposes justice. Without justice, love degenerates into vague feelings, unreflective passion, or ineffective desire. A husband may claim to love his wife sincerely, but if he fails to give her the quality time that she deserves, he is not only unjust toward her but also unloving. If a father takes no interest in his children's education, his love lacks something essential. If an employer demonstrates great compassion toward his injured employee but at the same time fails to pay him a just salary, his love for the employee is certainly doubtful. Many people, in fact, prefer to show love and generosity when and where they choose, while neglecting to fulfill the duties of strict justice. We should beware of behaving like the young man who enthusiastically organized a summer school for needy children but refused his parents' request that he tutor his younger brother, who was failing in school.

True love, then, must include justice, even though love is much greater than justice. To see how much greater love is than mere justice, consider the husband who showers his wife with gifts and is attentive to her needs and polite in conversation but does not love her. While we say that love cannot be measured, seen, heard, or touched, we cannot fail to notice when love is missing. When a husband loves his wife, he admires and appreciates her; he receives her into his own being and allows her to receive him into herself. A wife who is not really loved and does not have the courage to love her husband without reciprocation might resign herself to a tepid coexistence with this man—or she might file for divorce. If she did the latter, her husband would probably not understand. "What haven't I given her?" he might ask. "I gave her everything she needed and wanted, more than I had to, yet she complains that I was a poor husband."

An old proverb captures this irony well: *Summa iustitia summa iniuria*—the greatest justice is the greatest injustice. In other words, if you behave toward another person with perfect justice, neither more nor less, then in fact you have failed to do real justice to that person. For every person, created in God's image and deemed so valuable by God that he gave his Son for him, deserves something more: to be loved. Anything less than true love is ultimately an injustice toward someone. Giving full justice to a person, therefore, paradoxically entails loving him.[44] By the same token, our love for other people demands that we fulfill the requirements of justice. The two virtues of love and justice are inseparably intertwined.

f. Prudence and Wisdom

Prudence is the virtue that inclines us to reach the right decision in a given situation.[45] In nearly every moment of our lives, we are offered a choice between values; they may seem equally attractive, yet conflicting. For some, deciding how to spend a Saturday night is complex enough; consider the complexities that are present when choosing a college, a profession, or a spouse. Prudence weighs the values involved, sorts out the choices insofar as they seem good for the person under the circumstances, and helps the person identify one choice as the best. Certainly, moral values enter into the equation, but there are also personal factors to consider, like talents, abilities, and interests. Everyone must also learn to listen to his emotions.

An important part of decision-making is the ability to live with one's mistakes. Andrew Greeley writes, "Prudence is not a virtue which will guarantee us that we will avoid mistakes. On the contrary, it's far more likely to guarantee us that we *will* make mistakes. There are not many certainties in the human condition. Most of the decisions we make in our lives (beside the basic commitments of faith) would

---

[44] While everyone deserves the love of every other person, prudence and justice will determine how and to what degree that love should be expressed. Not all people can or should be loved in the same way. For example, a mother should love both her own children and those of a friend, but she cannot and should not love the latter equally with her own children.

[45] Josef Pieper, *Prudence: The First Cardinal Virtue* (New York: Pantheon, 1959).

best be based on a high degree of probability."[46] We should have enough self-confidence to live with our mistakes and eventually to learn from them. By postponing decisions, the indecisive man forfeits many of his choices. For instance, if he misses the deadline for applying to the country's best colleges, the school he ultimately attends will necessarily be second-rate. If, feeling love and admiration for a particular woman, he hesitates to commit himself to her, he should not be surprised when she chooses someone else for a husband.

Prudence becomes much easier for us when we are part of a community of faith and love or when we have good friends whose judgment we respect. In Greeley's words,

> The more open our relationships are with other human beings, the easier prudence becomes. As we understand them and they understand us, we come to understand ourselves better. In the marvelous interaction of self-revelation and mutual appreciation, we become more firmly grounded in reality and freer of the distorted fantasies that our frightened imagination has generated. A close friendship, a deeply meaningful and happy marriage, a satisfying web of personal relationships are the best guarantees of prudence, because such relationships immerse us in the bright dawn of reality and clear away the fog of self-deception. We see things as they are, because the love of others enables us to see ourselves as we are. We make our decisions, indeed, by ourselves, perhaps in a moment of cold isolation, but we also make them as part of a community, a community whose love and concern for us generates a wisdom that by ourselves we could never attain.[47]

This, indeed, is true wisdom: to see ourselves, other people, and things in general as they really are, according to

---

[46] Greeley, *Life for a Wanderer*, 101.
[47] Greeley, *Life for a Wanderer*, 109–10.

their real value. We can possess such wisdom only in a very limited way here on earth and only if we learn to love and value things as God loves and values them. But God will not deny us such a gift in the long run if we pray for it, study the wisdom of Christ and the saints, become part of the church community, cultivate good friendships, and dare to practice our own reasoning power.

Saint Bernard describes the wise man as *cui quaeque res sapiunt prout sunt*: he "to whom all things taste (exactly) as they are."[48] In other words, the wise man has a spiritual "sense of taste": he appreciates everything according to its real value. His affections correspond to reality. For example, he has greater affection for God than for man, for a saint than for a hypocrite; yet, on the level of action, he might spend more time and energy helping a hypocrite than enjoying a conversation with a saint. Having developed this "taste" for the good, he chooses what is truly good by this cultivated instinct rather than by a tiresome process of reasoning. Of course, Saint Bernard recognizes that this is an ideal we strive for here on earth, even if we will never fully realize it.

---

[48] Bernard of Clairvaux, *Sermones de diversis*, sermo 18, chap. 1, in *Sancti Bernardi Opera*, vol. 6, bk. 1, pp. 157–58.

7

The Sacraments

All virtues in the full sense of the word are rooted in, and built up, by grace; and all grace comes from Christ crucified and risen, present in the Eucharist of the Church. For this reason Saint Thomas declares, "This sacrament has the power to confer grace by itself and no one has grace before receiving this sacrament except by its desire."[1]

All the other sacraments have grace from the Eucharist and are ordained toward the Eucharist. Each of them conforms an aspect of our human existence to an aspect of the mystery of Christ. Baptism sanctifies the beginning Christian life by conforming the new member of the Church to Christ's death and Resurrection. Confirmation endows him with the threefold dignity of Christ: prophet, priest, and king. The sacrament of penance, or reconciliation, restores or improves the broken or wounded relationship between Christ and the sinner. In the anointing of the sick, the sick person is conformed to the sufferings and Resurrection of Christ so that he can overcome the despair and apathy caused by the illness. In marriage the couple shares in the relationship and love that unites Christ and the Church. And in holy orders the candidate is called to represent Christ, the head of his body, the Church. We see how all pre-sacramental and sacramental grace is not just some impersonal power

---

[1] *ST* III q. 79, a. 1, ad. 1. The Latin word for "desire" is *votum*, meaning the reception of a sacrament by desire.

mediated to us through words and gestures. Instead, the sacraments initiate, strengthen, deepen, and qualify our personal conformation to Christ, while in the Eucharist we become one body and one spirit with him.

In what follows we intend not to give a full treatise on the sacraments but only to focus on what is closely connected with the birth, growth, and restoration of spiritual life. In doing so, we will pay special attention to how the sacraments are symbolic expressions of Christ's sanctifying actions (while also actually bestowing the grace that they symbolize). The material aspects of the sacraments reveal spiritual realities: for example, water means the purification and new life of a soul; bread and wine mean its nourishment; ointment means healing; and the imposition of hands means a communication of power.

The Sacrament of Baptism

> Go therefore and make disciples of all nations, baptizing them in the name of the Father and of the Son and of the Holy Spirit, teaching them to observe all that I have commanded you; and behold, I am with you always, to the close of the age.[2]

The Greek text that is translated here as "in the name of" is *eis to onoma*—that is, "unto the name" of the Father, the Son, and the Holy Spirit. The context of the phrase is most likely the language of a property transaction: a thing (*res*), including slaves in Roman law, is transferred into the possession of the person named. The baptized person is "transferred" into the possession of the Triune God, joins the original

---

[2] Mt 28:19–20.

disciples of Jesus, and obligates himself to observe all that Jesus has taught. Jesus also extends his presence to him.

a. Baptism as a Participation in the Death and Resurrection of Christ

Saint Paul enriches the theology of baptism in the New Testament by declaring that baptism is a participation in the death and Resurrection of Christ and an incorporation into the Body of Christ, which is the Church.

> Do you not know that all of us who have been baptized into Christ Jesus were baptized into his death? We were buried therefore with him by baptism into death, so that as Christ was raised from the dead by the glory of the Father, we too might walk in newness of life.
>
> For if we have been united with him in a death like his, we shall certainly be united with him in a resurrection like his.[3]

This aspect of baptism is easiest to see when it takes the form of full immersion into water: "into Christ Jesus." In addition to becoming the possession of Christ, the baptized person is "baptized into his death." What immersion symbolizes truly happens: the old self is buried under the waters and a new man rises with the risen Christ, enabled to live in the newness of life. Participation in the dying and rising of Christ is carried out through the daily life of the Christian until it is completed at his physical death. Every time we resist a sinful tendency and choose to do God's will, our dying to sin progresses and the newness of life is strengthened in us.

This needs some explanation. The Christian not only

[3] Rom 6:3–5.

shares in the death of Christ through baptism but by the same rite also shares in his Resurrection. Neither sharing is a mere metaphor that refers only to a change in outlook or moral conduct. Paul means a real introduction into the death of Christ and a real share in the Resurrection of Christ. The resurrection of the Christian is effected by the same almighty power of the Father who raised Jesus from the dead. "The newness of life" that the baptized Christian receives from the risen Christ is so radically new that Paul expresses it as a "new creation": "Therefore, if any one is in Christ, he is a new creation; the old has passed away, behold, the new has come."[4] The Christian who emerges from the baptismal pool is as different from what he was before as the world was different after Creation from the nothingness that preceded it. This newness of life, however, is merely a beginning, a "seed," to use Saint John's expression.[5] In order to unfold its full potential, we must "walk in newness of life"; that is, our daily living should be transformed so that the new life we received may release its full power in us: "For if we have been united (*symphytoi*) with him in a death like his, we shall certainly be united with him in a resurrection like his. We know that our former man was crucified with him so that the sinful body might be destroyed, and we might no longer be enslaved to sin."[6]

The Greek word *symphytoi* means "grown [into union] with [him]," like a branch is grafted onto the trunk of a tree: it underlines the reality of our union with Christ that takes place by means of our baptism. The "former man"—literally our "old man"—means the man we once were, our person under the dominion of sin. "The sinful body" is lit-

---

[4] 2 Cor 5:17.
[5] 1 Jn 3:9.
[6] Rom 6:5–6.

erally "the body of sin," synonymous with "body of death" and "body of flesh"[7]—the grammatical structure refers to the force that dominates unredeemed man: "body" does not mean the material element alone but the whole earthly man. In baptism, this old self we once were, this breeding ground of sin, has been put to death; since our old self, which was under the dominion of sin, has been destroyed, we are freed from slavery to sin.

Yet just after Saint Paul speaks of being set free from the slavery of sin, he writes, "Let not sin therefore reign in your mortal bodies, to make you obey their passions."[8] This exhortation seems to contradict what he stressed so much before: that we have died to sin's dominion and are now alive with the life of the risen Christ. Why must we still struggle lest sin reign over us? With a closer look, however, the apparent contradiction simply expresses the tension inherent in Christian existence: we are "a new man," yet we must still "put off the old man"; we are raised to a new life with Christ, yet we must still be "renewed" in our minds and hearts.[9] This tension is even expressed in the grammar he uses: he begins with a statement ("you have died") but immediately transitions to a command ("put to death therefore what is earthly in you"[10]). The Christian is already dead to sin and alive with the life of Christ, but he has to live daily according to this new source of life (the Holy Spirit) in order to unfold into full maturity what he has received. This means dying daily to a self-centered existence and opening up to God again and again in trust, love, and obedience.

What Christ has done and suffered for us (climaxing in his

[7] Rom 7:24; Col 1:22.
[8] Rom 6:12.
[9] Eph 4:22–23.
[10] Col 3:3, 5.

death and Resurrection) are historical events that took place in time and space. Yet they are not mere ordinary human acts but acts of the God-man (*theandric* acts). As such, their efficacy transcends the limits of time and space. Since through these acts Christ wanted to redeem the entire human race, their efficacy extends to the whole of human history and reaches everyone. Thus, in baptism, the suffering, death, and Resurrection of Christ are not made present again in their historical-temporal reality; in other words, Christ does not die or rise again whenever a baptism is administered. But the death and Resurrection of Christ do produce their effects in history so that every baptized person participates in the one death and Resurrection of Christ by undergoing a process similar to that of Christ: he dies to his old self dominated by sin and receives a share in the life of the risen Lord.

b. Baptism as an Incorporation into the Body of Christ, the Church

Baptism incorporates us into the Church, the people of God, which is continuous with Israel and yet, at the same time, has its own new and distinct reality. We see this continuity in 1 Corinthians 10:1–3, which unites the foreshadowing of baptism with baptism itself, just as the old people of Israel and the new are considered one. Colossians calls baptism the "circumcision of Christ"; Galatians explains that by belonging to Christ through faith, Christians are "Abraham's offspring, heirs according to promise."[11]

At the same time, though, the Church is also distinct from Israel, since by baptism we are incorporated into the Body of Christ. "Just as the body is one and has many members,

---

[11] Col 2:11; Gal 3:29.

and all the members of the body, though many, are one body, so it is with Christ. For by one Spirit we were all baptized into one body—Jews or Greeks, slaves or free—and all were made to drink of one Spirit."[12] The same life of the Spirit that animates Christ is present, active, and visible in the Church, which, in this way, becomes the extension of Christ's personal risen body.

In the Letter to the Galatians, Paul further articulates the union among those classes of people that constituted the great social barriers in the ancient world: "For as many of you as were baptized into Christ have put on Christ. There is neither Jew nor Greek, there is neither slave nor free, there is neither male nor female; for you are all one in Christ Jesus."[13] The Greek word he uses here for "one" is the masculine singular *heis*, which stresses the all-transcending reality of our oneness in being with Christ and in Christ with one another. Consequently, whenever a local church identifies herself exclusively with one class or excludes any social group from full participation, it betrays the reality of the Church.

c. Sacramental Character

When the New Testament writes about baptism as a sealing, it indicates its permanent character.[14] The ancient Church gradually realized that baptism, confirmation, and holy orders may be received only once because these three sacraments mark the recipient with an indelible spiritual mark, the sacramental character of which, even if sanctifying grace is lost, cannot be erased by mortal sins. Theologians explain the meaning of the sacramental character of baptism

[12] 1 Cor 12:12–13.
[13] Gal 3:27–28.
[14] See 2 Cor 1:22; Eph 1:13; 4:30.

and confirmation in the following way. In ancient times soldiers were branded on their skin with the name of the emperor to make it obvious to everyone that they belonged to him. In a similar way baptism (as well as confirmation) marks one as belonging to Christ as his brother or sister and as belonging to the Father as his son or daughter. This indelible mark is a pledge of God's unconditional fidelity to that person: God will give the baptized and confirmed person all the graces he needs to develop into a mature Christian. Even if the person sins, God's commitment remains: as soon as the sinner asks sincerely for forgiveness, God renews his life in him and helps him grow. (If someone remains obstinate in sin until the end of his life, the character of baptism and confirmation will mark him out even in hell as a lost child of God, one who has chosen to be lost in spite of all the graces God offered to him.)

This permanence of sacramental character manifests God's permanent fidelity to the Christian, but each sacrament has a different way of conforming the Christian to Christ and enabling him to act accordingly. For example, baptism enables the Christian to act as a child of God both in the liturgy and in daily life. Confirmation enables him to become an adult spiritually and act accordingly, pursuing that which promotes not only his own salvation but also the salvation of others by confessing his faith and defending it against its enemies. Holy orders enables the Christian to represent Christ as head of his Church.

d. Infant Baptism

The New Testament records that entire households received baptism, which may have included children and infants,[15]

---

[15] See Act 16:15, 33; 18:8; 1 Cor 1:16.

and we have explicit testimony about infant baptism from the second century. Infants have not committed personal sins but, as a result of mankind's first sin, they are born with original sin—that is, they are conceived without God's sanctifying grace and therefore are not yet adopted children of the Father. Reflection on the practice of infant baptism helped the Church work out the doctrine of original sin (for if the child were born in sanctifying grace, there would be no need to baptize him before the age of reason), and our reflection on it here will help us understand the absolute priority of grace in relation to any human response. The development of the mother-child relationship provides a convincing analogy. The infant's mother does not wait for the first smile of her baby to happen on its own but tries her best to elicit the baby's response to her love. The child's first gesture of love is a response to the mother's initiative. In a similar way, God called us into being and called us to become brothers and sisters of Christ and children of his Father without our consent or decision. Infant baptism is a tangible sign of God's *prior* love for the child and will gradually enable the child to respond freely to that love.

The practice of infant baptism also manifests what theologians call the "law of salvation in community." In God's plan the entire ecclesial Body of Christ, in heaven, on earth, and in purgatory, is intimately interconnected in promoting one another's salvation. Children are baptized in virtue of the faith of those who present them for the sacrament. The supernatural communion we all have in Christ enables us to "substitute" ourselves for one another. As they grow, young children will experience the sincerity of their parents' faith and participate in it.

Finally, the practice of baptizing children before they are capable of mature decision sheds light on the nature of faith.

It is not a set of theories but rather personal communion with the Son of God. Therefore, if the adolescent cannot commune with Christ in the Eucharist and cannot receive the fullness of the Spirit in confirmation or hear Christ's words of forgiveness in sacramental absolution, he remains an outsider and does not really know the value of what he is missing. He will need a special grace to seek out the Church.[16]

The Sacrament of Confirmation

a. The Holy Spirit in Salvation History

Since the sacrament of confirmation imparts the gift of the Holy Spirit, we should first survey the role of the Holy Spirit in the economy of salvation and in God himself.[17] In the Old Testament we read about the Spirit of God. He is not yet revealed as a distinct subject in God, but he acts as God's life-giving and guiding presence that brings forth life in creation, guides the judges of Israel, and inspires its prophets. The Spirit's presence is not permanent or complete but transient and inchoate. The prophets, however, announce that the Spirit will rest on the Messiah and will be poured out on all peoples at the end of times.[18]

This promise of the full and permanent outpouring of the Spirit is fulfilled in Jesus. He is conceived by the Holy Spirit in the womb of the Virgin Mary. At his baptism Jesus hears the Father's words as the Holy Spirit descends upon

---

[16] Everett Ferguson, *Baptism in the Early Church: History, Theology, and Liturgy in the First Five Centuries* (Grand Rapids, Mich.: Eerdmans, 2009); Jean Mouroux, *From Baptism to the Act of Faith* (Boston: Allyn & Bacon, 1964).

[17] The following provides a rich collection of texts: Yves Congar, *I Believe in the Holy Spirit*, 4 vols. (New York: Seabury, 1983).

[18] See Is 11:1-2; 61:1; Ezek 36:25-27; Joel 3:1-2.

him. His public ministry is directed by the Father, who communicates with Jesus through the Holy Spirit. Jesus is led into the desert by the Spirit and returns in the power of the Spirit to Galilee.[19] He drives out demons by the Spirit of God; he gives thanks to the Father, rejoicing in the Holy Spirit; and he offers himself to God in sacrifice by the eternal Spirit.[20] In addition, Jesus promises the Holy Spirit to those who believe in him.[21] It is in the Holy Spirit that the risen Jesus will return to his disciples and remain with them.[22] The risen Lord breathes his Holy Spirit upon the disciples, which makes their mission of forgiving and retaining sins effective.[23]

From the role of the Spirit in the economy of salvation, we can draw conclusions about his role in God himself—that is, his role in salvation reveals his role in the immanent Trinity. Just as Jesus and the Father are united and communicate in the Holy Spirit here on earth, so is the Holy Spirit the one in whom Father and Son are united in eternity. And as the Holy Spirit unites the members of the Church with one another, with Jesus, and with the Father while preserving their personal uniqueness, so, too, does he unite Father and Son while preserving their personal distinctions.

b. The Development of the Sacrament of Confirmation

The Acts of the Apostles shows that Philip, one of the seven helpers chosen by the community, baptized the converting Samaritans, but then two of the apostles were sent to them

---

[19] See Mk 1:12; Lk 4:14.
[20] See Mt 12:28; Lk 10:21; Heb 9:14.
[21] See Lk 24:49; Jn 7:37–39.
[22] See Jn 14:15–29.
[23] See Jn 20:19–23.

so that, by the laying on of their hands, the baptized Samaritans might receive the Holy Spirit: "Now when the apostles at Jerusalem heard that Samaria had received the word of God, they sent to them Peter and John, who came down and prayed for them that they might receive the Holy Spirit; for the Spirit had not yet fallen on any of them, but they had only been baptized in the name of the Lord Jesus. Then they laid their hands on them and they received the Holy Spirit."[24]

We do not have much documentation from the first two centuries attesting to the existence of a second sacrament of initiation that is separate from baptism. The two—baptism and confirmation—seem to have always been performed together. From the third century on, we see that the laying on of hands was separated from baptism, since confirmation had been reserved for the bishop and he could not be present at every baptism.

We may wonder why confirmation needs to be completed, since baptism unites us to Christ and incorporates us into his Body, the Church. As Saint Ambrose says, "After the fountain (baptismal bath) there remains that perfection be made," the perfecting of Christian initiation.[25] God is never sparing or parsimonious in his gifts, either in nature or in grace. He always gives more than we ask for or can comprehend—the infinite riches of Christ in the Eucharist and his sevenfold Spirit in confirmation. Moreover, the needs of the supernatural life exhibit a certain similarity to the needs of the natural life, writes Saint Thomas: just as baptism corresponds to natural birth, so confirmation corresponds to growth into adulthood.[26]

---

[24] Acts 8:14–17; cf. 19:1–7.
[25] Ambrose, *De sacramentis*, bk. III, chap. 2, no. 8.
[26] *ST* III, q. 72, a. 1.

THE SACRAMENTS 149

The post–Vatican II rite of confirmation combines the traditional imposition of hands and chrismation (which was a later rite) into one gesture. The bishop (or his delegate) lays his hands upon the confirmand and anoints his forehead with a special aromatic oil called a chrism, while saying, "N., be sealed with the Gift of the Holy Spirit."[27] These words come from the Eastern Rite. While anointing the candidate, the bishop draws the sign of the cross on his forehead. This shows that the confirmed Christian accepts sharing in the Cross of Christ and agrees to bear witness to the crucified and risen Christ to others.

This essential rite is preceded by the renewal of baptismal vows. For those who were baptized before the age of reason, parents and godparents did this in their place; now the confirmands themselves make a personal commitment to the Catholic Christian faith. The anointing is followed by a solemn prayer of the bishop over the newly confirmed:

> All-powerful God, Father of our Lord Jesus Christ,
> by water and the Holy Spirit
> you freed your sons and daughters from sin
> and gave them new life.
> Send your Holy Spirit upon them
> to be their Helper and Guide.
> Give them the spirit of wisdom and understanding,
> the spirit of right judgment and courage,
> the spirit of knowledge and reverence.
> Fill them with the spirit of wonder and awe in your
>   presence.

---

[27] The International Commission on English in the Liturgy, *The Rites of the Catholic Church* (New York: Pueblo Publishing, 1976), 310.

We ask this through Christ our Lord.
Amen.[28]

c. The Grace of Confirmation

Saint Thomas Aquinas claims that the sacrament of confirmation offers us the fullness of the Holy Spirit for the strength (*ad robur*) to live a full Christian life and to overcome temptations.[29] We find the most perfect illustration of the effects of the Holy Spirit's works through this sacrament in the event of Pentecost[30] and in the rest of the Acts of the Apostles. The Gospel of John[31] and the letters of Saint Paul provide a deeper theological explanation.

Even though the apostles' hearts were clean[32] and they all believed in Jesus, the descent of the Spirit transforms their entire being.[33] An overwhelming power of love and understanding drives them to communicate the new life and joy that fill them. The words of Jesus are no longer just painful or happy memories but are spirit and life, a source of a new energy that gives them the assurance that they can carry the word of Jesus to the ends of the world. The mystery of the death and Resurrection of their Lord becomes more than just an event of the recent past; they experience his Resurrection as the power of their own new lives.

Obtuse and slow to understanding before, the apostles, especially Peter, now show a deep understanding of the Scriptures. In his first speech, Peter joins with ease and insight the texts of Joel 3:1–5, Psalm 16:8–11, and Psalm 110:1 into

---

[28] International Commission on English in the Liturgy, *The Rites*, 309.
[29] *ST* III, q. 72, a. 1, ad. 2; *ST* III, q. 72, a. 7.
[30] See Acts 2.
[31] See especially Jn 14:15–31.
[32] See Jn 13:10.
[33] See Acts 2:1–41.

a masterful exposition of God's plan of salvation.[34] Earlier, when he was brought before the Sanhedrin, he was fearful and moody; now he speaks with a serene firmness and boldness that strikes the members of the council: "Whether it is right in the sight of God to listen to you rather than to God, you must judge; for we cannot but speak of what we have seen and heard."[35] The apostles eat their meals with exultation and, when flogged, they rejoice that they have been found worthy to suffer dishonor for the sake of the name of Jesus.[36]

The descent of the Spirit reverses the scattering of the nations that occurred when the tower of Babel was built. On Pentecost, Jewish pilgrims, coming from many countries and speaking many languages, all understand the preaching of the apostles.[37] Those who convert and receive baptism at the preaching of Peter become one heart and mind, sharing their goods and their meals. They pray together daily in the Temple; celebrate the breaking of the bread, the Eucharist, in their homes; and proclaim with great power the Resurrection of the Lord Jesus.[38] Thus, the Holy Spirit fills the Church with life and all the gifts needed for her unity and growth.

No other unity on earth compares with the unity brought about by the Holy Spirit. It is based not merely on common interests, values, ideals, or personal attraction but on the presence and activity of the very same Spirit in every member. Only our resistance can frustrate and prevent his action. The Spirit also transforms the moral life of every Christian:

---

[34] See Acts 2:14-36.
[35] Acts 4:19-20.
[36] See Acts 2:46-47; 5:40-41.
[37] See Acts 2:5-12.
[38] See Acts 2:42-47; 4:32-37.

"The law of the Spirit of life in Christ Jesus has set [us] free from the law of sin and death," says Paul.[39] The Old Law only pointed out what leads to sin and death but could not give us the power to avoid sin and follow God's will. But if the Christian allows the Spirit to animate his life, he will not need the prescriptions of the external law, for the "law of the Spirit of life" will inspire him to every good work.[40] The fruits of the Spirit will be "love, joy, peace, patience, kindness, goodness, faithfulness, gentleness, self-control."[41]

In brief, the entire life of Paul is summed up in this statement: "It is no longer I who live, but Christ who lives in me."[42] The same Spirit is given to each confirmand, but the extent to which the gifts of the Spirit will be at work in him depends on his openness to the Spirit and the needs of his life situation. Sadly, very few even know the infinite power and potential for action and joy that are offered to them.[43]

d. The Sacrament of Confirmation and the Holy Eucharist

There is an enriching mutual causality between the Eucharist and confirmation that is analogous to the relationship between Christ and the Holy Spirit. It is always Christ who gives the Holy Spirit; thus the Spirit's gift in confirmation comes from the Eucharist. The Spirit, on his part, then enlarges and deepens the capacity of the confirmed person to

---

[39] Rom 8:2.

[40] Rom 8:2; cf. 1 Tim 1:8–9.

[41] Gal 5:22–23. See also the charisms in the letters of Paul (Rom 12:4–8; 1 Cor 12:4–11; 12:27–31; 14:1–40).

[42] Gal 2:20.

[43] Burkhard Neunheuser, *Baptism and Confirmation*, trans. John Jay Hughes (Eugene, Ore.: Wipf and Stock, 2018); Liam G. Walsh, *The Sacraments of Initiation: Baptism, Confirmation, Eucharist* (London: Chapman, 1988).

receive Christ in the Eucharist more fruitfully. The Spirit of Jesus also helps us attain a better, more existential understanding of the Eucharistic mystery and gives us the courage and assurance to bear witness to its reality.

The traditional order of the sacraments of initiation places confirmation after baptism and before the first reception of Holy Communion. However, the Church also allows children to receive confession and Holy Communion at an early age before the reception of confirmation. This change was made on the basis of religious psychology, which suggests that the best age for receiving the sacrament of confirmation is thirteen or fourteen, when children have not yet entered the turbulence and confusion of adolescence but are capable of appreciating the power of the Holy Spirit to overcome the lure of the flesh, the lies of the world, and the conceit of arrogance. Some dioceses, though, apply the traditional liturgical order of initiation not only to adults but also to children, confirming them at the age of reason (six or seven) before First Communion. In this case, when the children reach puberty, they should be reminded that they have the grace of confirmation to fight the spiritual battles of adolescence.

The Sacrifice of the Holy Eucharist

The Holy Eucharist is the redemptive sacrifice of Christ made present by the Church so that the members of the Church may unite themselves with him, and their sacrifice with his.[44] In a general sense, a sacrifice is a tangible gift to

---

[44] See in more detail Joseph Cardinal Ratzinger, *God Is Near Us: The Eucharist, the Heart of Life* (San Francisco: Ignatius Press, 2003); Roch A. Kereszty, *Wedding Feast of the Lamb: Eucharistic Theology from a Historical, Biblical, and Systematic Perspective* (Chicago: Hillenbrand Books, 2004).

God that symbolizes the one making the offering—his free will, love, and obedience. Jesus Christ offered to God not a material gift but his whole earthly life, which culminated in accepting a violent death for our sake on the Cross. What made the sacrifice of God's Son infinitely precious and valuable for the Father was the infinite love expressed in it.[45]

It is Christ's crucified and risen body given up for us and his blood poured out for us that become present in the Eucharist under the signs of bread and wine. Of course, if his risen body is present, then the living Jesus Christ, the Son of God become man, is present for us. He is present not only to be worshipped and adored but also to be consumed as food so that he may transform us into himself.[46] (This is one of the differences between regular food and the Holy Eucharist: regular food is assimilated by our organism and becomes part of it, while the Eucharist assimilates us to itself and we become members of the Body of Christ.) Then our love and obedience—in other words, the gift of our own selves—will become, "through Him, with Him, and in Him," a pleasing sacrifice to the Father.

a. An Excursus on the Real Presence of Christ in the Eucharist

The Roman Catholic Church and the Orthodox churches have from the beginning believed in the real presence of Christ under the sign of the Eucharistic bread and wine. Some Protestant denominations, however (for instance, the

---

[45] God the Father could not be pleased by the suffering and death of his Son *as* suffering and death. They were pleasing to him in the sense that the Son's free acceptance of death for our sake revealed his love in the most perfect way. This death, accepted out of infinite love, conquered death and became the source of life for all who join the Son in faith and sacraments of faith.

[46] See Jn 6:27, 51–56.

Baptists and the Churches of Christ), consider their Holy Communion service merely a reminder of the life-giving death of Jesus; they consider the Eucharistic elements regular food that merely symbolize the body and blood of Christ. They point out that the words of the institution ("This is my body. . . . This is my blood of the covenant, which is poured out for many for the forgiveness of sins"[47]) suggest a mere symbolic interpretation. Jesus also said, "I am the good shepherd"[48] and "I am the door of the sheep,"[49] yet no one thinks that Jesus was actually a shepherd or a door.

However, in the Gospel of John, Christ himself interprets the words of the institution in a literal sense:

> Do not labor for the food which perishes, but for the food which endures to eternal life. . . . I am the living bread which came down from heaven; if any one eats of this bread, he will live for ever; and the bread which I shall give for the life of the world is my flesh. . . . Truly, truly, I say to you, unless you eat the flesh of the Son of man and drink his blood, you have no life in you; he who eats my flesh and drinks my blood has eternal life, and I will raise him up at the last day. For my flesh is food indeed, and my blood is drink indeed. He who eats my flesh and drinks my blood abides in me, and I in him.[50]

In conjunction with the institution accounts of the Eucharist (which the reader of John knows about from the Synoptic Gospels), these words express clearly the fact that Christ himself is the Eucharistic bread and that in and through the Eucharist he gives his own flesh as food and his own blood as drink to the believer.

[47] Mt 26:26, 28.
[48] Jn 10:11, 14.
[49] Jn 10:7.
[50] Jn 6:27, 51, 53–56.

It also becomes clear from this passage that Christ is present as food to nourish us for eternal life and to unite us to himself so that he may dwell in us and we in him. Yet Jesus does not speak about a cannibalistic eating of human meat. When the Jews protest, "This is a hard saying; who can listen to it?" he does not retract what he said but explains that his words are "Spirit and life."[51] His crucified and risen body becomes for us the source of the Holy Spirit, the Spirit of eternal life.

Saint Paul's First Letter to the Corinthians is the earliest written record of the way in which the apostolic Church interpreted the Eucharistic words of Jesus. (Paul wrote 1 Corinthians in A.D. 56–57—much earlier than the Gospel of John was composed.) The rhetorical question Paul asks his readers presupposes that the Corinthians are aware of the real presence of Christ in the Eucharist: "The cup of blessing which we bless, is it not a participation in the blood of Christ? The bread which we break, is it not a participation in the body of Christ?"[52] Yet just as in the Gospel of John, the presence of Christ is not the ultimate goal for Paul: "Because there is one bread, we who are many are one body, for we all partake of the one bread."[53] Christ is present so that by partaking of the Eucharistic bread, we may become united with him and with one another into "one body."

If someone is scandalized by the apparent absurdity of such a belief, we can point out to him that belief in the real presence of Christ in the Eucharist is no more absurd than belief in the Incarnation. If God could become a Jewish rabbi from Nazareth, this same God-man could offer himself to us as food under the sign of bread and wine. Both mysteries, the Incarnation and the Eucharist, reveal the same divine

[51] Jn 6:60, 63.
[52] 1 Cor 10:16.
[53] 1 Cor 10:17.

logic of love. God became man in Jesus so as to bridge the infinite gap between himself and sinful mankind, and this Jesus offers himself as food to us so that he may not only be *near to us* but also *inside us* and can re-create us into his likeness.

And if someone wonders how one and the same Christ —and the whole Christ—can be received by such innumerable multitudes, he should again reflect on the nature of love. Material realities diminish by being divided and distributed, while the spiritual reality of love does not. God gives his whole undivided self to everyone who opens himself to him. The glorified and risen body of Christ, in turn, becomes truly "Spirit and life," a completely docile and pliable medium through which Jesus Christ can give himself, whole and entire, to everyone.

b. Participation in the Eucharist

Participation in the Eucharist does not simply mean receiving Holy Communion, saying some prayers, and singing some songs. The action is both external and internal. Christ first nourishes our faith with his Word (in the Liturgy of the Word) so that we may become ready to receive his Body and Blood, his full divine-human reality, in the Liturgy of the Eucharist. Just as in his sacrifice on the Cross, Christ's purpose is twofold in the Eucharistic celebration. He wants to unite to himself all believers at every time and place so that "through Him, with Him and in Him" we may give ourselves over in praise, thanksgiving, and atonement to the Father. But he also wants to unite us with one another in himself so that all believers may become "one body" and "one spirit" in him.[54]

---

[54] 1 Cor 10:17; 6:17.

These two purposes of the Eucharist, to worship the Father and build up the Church, are inseparably linked: we can worthily worship the Father only to the extent that we become incorporated into the Body of Christ that is the Church. On the other hand, the purpose of building up the Church community is to unite all mankind into Christ and into Christ's worship of the Father. Yet, in practice, one of these two purposes has often been emphasized at the expense of the other. Before the liturgical renewal (which culminated in the Second Vatican Council), the prevailing danger had been to stress the aspect of worship while forgetting or de-emphasizing the communitarian dimension of the Eucharist. In the postconciliar era it is rightly emphasized that Christ is present not only in the form of consecrated bread and wine but also within the celebrating community. Many, however, have forgotten today that it is Christ's Eucharistic presence that nourishes and intensifies his presence in the community. The center of the Eucharistic celebration should never be misplaced in the community itself. In other words, we should not worship one another or the community as a whole but only the Eucharistic Christ and, in union with him, God the Father.

Yet it remains true that liturgical worship presupposes an existing Christian community. In fact, it can build up the community only if a community of faith has already been established prior to the liturgical celebration. This community of faith ought to be expressed in some perceptible way that takes into account the needs of human nature. The forms of liturgical prayer cannot fulfill their role if they do not express the faith of a community—if instead the participants merge into a faceless, impersonal mass of people so characteristic of modern city life. The individual consumer goes shopping in big crowds, but he cares about his fellow shoppers only to the extent that their latest fad determines his own desire for what to buy for himself. He also goes to church to satisfy his own religious needs, shopping around to find the church that seems to fit his needs best; if his expectations are not met, he quickly switches attendance or quits altogether. Christian formation, both outside and within the liturgical celebration, should counteract this consumerist tendency. We have to educate ourselves to understand that the Eucharistic celebration is a share in Christ's gift to the Father and to mankind. Unless we are ready to join ourselves to this twofold gift, our participation remains insincere. Uniting ourselves to the will of Christ, then, demands both worship of God and commitment to one another. Deepening this spirit of adoration of God and service to one another, as well as helping those in need, is essential both as preparation for and as a goal of the Eucharistic celebration. This integration of the two dimensions of the Eucharist is truer to the nature of the liturgy than the promotion of an artificial "high" brought on by community fellowship or the creation of an atmosphere in which the liturgical action becomes subordinate to a music concert.

However, no matter how much we may try to shape the right attitude in ourselves and in others, we will not find an ideal liturgical celebration on this earth. If we are disturbed by the eccentricities or imperfections of the participants, we must realize that through such distressing encounters we are brought face-to-face with the reality of our own ecclesial community. This experience calls for both a realistic acceptance of our community (just as we must accept ourselves in spite of our own sinfulness) and a serious effort to improve it. Someone who reacts to a disturbing liturgical situation by escaping into his own private devotions helps neither himself nor others. The words of the institution of the Eucharist in the First Letter of Paul to the Corinthians[55] are worth pondering: "The Lord Jesus on the night when he was betrayed took bread."[56] The Last Supper, the first Eucharistic gathering, was full of distracting features that would have disturbed anyone seeking the peace of quiet recollection. Not only the distasteful rivalry of the apostles (about who will be the greatest in the kingdom[57]) but especially the scandal of the betrayer's presence should be an effective warning for us: the community of Christ's disciples will be perfect only in heaven. Instead of looking for an entirely gratifying "worship experience," we may recall another passage from Saint Paul's letter: "As often as you eat this bread and drink the chalice, you proclaim the Lord's death until he comes."[58]

The Sacrament of Reconciliation

Christ accompanies us on the way of conversion that leads us to the Father's home in many ways, but especially through the sacrament of reconciliation. Since conversion is a lifelong task, the experience of the saints shows us that we need this sacrament at every stage of our lives. God inspires sorrow in us, forgives us, strengthens us, and lifts us up whenever we return to him with the sincere resolution to start over again.[59]

---

[55] He introduces his directives to correct the Eucharistic abuses of the Corinthian church by recalling its institution by Christ (see 1 Cor 11:17–34).

[56] 1 Cor 11:23.

[57] See Lk 22:24–27.

[58] 1 Cor 11:26.

[59] For further studies see Pope John Paul II, apostolic exhortation "Reconciliation and Penance" (December 2, 1984); Bernard Häring, *Shalom: Peace;*

a. Foundations in the New Testament

> On the evening of that day, the first day of the week, . . .
> Jesus came and stood among them.[60]

In John's Gospel this is the first appearance of the risen Christ to his disciples. In the Creation story of Genesis, the first day is the creation of light. In the new creation of redemption, the light of the Resurrection shines into the old world. A new age of reconciliation, forgiveness, and peace dawns on the disciples: "Jesus came and stood among them and said to them, 'Peace be with you.' When he had said this, he showed them his hands and his side. Then the disciples were glad when they saw the Lord. Jesus said to them again, 'Peace be with you.'"[61]

"Shalom—peace" is even today the customary greeting among Jews. During Jesus' time the Messianic overtones of the greeting were clearly understood. To offer another person "shalom" was the Jews' way of wishing him the peace that the Messiah would one day bring, a peace that would embody all the blessings of the new age.[62] At that blessed time, Israel's infidelities would be forgiven and God would draw so close to his people that "the earth shall be full of the knowledge of the LORD as the waters cover the sea."[63] Because Israel was to be reconciled to God when this happened, peace would reign among all the nations: "They shall beat their swords into plowshares, and their spears into

---

The Sacrament of Reconciliation (New York: Farrar, Straus, and Giroux, 1968); Robert L. Fastiggi, *The Sacrament of Reconciliation: An Anthropological and Scriptural Understanding* (Chicago: Hillenbrand Books, 2017).

[60] Jn 20:19.

[61] Jn 20:19–21.

[62] See, e.g., Is 9:1–6; 11:1–9; Mic 5:1–5: "this shall be peace."

[63] Is 11:9.

pruning hooks"[64] and "they shall not hurt or destroy in all my holy mountain."[65] In the episode that John recounts, Jesus twice repeats "shalom" to his disciples. He does not merely wish them this peace; he bestows it upon them. And this peace summarizes and incorporates *everything* that Jesus gives. Next, showing them his pierced hands and wounded side, he reveals that this peace is the fruit of his suffering and death on the Cross. Through his death we now have, first, peace with God; second, peace with ourselves since our consciences no longer condemn us; and finally, peace with one another.

Thus, the tiny band of disciples becomes the seed of the Church, the community of peace. Whoever enters this community enters a community of peace. If someone perseveres within the loving communion of the Church, even if he sins, he should ask for forgiveness and he will be forgiven:[66] " 'As the Father has sent me, even so I send you.' And when [Jesus] had said this, he breathed on them, and said to them, 'Receive the Holy Spirit. If you forgive the sins of any, they are forgiven; if you retain the sins of any, they are retained.' "[67] With these words, Christ commissions his disciples to continue the same mission he himself has received from the Father. In fact, John's Gospel characterizes the entire mission of the Church this way: to transmit the peace of Christ, the forgiveness of sins. This is not something the disciples could have hoped to accomplish on their own; it is brought about by the Holy Spirit, received from Christ, who lives within them. All who believe will be "reborn of water and the Holy Spirit" in baptism, and they shall receive this peace,

---

[64] Mic 4:3.
[65] Is 11:9.
[66] See 1 Jn 1:7–10; 5:13–19.
[67] Jn 20:21–23.

which is the forgiveness of their sins and life in the Spirit. Conversely, all who reject the Word of Jesus, preached by the disciples, will remain in their sin.

What about those already within the Church who commit sin after being baptized? The apostles are charged to mediate forgiveness to these people as well. But while the Scripture mentioned earlier establishes the sacrament of penance, it does not explain how the sacrament is to be administered. For guidance on this point, let us look to the Gospel of Matthew. Christ tells the apostles, "Truly, I say to you, whatever you bind on earth shall be bound in heaven, and whatever you loose on earth shall be held loosed in heaven."[68]

Grave sin means the loss of the life of the Holy Spirit. When a member of the Church commits a serious wrongdoing with full knowledge and consent, he is in a state of mortal sin; he has, in effect, become a "dead member" of the Body of Christ and must therefore not receive Communion. But if he regrets his sins and expresses this sorrow by seeking forgiveness in the sacrament of reconciliation, the Church will readmit him to Communion, which, as we saw earlier, unites us not only to Christ but also to all other believers. This reconciliation with the Church obtains for the penitent God's forgiveness. Through the Church Christ prays for the penitent's forgiveness, which the Father always grants because he wants the sinner to again become a living member of the Church, filled with the Holy Spirit.[69] An instructive example of this process of the loss and then regaining of communion with the Body of Christ appears in 1 Corinthians 5:1–5, where Saint Paul—in the name of Jesus and by his power—excludes from the community a

---
[68] Mt 18:18.
[69] See 1 Jn 5:16.

man who has committed incest. Paul does this in order to promote the sinner's eventual reconciliation: he must suffer this exclusion so that "his spirit may be saved in the day of the Lord Jesus."[70]

While the shape and practice of this sacrament have undergone some dramatic changes over time, its essential elements remain remarkably consistent with their New Testament origins. A person in the state of mortal sin is barred from Holy Communion until he receives sacramental absolution. Moreover, we are encouraged to go to confession and receive absolution also for venial sins. This sacrament is very helpful at every stage of spiritual growth. The *Catechism of the Catholic Church* tells us that regular confession even when we are not in mortal sin "helps us form our conscience, fight against evil tendencies, let ourselves be healed by Christ and progress in the life of the Spirit."[71]

Even when we are in a state of serious sin, we remain moral beings. Thus, we defend ourselves by rationalizing our motivations and actions. We tell ourselves that what we did was not evil at all, that it was not as evil as it seemed, that our motive was decent, or that we have grown beyond our former childish inhibitions. Even if we are sincerely trying to improve, we are tempted to shift the focus from our actual sins to our general good intentions, saying to ourselves, "I am a sinner like everyone is a sinner, but I still have a general intention to do better in the future." Most of the time the result of such vague self-assessment is moral stagnation. The need to confess our sins conflicts with this general human tendency to hide behind generic confessions and sweep under the rug our actual sins in their shameful

---

[70] Cf. 2 Thess 3:13–15; 1 Tim 1:19–20.
[71] *CCC* 1458.

concreteness. Each of us feels the impulse to deny, forget, or at least explain the evil that we have done. In confession, however, we are forced to face the reality of our sins. We have to dig them up, bring them out into the open, and acknowledge them without any hollow excuses. Confessing them is a first step toward separating ourselves from them. "Yes, I have done or omitted this or that, but I reject and condemn these acts. I no longer want to be identified with them. On my own I cannot separate myself from my own guilty self; only God, who reconciles the world in Christ to himself, can in truth re-create me. So I need the forgiveness of Christ."

Because, as we have seen, following Jesus is not just an individual commitment but immersion in community—the Body of Christ—we also need the forgiveness of the Church, which we have wounded by our sins. As members of the Church, our vocation is to be images of Christ to the world and to our fellow Christians. Only through us can the light and the fire of Christ's love be made visible in the world. In the state of mortal sin, I become a counterwitness to him—darkness rather than light. Just as the impact of one good act calls forth a wave of goodness, so does one evil act produce a wave of negative responses. Even what we call venial sins are harmful for the Church and thereby for the world. Half-hearted attitudes toward prayer, neglecting to go beyond the limits of strict duty, merely superficial kindness, and other failings are all counterwitnesses to Christ. We must make our confession to the representative of the Church we hurt and disfigured; through her ministry, we receive from Christ forgiveness and healing. Through the act of faith, we recognize Christ in our encounter with a priest in the sacrament of confession. In his absolution, we meet the same person who told the paralyzed man, "Take heart, my son; your sins are forgiven."[72] We hope our preparation is adequate to receive Christ's forgiveness, but we know with the certainty of faith that Christ offers his forgiveness to us.

As mentioned previously, this sacrament remains a great help to us not only early on in conversion but during every stage of our journey on earth. The more sensitive we become to the operations of the Holy Spirit within us, the more realistically we begin to confront our sinfulness. God is gentle and patient. He gradually reveals to us the real state of our soul in such a way that we are able to cope with this knowledge. Saint John Vianney asked God at the beginning of his ministry to show him his soul as God sees it. He saw it and became frightened. So he begged the Lord not to do it again. As Saint Bernard explains, God shows us first the sins of the flesh, such as sensuality, gluttony, sloth, greed, and violence. Only later do we begin to discover the direct sins of the soul, such as conceit, vanity, uncharitableness, resentment, hatred, and jealousy.

At the beginning of the spiritual life, very often fear of God's punishment accompanied by some vague awareness of God's goodness to the repentant sinner dominates the act of repentance. We should not underestimate the salutary effects that fear has on our conversion, because it provides a more powerful force for breaking an addiction to a sinful life than does our weak love on its own.[73] There are, of course, exceptional cases in which the overwhelming sweetness and

---

[72] Mt 9:2.

[73] We call such contrition, motivated by fear of punishment, "imperfect contrition," which is sufficient for forgiveness in the sacrament. Contrition motivated by the love of God is called "perfect contrition," which immediately obtains forgiveness for sin, although mortal sins must still be confessed later.

power of divine love predominates from the beginning and enables an immediate surge of a radically new life of loving devotion. But even where fear prevails at the start, the freedom and vigor that develop from observing God's commandments begin to open up the soul to appreciate God's goodness. If we do not stop here but respond with gratitude to the accumulating signs of divine love in our daily lives, we begin to taste that the Lord is good and that his yoke is easy and his burden is light. Then, parallel to the growth of love and gratitude, our conscience is gradually refined. A saintly monk describes perfect contrition motivated by love in these terms:

> The only person who knows true sorrow is the one who has already suffered because of his sin. He is not surprised by God's forgiving mercy since his sin hurts him exactly because he has experienced God's goodness. Sorrow is a great grace; blessed is the suffering of those who are hurting because they have hurt Goodness Itself. This sorrow cleanses the soul. The forgiveness is only the kiss that God gives to the purified soul.[74]

A gesture between lovers that is barely noticeable to outsiders, such as the tone of a voice, a twitch of the cheek, or a casual remark, can cause hurt feelings and result in a heartfelt act of sorrow and renewed kindness. This is so between Christ and the sensitive Christian as well. We want to love Christ and other people with the very love of Christ. In the words of Thérèse of Lisieux, we try to "borrow" the love by which Christ loves us. Whenever we fall short of this standard—and this happens most of the time—we beg for forgiveness and start all over again. Thus, periodic confession

---

[74] See Rókus Kereszty, *Sugárzó lelke tovább világit: 'Sigmond Lóránt írásai* (Budapest: SZIT, 2000), 238.

is for us a God-sent means for expressing our sorrow and asking Christ for the grace to start anew.

b. Spiritual Guidance

We treat spiritual guidance or spiritual direction here in connection with the sacrament of reconciliation, since in practice the two are often connected. In principle, however, every qualified Catholic, man or woman, may become a spiritual guide or director, since guidance does not require the use of the sacrament of reconciliation. A Catholic always has the freedom to go to confession to any priest of his choice, even if the priest cannot provide spiritual direction. It is, however, strongly recommended, especially for beginners in the spiritual life, to choose one spiritual director or, more accurately, a spiritual guide.[75] The word "director" connotes someone who requires strict obedience imposed from the outside. Spiritual guidance may indeed include obedience in certain cases, when, for instance, the guidee is contemplating a sinful act or needs to be liberated from the chains of a scrupulous conscience. Most often, however, the spiritual guide will aim at inspiring free and creative cooperation.

The most important qualities of a trustworthy guide are theological and psychological knowledge, empathy, the ability to make prudent judgments, and holiness. By holiness, I do not mean the guide must be ripe for canonization but that he is a Catholic who sincerely strives to do God's will in everything and lives his faith. A good guide is more than

---

[75] See in more detail Thomas Dubay, *Seeking Spiritual Direction: How to Grow the Divine Life Within* (Cincinnati, Ohio: Servant Books, 1993); Timothy M. Gallagher, *The Discernment of Spirits: An Ignatian Guide for Everyday Living* (New York: Crossroad, 2005); Roch A. Kereszty, *Rekindle the Gift of God: A Handbook for Priestly Life* (San Francisco: Ignatius Press, 2021), 226–34.

a teacher and a counselor. He resembles Paul, who was in birth pangs until Christ was being formed in his faithful.[76] Spiritual life is the birth and growth of the likeness of Christ in the believer, and a good spiritual guide strives to become both a mother and father to the guidee, taking as examples Mary and Joseph. Joseph loved Jesus more than if he had been his biological son, but he gave him back to the Father every day of his life. Both intimacy and detachment are essential qualities of the guide. We outline here only some of the basic duties and functions of the spiritual guide.

1. The guide and guidee clarify together the goal of the guidance. In general terms, of course, the goal is to seek holiness of life, but it can be concretely formulated in different ways. The goal of the guidee may be to find out God's plan for his life and fulfill it daily. Or it may be to hear at the end of his life, "This is my beloved [child], with whom I am well pleased."[77] Or it may be to strive to die to himself and allow Christ to live in him. In order to inspire such seemingly unattainable goals, the spiritual guide should show by his personality a foretaste of the peace and serenity that awaits us if our will is united with God's will.

2. The guide helps the guidee acquire self-knowledge, which is indispensable to this journey. Most of us do not like to face ourselves, so we distract ourselves almost ceaselessly by external sensory stimulation or internal fantasies of our imagination. As a result, we are familiar only with some of our obvious faults, but the deep-seated roots of what prevents the transforming work of grace in our souls remain unrecognized. The guide should help the person bring back his escaping self in order to face himself and acknowledge his real faults

[76] See Gal 4:19.
[77] Mt 3:17; 17:5; 2 Pet 1:17.

and their roots. Very often this is a gradual and delicate process that requires of the guide gentleness, firmness, and the ability to know the convolutedness of the human heart.

3. The guide helps the guidee discover behind thick masks of pretenses and rationalizations the roots of sin and, at a deeper level, the longing of the human heart for true love, for true joy, and ultimately for God. To do this, the guide must have faced his own tortuous soul before working with others. Someone who has faced the demons in himself will not talk down to the guidee but will develop a deep solidarity with him. He may even share some aspects of his own journey in order to encourage the guidee in his personal struggle. A basic equality should be acknowledged between them—their goal is the same, although they are at different points on the road—and they should discover and admire God's grace working in each other's lives. Feeling solidarity with someone who suffers should never degenerate into sheer commiseration, however. It is true that misery loves company, but compassion is most helpful when the sufferer finds hope and peace in a friend who lifts him up. Thus, Jesus alone is the perfectly compassionate one. He feels our suffering more deeply than we do, but his peace and intimacy heal all our wounds.

4. The guide helps the guidee discover the signs of God's work throughout his life: how God tried to get his attention by blessings and hardships and how God, at times gently and at other times harshly, suggested something but the person remained deaf and blind to it. A sensitive guide can show how much gentle and tough love God has showered upon this person and how helpful God's apparent periods of silence have been in his life.

In this way, the guide helps the guidee understand the current dynamics of his spiritual life. After the first struggles to put order, direction, and prayer into his life, the beginner often feels intense joy and enthusiasm in prayer. God wants to lure him closer to himself and away from the sinful practices of his previous life. The guide should encourage him to be grateful but also help him keep in mind the ebb and flow of consolation and desolation as he progresses. Uninterrupted spiritual delights would lead to stagnation. The beginner might come to seek his own consolation, rather than God himself, in prayer. The times when a feeling of closeness to God is absent and prayer becomes arid, difficult, or even repugnant should be equally, if not more, valued than the times of consolation. The will, the perseverance, and the love of the beginner are tested by feeling the absence of God. His faith tells him that God is close, but he feels only distance and disgust in prayer and no hope for the future. The guide should tell him that these high and low periods are a regular feature of the spiritual life and encourage him to add something special to his daily routine of prayer or work to show God that he loves him more than the enjoyment of his consolation. When Teresa of Avila asked Jesus after a very long period of abandonment, "Where were you, Lord?" he responded, "I was hiding in your heart." Simone Weil, the great French mystic, tells us that if you endure the void, you will receive the supernatural bread.[78]

5. The guide helps the guidee understand that sometimes God withdraws his felt presence because the soul is not quite free for him but still clinging to some imagined or real possession. The following children's tale illustrates the Achilles' heel of many devout persons. Burning with love for Jesus, a little boy began his prayer with these words: "Jesus, I love you very much because you are so good to me. I also would like to show you that I am very grateful to you. I want to give you my

---

[78] Simone Weil, *La pesanteur et la grâce* (Paris: Plon, 1948), 20–21.

best friends, my little sister, my mom and my dad, even my . . . rubber cat. But no, Jesus, forgive me, let me keep my rubber cat." Most of us cherish a rubber cat of some sort, something or someone we would not be able to give up for anything else in the world. But in the divine-human game that Jesus is playing with those who want to be his friends, he very often asks for our rubber cats. For instance, the spiritual guide might explain why Jesus wants a man to break up with his girlfriend whom he cannot and does not want to marry, or why Jesus wants him to quit a dream job that requires long absences that hurt his family life. Once the cherished rubber cat has been given up, the pain of loss is followed by freedom and joy.

6. *The guide helps the guidee discover his personal "demons" or beastly energies.* If the shock is too disturbing or the beast too unruly, the help of a psychologist might also be needed. The first step is to help restore trust and self-confidence. It is important to know what raw energies are dormant within us, but it is even more important to be aware that, with our conscience open to God's guidance and our will ready to follow our conscience, we will win the battle. At the beginning it is enough to chain the beast—that is, to gain mastery over our instincts. The next step, however, is to tame the beast—that is, to use our vital, instinctual energies to support our goal-oriented activities. For instance, the serial killer, the butcher, and the surgeon use the same instinct of aggression. The same vehement sexual energy may vitalize a Don Juan and fuel the ardent prayer of a monk. The prevailing or lacking instincts, however, set clear limits to our choices. A psychologist once presented the family tree of a person in which every member but one was a pyromaniac —and that one was a firefighter. The psychologist pointed

out that the firefighter made the one positive choice open to him: instead of starting fires, he chose to put them out.

7. *The guide helps the guidee sort through his mixed motivations.* Guides often hear complaints like these: "I like to serve, and I like to be generous, especially when people notice it" or "I love to talk when I have something worthwhile to say, but I become depressed if people disagree." The guidee wants to know what to do when his objectively good action has a mixed motivation—good and not so good at the same time.

If we acted only when our motivation was 100 percent pure, we would never act, which would, in fact, be the worse choice. Nevertheless, there are ways by which we can purify—to some extent—our motivations. In the first case, the guide teaches the guidee that he must remain just as generous and ready to serve, if not more so, when nobody notices him as when people do. He must do so even in situations in which he foresees ridicule or disapproval. If, however, people do see and compliment him, he should be happy and be grateful to God, who enabled him to give.

8. *Once the spiritual guide has come to know the history and personality of the guidee, he helps him discover God's plan for his future.* Help he can, but he should refrain from trying to decide for him or even from gentle pressuring. The Ignatian discernment of spirits is a very reliable guide to such a discovery, provided it is not misunderstood or misused. Above all else, the guidee should seek with his whole heart to fulfill God's plan in his life. To obtain such a disposition, he should free himself from attachment to any of the choices open to him. Then, placing himself in each of the alternative positions, he should watch his reactions: in which choice does he find a greater and lasting peace, even if that alternative includes

greater difficulties and sufferings? It is this alternative that is probably the right choice.

Suppose one is attracted to a priestly or religious vocation but cannot decide to pursue it. The spiritual guide should help him realize that a free, personal decision is an integral part of the vocation—in fact, an integral part of becoming a mature person. It is like stepping off a wooden plank into a turbulent sea or jumping out of an airplane trusting in the parachute of faith. This leap can cause great fear but also great joy if done out of love for God. T. S. Eliot describes beautifully this act of making a life-altering decision:

> What have we given?
> My friend, blood shaking my heart
> The awful daring of a moment's surrender
> Which an age of prudence can never retract
> By this, and this only, we have existed.[79]

The Sacrament of the Anointing of the Sick

In contrast to those for whom this life on earth is the only reality, Christians look at their lives on earth as a preparation, a school through which they develop and train for eternal life with God in the communion of the saints. Many believers, however, become so attached to this world that they live as if they will never die. When someone learns that he has a terminal disease and will shortly die, he may be jolted awake from a life of self-deception. He might then admit to himself that he is not an immortal god but a creature whose life hangs on a thin thread and who will soon fade away. He may develop a new outlook on his past, on

---

[79] T. S. Eliot, "The Waste Land," lines 403–9, in *The Complete Poems and Plays: 1909–1950* (San Diego: Harcourt Brace, 1962), 49.

his successes and failures, and on what he has done and what he has omitted. He may realize how many chances he has missed to love those whom God gave him to love and how much energy and effort he has wasted on useless trivialities. This discovery may be followed by sincere repentance and a desire to put to good use the time left to him. He may renew and deepen his love for his family and friends and strive to make up for the hurts and offenses he has caused. As his pain grows and he experiences the gradual deterioration of his body, the fear of total annihilation will intensify. His challenge at this point will be to trust and love God when he feels most forsaken by him. By facing this challenge, he will come closer to Christ, who took upon himself our sufferings and shared the agony of our dying. Thus, the most terrifying reality—death itself—may become for him a blessing: a powerful therapy that brings him back to reality and self-knowledge, to loving others and trusting and loving God. However, this process of reality therapy is not smooth and certainly not effortless. The dying person needs the grace of the sacrament of the anointing of the sick—as well as the help of his family, his friends, and the Church—to make sense of the terrible things that are happening.[80]

Here are the essential words the priests says as he celebrates this sacrament and anoints the person's head and hands:

> Through this holy anointing
> may the Lord in his love and mercy help you
> with the grace of the Holy Spirit.
> Amen.

[80] Karl Rahner, *The Anointing of the Sick* (Denville, N.J.: Dimension Books, 1970); Kevin Tripp et al., *Recovering the Riches of Anointing: A Study of the Sacrament of the Sick*, ed. Genevieve Glen (Collegeville, Minn.: Liturgical Press, 2002).

May the Lord who frees you from sin
save you and raise you up.
Amen.[81]

Most importantly, people should understand that this sacrament is not just for the terminally ill but also for every seriously sick person and even for the elderly who suffer from the debilitating effects of old age. If the sacrament is received in faith, the sick person is united with the suffering Christ so that he might conquer his illness with Christ. Overwhelmed by the suffering of their illnesses, sick people are tempted to think only of themselves, to focus on their pain, and to forget about God and other people. The sacrament helps them overcome this lethargy and raises them up so that they anticipate their resurrected life by renewing their trust and developing their courage to suffer in union with Christ. Oftentimes, a visible alleviation of the pain follows the anointing, and at times, bodily healing may ensue. One possible cause of this healing is that the sacrament restores or deepens the sick person's peace with God and with his fellow men, and it provides spiritual energy. The peace and strength of the soul can strengthen the natural processes of the body to overcome the disease.[82] However, if the person is dying, the sacrament helps him unite with the dying of Christ.

In light of this Christian understanding of death and the way God's grace works through it, here are a few recommendations for the priest and the relatives and friends of the dying person: First, rather than projecting an artificial and evasive cheerfulness, they should be willing to listen

---

[81] International Commission on English in the Liturgy, *The Rites*, 603.

[82] Modern medicine takes more and more seriously the psychosomatic unity of man and acknowledges that the state of a person's soul often determines how successful medical treatment is.

when the dying person wants to talk about his pain and anxiety. They can do this only if they have accepted their own death at least to some degree. Second, they should show their closeness rather than being afraid of sharing the person's fear and despair. Physical signs of care and love, such as holding the dying person's hand, kissing, and hugging, may be more effective than words. Finally, they should pray with the person, expressing their union with him and their trust in God. The Rosary and the Litany of the Saints can be very helpful in this situation.

The person's friends and relatives should not hide from him the fact that he is terminally ill. Everyone has the right to know the truth about his condition. By lying or by silence, friends and relatives deprive the sick person of an opportunity to prepare for the final encounter with God. As long as there is hope for a physical recovery, they should strengthen the sick person's hope, since recovery depends partially on his inner disposition. But if there is no medical hope, the truth must be told with tact and love. Some doctors declare the terminal condition in an abrupt, matter-of-fact way and leave the room before the patient can ask questions, such as "How soon? How much pain will there be? How will it happen?" The doctor should assure the dying person that he will remain available to him and inform him of the many ways the pain can be alleviated. If these tasks fall to members of the family, they should act in a similar way, always speaking the truth and reassuring the dying person of their closeness.

8

Prayer and Religious Experience

The converting person who is led by grace to the love of Christ experiences, in and through the act of faith, God's presence as a reality at work in his life. This awareness of God's presence in one's life is the first stage of Christian experience; in other words, this is the fundamental mystical experience well known to every believer who consciously lives his faith. Thus, every life of faith is accompanied by an experience of faith: the facts and truths of faith are known to the believer not only by the way of abstract knowledge but also by some immediate, experiential contact. Such an experience is not an extraordinary grace, nor does it provide a direct access to supernatural realities—an access that would transcend the act of faith. Touched by grace and conformed to Christ by grace, the believer experiences in himself the effects of this grace; he is aware of being transformed, and he experiences this transformation as both trying and uplifting, fulfilling yet stretching his humanity beyond its utmost limits. The theology of spiritual life must examine the basic forms and the dynamics of this spiritual experience.

The experience of faith demands the practice of prayer.[1] He who reflects on his faith not only accepts abstract truths

[1] Yves Congar, *Faith and Spiritual Life* (New York: Herder & Herder, 1968); Bernard Bro, *Learning to Pray*, trans. John Morriss (New York: Alba House, 1966); Pope Benedict XVI, *A School of Prayer: The Saints Show Us How to Pray* (San Francisco: Ignatius Press, 2013); Romano Guardini, *Meditations before Mass* (Manchester, N.H.: Sophia Institute Press, 2013).

but also becomes aware of a Personal Reality, the absolute Source and Lord of his life. But this Sovereign Lord does not want to impose his dominion by force; he rather lures and invites and calls for a free response. This dialogue with God is prayer. He who believes, prays. Without prayer he could not conceive and utter the Yes of faith to God. The Acts of the Apostles presents Paul—after his conversion and before his baptism—as a man at prayer: "Behold, he is praying," says the Lord to Ananias.[2] Quite a few commentators point out in this scene the natural link between the beginnings of faith and prayer.

Faith needs prayer for its beginnings, survival, and development. Prayer is to faith as oxygen is to a human being and soil to a plant. Without prayer, faith would wither and die. The most important role of prayer is to make us aware again and again of the One in whom we believe. At the many turning points and in the changing situations of our lives, we activate our faith and face up to the Reality in whom we believe. When filled with joy or facing a crisis, pondering a decision or undergoing a shattering upheaval, the believer most naturally turns to prayer. He whose desire for God spurs him to let Christ occupy the center of his life will also strive to extend his prayer consistently and methodically to all the areas of daily life. Thus, the desire and the task to develop one's prayer life lead naturally to questions regarding the forms, methods, impediments, and degrees of prayer.

The Dynamics and the Many Forms of Prayer

According to traditional terminology, we differentiate between external and internal, as well as public and private

[2] Acts 9:11.

prayer. Such divisions are valid and useful provided that we are aware of their relativity, for none of these divisions can be applied exclusively. An exclusively external prayer is no prayer at all. If someone goes through the external motions of prayer out of sheer hypocrisy or simply playing a part on the stage without his heart being involved, he does not really pray. On the other hand, it is hard to imagine an exclusively internal prayer since, as a rule, our inner acts are accompanied by reflection: even if our lips do not move, even if we do not express our prayers in words, we at least express to ourselves what is going on in our consciousness —that is, we give an account to ourselves of our prayer. It is, however, important to notice that, according to the degree of the realization of external and internal elements, the different forms of prayer extend over a wide range of possible variations: from a strictly structured verbal prayer combined with definite postures and gestures to an almost passive quiet contemplation in which one does not concentrate on any idea or image but simply spends time in the presence of God.

The dividing line between private and common prayer is also somewhat blurred. Individuals who silently worship the Blessed Sacrament together, especially if they know one another and purposely pray together at the same time and place, perform a "common prayer," even if none of them knows what the other is thinking at a given moment; their prayers are joined together by space, time, and their common faith in the Holy Eucharist. At the same time, the Church has often insisted that "the private Mass" of a priest is not actually private prayer: although he is separated from others by time and space, the sacramental acts join him in a manifold way to the universal Church. Thus, the reality of prayer is much more complex than a simple classification into different kinds would indicate. In fact, even when we perform a common prayer, we feel the need to pause at times. When people say a prayer aloud together, the identity of words, gestures, and thoughts unites the participants, while the silent pause in the midst of common recitation allows for individual meditation. But the meditative silence, if used well by the individual, will only intensify his personal involvement in the common prayer.

There is another borderline case that occurs quite often and defies easy classification: an individual believer—priest or layperson—may share with others his own "private prayer"; he prays aloud while the others follow him silently and make his faith, mind, and heart their own to varying degrees. When parents teach their children to pray or when we pray with a dying person, we practice this kind of "common prayer." To what extent this prayer is truly common, God alone knows. Nevertheless, there are many situations that call for this way of praying in which we directly share in one another's faith. Someone whose faith has become weak, shaken, or simply tired may be helped in this way to rekindle his faith by the strength of another's and to find his way back to personal prayer.

The forms of prayer, then, display a wide spectrum of various combinations. To set a limit to possible variations and rank them according to their respective value would be practically impossible and theologically questionable. Nevertheless, certain forms of prayer can be found in almost every Christian's prayer life since these are necessary consequences either of human nature or of God's plan of salvation.[3]

---

[3] Of course, these two reasons intertwine: in his plan of salvation God adjusted to the needs of fallen human nature.

Liturgical Prayer

Liturgical prayer is the official public prayer of the Church.[4] Since the Church is not a mere human organization but is united to Christ as the body to its head—as the branches to the vinestock—her official prayer participates in the prayer of Christ himself in varying ways and to different degrees. As God's only Son, Christ alone knows fully the Father's goodness and holiness, and he alone loves and worships the Father as the Father deserves to be loved and worshipped. The Father always hears the Son and grants what he asks for: relief of a physical need, forgiveness of sins, bestowal or increase of divine life. This explains why the sacraments are so central to the life of the Church and her members: they are the prayer of Christ in an eminent sense of the word, and the Father's response to that prayer, which the Church applies to the different needs of her members.

As discussed earlier, the sacrament par excellence, the center and source of the Church's liturgical life (as of all her activities), is the Holy Eucharist, which is more than prayer. All the Church's liturgical prayer is thus linked to the Eucharist. The Liturgy of the Hours, or Divine Office, which extends the prayer of the Church through the span of a day, is similar in nature to the first part of the Mass, the Liturgy of the Word.[5] This link with the Eucharist is brought to light

---

[4] Cipriano Vagaggini, *Theological Dimensions of the Liturgy* (Collegeville, Minn.: Liturgical Press, 1959); Joseph Cardinal Ratzinger, *The Spirit of the Liturgy* (San Francisco: Ignatius Press, 2000); Thomas Merton, *Praying the Psalms* (Collegeville, Minn.: Liturgical Press, 1956).

[5] The Roman Liturgy of the Hours consists of Morning Prayer, or Lauds; Midday Prayer (with an option of two additional Hours, Midday Prayer and Midafternoon Prayer, for contemplative communities); Evening Prayer, or Vespers; and Night Prayer, or Compline. The Office of Readings was traditionally recited at night or dawn, but now it may be celebrated at any time of the day.

by the Holy See's recent instructions that allow and even encourage the insertion of the respective liturgical hour of the day into the celebration of the Eucharist. An important characteristic of the Liturgy of the Hours is the almost exclusively biblical provenance of its components. Only the hymns, prayers, and second reading of the Office of Readings (which is taken from an ecclesiastical author) are exceptions. This biblical focus is not the result of a mere historical contingency. Before it became a permanent tradition, the Church repeatedly examined the issue and always decided in favor of the inspired texts of Sacred Scripture, allowing only a very limited space for more recent or contemporary prayers. In spite of its explicit intention to bring the Church up to date, the Second Vatican Council left this traditional principle intact; in fact, no one rose to contest it during the Council.

About half of the daily Liturgy of the Hours consists of psalms. If we recall that the psalms were composed during the period of the Old Testament, the importance of the principle of salvation history—as we have explained previously —appears in full light. To appreciate the liturgical prayer of the Church, we must understand the relationship between the two testaments: the full meaning of the Old Testament texts is disclosed only in the light of Christ, while our understanding of Christ becomes distorted unless it is formed in light of the preparation for and anticipation of him that we see throughout the history of the Old Testament. This understanding, however, requires much reflection and study; the historical reality and complexity of salvation history also necessitate the application of the historical-critical method as a means to penetrate into the Christian religious meaning of the texts.[6] Since the longest part of the Divine Office

---

[6] Of course, as emphasized before, the historical-critical method is a necessary but insufficient condition for a Christian hermeneutics. In fact, its

consists of the Psalms, we hear most of the time about the experiences, events, and figures of the Old Testament that promise, prepare for, and anticipate the person and redemption of Christ. Thus, our prayer is a constant remembrance of and thanksgiving for the fidelity of God, who fulfilled his promises.

At the same time, the Psalms express in astounding depth and breadth the dimensions of the human soul; they faithfully reflect all the desires, joys, and complaints of religious men and women throughout history. Precisely because these poems that express such typically human attitudes are part of God's inspired Word, they provide a great consolation for us. We begin to see the wisdom of the Church's option in favor of the Psalms: these deeply human songs that each of us can so easily identify with in the different situations of our lives are divinely inspired prayers; thus, by making them our own prayer, we both conform to the intentions of the Holy Spirit and widen our prayer to include all the different needs of mankind. This, then, is the right way of praying the Divine Office: to express the intentions of the Holy Spirit, who dwells in us when we pray the biblical Word that has

---

own logic demands that we transcend it: we cannot understand the intention of the author of the sacred text unless we understand it as the expression of his faith in the God of the covenant. This God, however, consistently asks for faith in his promises of definitive salvation and promises that he is going to fulfill them with unbreakable fidelity in spite of the constant infidelities of his people. Thus, the act of appropriating the faith of the sacred author also includes the acceptance of a God who carries out his promises in a sacred history, which culminates in the "Christ event." See more in Denis Farkasfalvy, "In Search of a 'Post-Critical' Method of Biblical Interpretation for Catholic Theology," *Communio* 13, no. 4 (Winter 1986): 289–307. See also two books by the same author: *Inspiration and Interpretation: A Theological Introduction to Sacred Scripture* (Washington, D.C.: Catholic University of America Press, 2010); *A Theology of the Christian Bible: Revelation, Inspiration, Canon* (Washington, D.C.: Catholic University of America Press, 2018).

been inspired by the same Spirit. When we try to identify with what we pray by making our minds and hearts agree with the biblical Word, we are approaching this goal.

Meditative Prayer

The need for meditation precedes faith, as it is rooted in man's desire to find and face his own reality. Meditation, then, originates from this effort to turn inside so that we may take a realistic look at ourselves. As an eminently spiritual activity, meditation provides an opportunity for us to actualize and develop our spiritual potential. The basic attitude and practice of meditation is not exclusive to Christianity; we find various forms of meditation in many religions and religious philosophies. In fact, meditation often has nothing to do with religion at all. Its goal may be nothing else but to become aware of one's own deepest reality without any effort to relate to a personal Absolute; in some forms of meditation, the meditator identifies Divine Reality with his own real self.[7] At times the goal is entirely practical: to rescue the individual from the turbulence and pressures of sense experience and bring him to a peaceful and quiet state of mind.[8]

The specific character of Christian meditation is determined by faith in Christ. As it is based on a universal human need, Christian meditation shares some of the basic features of meditation outside Christianity; yet it also differs from any other form of meditation because it is transformed by faith in Christ. It is more than a state of recollection and a deepened self-awareness. The Christian meditator strives

[7] Cf. the philosophy of Yoga and certain forms of Buddhism.
[8] For instance, the practice of transcendental meditation.

to meet Christ the incarnate Son of God, and he comes to know the Father through Christ in the Holy Spirit. He wants to know and carry out the Father's will. As a consequence, Christian meditation always remains linked to the concrete material world. Thus, the main features of Christian revelation—the Word of God in Scripture, the fact of the Incarnation, the love of the Father for his creation, the threefold direction of love (toward God, neighbor, and oneself), and the inseparable unity of action and contemplation—assure that the Christian meditator does not end up in a spiritual vacuum by trying to deny the existence of the material world, his own individual self, and that of his fellow men.[9]

When the Christian meditator looks at himself, he does not simply rely on his own natural resources of self-reflection and evaluation. He wants to see himself in the light of faith—that is, he wants to know what God thinks of him and what God wants from him. It is for this purpose that he opens the Bible, the document that contains God's plan of salvation and God's intentions for mankind and for each individual. As Saint Gregory the Great puts it, the Christian seeks in these pages, as in a mirror, his own true face. He actually seeks Christ, the true, fully developed face of man, into whose likeness he is to be transformed by "the Lord who is the Spirit."[10] Introspection, looking at Christ and at oneself, and uniting one's will to the will of Christ lead necessarily to action, the carrying out of God's will in every area of one's life. In Christian meditation, then, turning inward and turning outward succeed each other with a rhythm as natural as the movement of inhaling air and exhaling it.

---

[9] Romano Guardini, *The Art of Praying: The Principles and Methods of Christian Prayer* (Manchester, N.H.: Sophia Institute Press, 1995); Hans Urs von Balthasar, *Prayer* (San Francisco: Ignatius Press, 1986).

[10] 2 Cor 3:18.

The few details we have about the prayer life of Jesus show this twofold dynamism at work. In describing the beginnings of his ministry, Mark reports that "in the morning, a great while before day, [Jesus] rose and went out to a lonely place, and there he prayed."[11] This time of prayer, however, followed a long tiring day with the crowds. Even more significant is the fact that after his disciples track him down and find him in a "lonely place," Jesus does not resent their interference but invites them on a missionary journey: "Let us go on to the next towns, that I may preach there also; for that is why I came out."[12] We find a similar pattern at the end of his ministry. He spends the last night of his life in prayer but concludes with a command to his disciples: "Rise, let us be going; see, my betrayer is at hand."[13] The prayer in which he subjected himself to the Father's will moves him to embrace his destiny of execution on the Cross.

Historians of Christian spirituality like to point out that in the first 1,500 years, Christian meditation was based primarily on the reading of biblical texts. Contrary to the Gnostics, who sought only the truth of their own selves in meditation, the first cultivators of Christian gnosis were all exegetes of the Bible. Above everyone else, we think here of Origen, whose hermeneutics has not yet been sufficiently utilized for contemporary exegesis and spiritual life. Origen expounds the correlation between knowing our own depths and knowing the depths of God, while emphasizing

---

[11] Mk 1:35.
[12] Mk 1:38. *Exélthon* literally means "I have come out." Several commentators point out the parallelism between this saying and the many Johannine statements that explain by this term the goal of the Son's Incarnation, the reason he came out from the Father into the world.
[13] Mk 14:42.

the interdependence between the different levels of spiritual growth and the corresponding levels of penetrating the meaning of a biblical text. Regardless of the imperfections of his system,[14] Origen and the patristic tradition of contemplation that depends on him resolutely avoid the dangers of an arbitrary subjectivism by remaining firmly anchored in the historical revelation of God as it is reflected in the books of the Bible. The medieval *lectio divina*, the monastic form of meditative prayer, continues the same biblical orientation. Based on reading the Bible or writings expounding the meaning of the Bible, *lectio divina* aims at both the intellectual understanding of the text and the spiritual transformation of the reader. Moreover, it often results in the composition of new biblical commentaries and homilies.[15]

The separation between exegesis and meditative prayer occurred only in modern times. Yet the link between the biblical text and meditation has to some extent been preserved even in modern Christian spiritualities, and the search for realizing God's will in the circumstances of a concrete human life usually preserve the meditator from being lost in a vague subjective experience. Unfortunately, however, recent tendencies in meditation display an unhealthy split between action and contemplation. On the one hand, emphasis on action to improve this world can lead to a depreciation of meditative prayer or degrade meditation to a technique of

---

[14] In the *Peri Archon* he establishes a parallelism between the three levels of human existence (body, soul, and spirit) and the three meanings of Scripture (the literal, moral, and mystical senses).

[15] For a careful comparison of Christian and Eastern forms of meditation and an explanation for why Christian meditation is always based on the life of Christ, see Joseph Cardinal Ratzinger, "Letter to the Bishops of the Catholic Church on Some Aspects of Christian Meditation," October 15, 1989, https://www.vatican.va/roman_curia/congregations/cfaith/documents/rc_co n_cfaith_doc_19891015_meditazione-cristiana_en.html.

decision-making. On the other hand, as a reaction against the complexity, fast pace, and nervous tensions of modern life, the cult of peaceful passivity, pure self-possession, and a state of calm without any emotional or intellectual content has become an attractive commodity. This trend regards with some suspicion the traditional forms of Christian meditation as too intellectual or too articulate since they impose a definite worldview on the meditator. Thus, many people who seek the peace of meditation but are not ready for a religious commitment turn toward the various Westernized forms of oriental meditation. These promise a variety of psychic or spiritual benefits, such as a state of complete relaxation, a release of almost limitless spiritual energy, and an indescribable experience of enlightenment. Christianity remains open to any form of human experience or religious meditation, and the theory of Zen Buddhism or Yoga may contain genuine values, just as Neoplatonism and the philosophy of Aristotle did in the first thirteen centuries; however, God's grace (which—along with sin and ignorance—has influenced to varying degrees all cultures, religions, and religious philosophies) found its pure and full expression in the person and work of Jesus Christ. Thus, the Christian will discern and transform every religious theory and practice in the light of Christ. The rejection of Christ would be a fatal loss, the attempt to transcend him a blind presumption.

Prayer of Praise, Thanksgiving, and Petition

This division of prayer is based on its content, and the problems each of the three kinds presents are well known. The self-centered person easily neglects praise and thanksgiving. The philosopher might find the prayer of petition absurd since the attempt to change God's predestining or permitting will appears not only unreasonable but naïve and futile as well. However, if we regard prayer as the practice and expression of faith, the importance of all three kinds of prayer comes to light. As explained before, personal faith is not simply consent to the abstract truth of God's existence or putting our signature on the Creed, whose statements we memorize and cherish in our mind as if they were the content of a highly esteemed lexicon. Faith becomes living when it becomes a personal confession: I accept God not only as the Lord of the universe but also as the Creator and Lord of my life, who creates and guides me, sets tasks for me, and tests, judges, and calls me to himself not only in a distant future but also in the here and now.

The prayer of thanksgiving expresses this living faith with joy and hope. He who is able to give thanks believes that his life is the gift of a caring God, even if it is burdensome and at times so unbearably difficult that, without faith, he would rather attribute his life to a cruel devil than to a benevolent Creator. In this perspective a prayer of thanksgiving appears as part of the victory of faith that conquers the world and Satan.[16]

In a similar way, a prayer of praise expresses obedience, recognition, admiration, and security, all likewise based on faith. To pray the psalms of praise daily always remains a task and a test: Do we really attempt to bring into harmony these songs of praise with our daily experience? Do we try to express our own praise through them? The prevailing pessimistic mood, often the result of a deterministic philosophy, that deeply influences the current outlook of both individual and society is for us a serious obstacle to expressing praise

---

[16] See 1 Jn 5:4.

and thanksgiving. We cannot thank and praise God unless we discover the power of faith that prevails over our feeling of helplessness when we confront the evil in our world.

Even a man of weak faith is capable of uttering a prayer of petition, although later he may think that he prayed not out of faith but only out of fear or perhaps superstition. Sometimes we feel that, if we had true faith, we would simply cast our cares unto the Lord and stop trying to bang on the door of heaven; we would just continue playing, as Saint Philip Neri said he would if he were told that he would be dead in an hour. However, in the face of man's real situation, such reflections appear hardly more than sophistry. If he is honest with himself, the believer knows that his faith does not insure him against the temptation of sin or even the eventual loss of this faith. Thus, in the prayer of petition, we express above all the limits or the deficiency of our faith, as the father of the sick boy in the Gospel of Mark did so dramatically: "I believe; help my unbelief!"[17] It is, therefore, imperative that our prayer of petition be aimed first of all at spiritual goods: to keep alive our faith, hope, and love. However, the needs of our daily lives and the worries that arise from personal responsibilities should also be brought into the Father's presence with the same simplicity and trust. Concerns about daily bread and liberation from sin, as well as fears and anxieties about temptations, all stir up our faith (which is never quite secure among the vicissitudes of this life) to petition God. God is our Father, and he loves for his children to turn to him in their needs. Every sincere prayer is heard and responded to, even if the response is different from the one we expected. In retrospect, in the light of faith, we often understand even in this life why God answers as he does.

---

[17] Mk 9:24.

We also have to consider what justifies our prayers for others. When we are moved to pray for the bodily and spiritual needs of others, not only do we express the awareness that, left to our own resources, we can do nothing or very little to provide relief, but we also accept solidarity before God with our fellow men. The first motivation simply acknowledges our finite, creaturely existence; the second goes much further: we present to God our faith and trust on behalf of the person we love because we know that this fraternal solidarity and acceptance of responsibility for one another is God's supreme will and pleasure. What would please a father more than his children treating one another as brothers and sisters? We know that, as a response to our faith, God will take care of the needs of our fellow men. What we have said earlier also applies here: we are truly enabled to participate in the redemptive work of Christ not only through suffering but also through every meritorious deed (a deed deriving from faith), not the least of which is an expression of faith in prayer.

The prayer of petition, however, does not try to change God's mind. When setting before us the examples of the man in need who bangs on the door of his neighbor until it is opened and of the widow who keeps bothering the unjust judge until he decides to take up her cause,[18] Jesus does not suggest that we could or should attempt to change God's will. On the contrary, he teaches us to pray that his will be done. But God has decided from all eternity to give us certain things on the condition that we ask for them. Thus, in his fatherly love, God has allowed our prayers to play a real part in his eternal plan. In this way, he shows how seriously he takes the requests of his children.

---

[18] See Lk 11:5–8; 18:1–5.

The Development of Prayer Life

People who have never prayed before may turn to prayer when disaster strikes. They may plead, beg, and cry, half believing, half doubting, turning to God as their last hope after everything else has failed. The deeper the misery (one's own or that of someone close to the person in prayer) and the more sincere the cry for deliverance, the more certainly God will heed such a prayer. Jesus promises everyone without exception: "For every one who asks receives, and he who seeks finds, and to him who knocks it will be opened."[19] Sometimes God will grant the request exactly as it was asked. Sometimes he expects us to wait and persevere, and at the end he will grant us something that we did not expect. Either way, the sincere beggar will realize sooner or later that he is dealing with a generous and wise Heavenly Being. Then, for the first time, he may thank God: at first, for the pleasant gifts; and later, for the trials and disappointments as well. Gradually, he will begin to find the Giver more attractive than his gifts and will desire to possess him more than any of his gifts.[20] Such a person understands the psalmist's invitation: "Taste and see that the LORD is good!"[21] Then he will be grateful for God himself; he will praise and thank God, not for some particular favor, but simply for the fact that God is God and for every past and present moment of his life. He can make his own the prayer of the Gloria of the Mass: "We give you thanks for your great glory."

Just as gratitude prompts God to overwhelm the grateful

---

[19] Mt 7:8.
[20] Bernard of Clairvaux, *De diligendo Deo*, nos. 23–33, in *Sancti Bernardi Opera*, ed. J. Leclercq and H.M. Rochais (Rome: Editiones Cistercienses, 1966), 3:138–47.
[21] Ps 34:8.

person with new and greater gifts, lack of thankfulness may stop the flow of favors. Saint Bernard raises the question, Why would God shower his gifts on someone who, by his ingratitude, only aggravates his guilt? According to Bernard, God's refusal to heed the prayer of the ungrateful man can be an act of mercy. He does not want to increase the man's guilt by bestowing upon him new favors that would only be ignored or taken for granted.[22]

Different Forms of Devotion

Here, our purpose is not to describe individual devotional practices but to discuss some basic principles that should govern our attitude regarding devotions. First, it is clear that particular devotions are not time resistant; they change from age to age. For example, we have been using the Rosary only since the thirteenth century, and the celebration of the first Friday of the month is only three hundred years old. At the same time, certain practices have become unusual today. Nowadays, when an epidemic occurs, we do not go around in a procession with the relics of the saints; nor is it common to touch coffins of the saints with our personal belongings. No form or practice of devotion is an absolute. No particular devotion is required as a necessary ingredient of Christian life. Not everyone has the same vocation or personality. We express and develop the same faith in a variety of ways according to the needs of different religious communities, cultures, epochs, and historical and sociological circumstances.

However, a healthy pluralism and freedom do not exclude the recognition that, in general, certain *types* of devotions are

[22] Bernard of Clairvaux, *Sermones de diversis*, sermo 27, chaps. 6–8, in *Sancti Bernardi Opera*, vol. 6, bk. 1, pp. 202–3.

indeed necessary for Christian life in every age and culture. For instance, one could hardly state that processions with the Blessed Sacrament are a necessary part of the Eucharistic devotion of a given parish or religious community today. However, every parish and religious community needs some form of Eucharistic devotion, or else its sacramental life and, consequently, the vigor of its spiritual life would suffer. Similar considerations apply to the realm of Marian devotions. The role of the Blessed Virgin Mary in salvation history is an integral part of our Catholic faith. This faith must, in some way and form, be expressed and nourished in every age and culture. Still, we cannot deduce from this general principle that the praying of the Rosary—albeit so widespread and so fruitful—must become a necessary part of everyone's spiritual life. Nor can we present a pilgrimage to a Marian shrine as an indispensable means to foster the growth of faith. (This respect for personal freedom should go hand in hand with the acknowledgment that precisely in our age the praying of the Rosary and Marian pilgrimages do result in a renewal and deepening of faith in many people.)

We must also see that more is not always better in this area, and not only because one's duties of life allow only so much time for devotional practices. Before we evaluate a concrete case, we need to take into account the vocation, personal characteristics, and needs of the individual. When someone omits a devotional practice from his daily schedule or inserts one into it, he should evaluate his motives. Whether the change in his devotional practices will result in the growth of his faith or its weakening depends on his motivation.

Generally, the masters of spiritual life emphasize the guidance of divine grace: we have "gifts that differ according to the grace given to us."[23] We have to build up our prayer lives in response to these gifts. This requires from us an openness and readiness and an active and unselfish search for God's will. But it would be wrong to assume that we receive God's guidance only in the form of inward inspiration. We are on much safer ground if we do not choose our devotions independently but with help from the directives of the universal Church, practiced at our local church. Moreover, marriage partners, friends, and the community in which we live may also, directly or indirectly, provide much incentive and direction, especially if we seek God's will in the events and turning points of our lives. By this, the searching soul finds the way of prayer that he personally has to travel. We should remember that the call in the gospels always addresses the individual: "Come, follow me."[24] Each of us must hear and follow this unique, personal call.

Religious Experience

In post-Tridentine Catholic theology (that is, theology after the Council of Trent in the sixteenth century), a significant trend denied any experiential knowledge of grace, a view that seemed to be the logical conclusion of the Tridentine decree denying the Protestant doctrine of the absolute subjective certainty of salvation.[25] The importance of religious experience was also de-emphasized because of the Catholic Church's traditional suspicion of the constantly emerging

---

[23] Rom 12:6.
[24] Mt 19:21; Mk 10:21; Lk 18:22.
[25] Cf. Vatican Council II, Declaration on Religious Freedom *Dignitatis humanae* (December 7, 1965), nos. 1533–34, 1562–64.

religious emotionalism in movements such as Montanism, Quietism, and the different forms of Protestantism.

On the other hand, the twentieth-century biblical, patristic, and liturgical renewal has brought to light the rich tradition of religious experience, in the Scriptures and in patristic and medieval theology. The apostles were privileged witnesses to the earthly Jesus; they heard and saw him and lived with him. After his Resurrection, however, their earthly senses alone were no longer sufficient to recognize him. Their faith had first to be awakened in order for them to identify Jesus in the breaking of the bread, at the shore of the Sea of Tiberias, and on the road to Damascus.[26] Paul goes one step further: not just the eyewitnesses to Christ on earth but all Christians can contemplate, through faith, the glory of the risen Lord.[27] Paul is aware that Christ lives and speaks in him and that he spreads the odor of the knowledge of Christ when he preaches the Gospel.[28] The fruits of life in Christ and in the Spirit are "love, joy, peace, patience, kindness, goodness, faithfulness, gentleness, self-control."[29]

Both in Paul and in John, one can know whether one is in Christ by the Spirit of God, and the Spirit of God is discerned by faith: "No one speaking by the Spirit of God ever says 'Jesus be cursed!' and no one can say 'Jesus is Lord' except by the Holy Spirit."[30] In John's Gospel, Jesus promises that he will send the Holy Spirit, and the disciples will know him because he will remain with them and in them. The world can no longer see Jesus, but in the Spirit the disciples

---

[26] See Lk 24:13–35; Jn 21:7–12; Acts 9:4–9.
[27] See 2 Cor 3:18.
[28] See 2 Cor 2:14; 13:32.
[29] Gal 5:22–23.
[30] 1 Cor 12:3; see also 1 Jn 3:24; 4:1–3.

will see him and know that Jesus is in the Father, the disciples are in Jesus, and Jesus is in them.[31]

As we survey the nature and finality of theology in the patristic age, we see that abstract reflection and striving for loving contemplation often merge into one. The first example, and one of the greatest, of this theology is that of Origen. From the careful description of the literary sense of Scripture, he proceeds, or at times jumps, to its spiritual meaning within the whole of the mystery of Christ. He is convinced that all Scripture aims at, and culminates in, the Church's loving union with the Logos, the bridegroom of the Church, and in his union with each soul within the Church. Origen seems to be the first theologian to have worked out a theory of the "spiritual senses" in order to show how Christ adapts his experience to the different needs of the soul:

> [Christ] is called the true Light, therefore, so that the soul's eyes may have something to lighten them. He is the Word, so that her ears may have something to hear. Again, He is the Bread of life, so that the soul's palate may have something to taste. And in the same way, He is called the spikenard or ointment, that the soul's sense of smell may apprehend the fragrance of the Word. For the same reason He is said also to be able to be felt and handled, and is called the Word made flesh, so that the hand of the interior soul may touch the Word of life. But all these things are the One, same Word of God, who adapts himself to the sundry tempers of prayer according to these several guises, and so leaves none of the soul's faculties empty of his grace.[32]

---

[31] See Jn 14:15–20.
[32] Origen, *Commentary on the Song of Songs*, bk. 2, chap. 9, in Johannes Quasten and Joseph C. Plumpe, eds., *Ancient Christian Writers: The Works of the Fathers in Translation*, vol. 26, *Origen: The Song of Songs; Commentary and Homilies*, trans. R. P. Lawson (New York: Newman Press, 1957), 162; cf.

The tradition of the five spiritual senses continued both in Eastern and Western forms of spirituality. Before we look at it in Saint Bernard, we want to understand more precisely the nature of spiritual experience and spiritual delight, which Saint Augustine explains in a way that even his rustic audience in the church of Hippo was able to appreciate. He asks a rhetorical question:

> So my brothers, does wickedness have its own delights and justice does not? Does evil delight and goodness does not? It does delight by all means, but it is the Lord who will give sweetness and our land will give its fruit. Unless he first gives sweetness, our land will be sterile. The Apostle has desired this justice and he was delighted. He remembered God and was delighted. His soul burned with desire for the courts of the Lord and all that he had highly esteemed lost their value, they became damage, loss, and trash.[33]

The idolizing of created things fills the heart with pernicious enjoyment, and only the greater delight of spiritual realities—the love of justice, truth, and goodness and ultimately the love of God—can expel it from the soul. God's grace enables the will to make this free choice, and the soul finds its delight in spiritual realities, as Augustine says: "Everyone who converts to God experiences the change of his enjoyments: they are not removed but changed."[34] Thus, enjoyment belongs to the very dynamics of Christian life, and the affection that liberates from the tyranny of evil desires and enables one to enjoy eternal spiritual realities, in-

---

Origen, *Commentary on the Song of Songs*, bk. 1, chap. 4, in *Ancient Christian Writers*, pp. 82–83.

[33] Augustine, *Sermo* 169, chap. 7, no. 8.
[34] Augustine, *Enarrationes in Psalmos* 74, no. 1.

deed God himself, comes from above; it is an undeserved grace.[35]

The symbols of the five spiritual senses are used less frequently by Augustine than by Bernard of Clairvaux. Hearing the Word of God with the external bodily ear and hearing the living Word in the heart transcend what the bodily eye sees, which is the external form of the earthly Christ and his extreme humiliation. Hearing with faith purifies the spiritual eye to see even in this life the glory of God in some initial way. Similar to the ascent from hearing to seeing is the movement from smelling the Word's fragrance to touching him. For Bernard, the soul smells the fragrance of the glorified Christ, her bridegroom, and is stirred up to seek him. She can touch him only by the "hand of faith" and taste him as Wisdom, the taste of truth, justice, goodness, and purity.[36]

But to see the full christological structure of spiritual experience in Bernard, we need to go beyond the images of the five spiritual senses. At the beginning of the spiritual journey, the soul can enjoy only fleshly, sensible, and material realities. When she encounters Christ, she can relate only to the earthly Jesus: the crying infant; the young man; the humiliated, suffering Christ:

> The love of the heart is in a some sense a fleshly love which affects the human heart by the flesh of Christ, and by what Christ has done and commanded in the flesh. Talk about these things easily moves the soul who is filled with this love. He listens to nothing more willingly, studies nothing

[35] Jean Mouroux, *The Christian Experience: An Introduction to a Theology*, trans. George Lamb (New York: Sheed and Ward, 1954).

[36] Bernard of Clairvaux, *Sermones in Cantica canticorum*, sermo 20, chap. 8, in *Sancti Bernardi Opera*, 1:120.

more eagerly, recalls nothing more frequently; no other meditation is as sweet to him. This provides the ointment for the holocausts of the soul's prayers, as it were, with the lard of the fattened bull. The sacred image of the Man God is present to the praying soul, as being born and nursed or as teaching, dying, rising or ascending to heaven.[37]

Such *amor cordis* (love of the heart) or *amor carnalis* (fleshly love) draws away the affections from vices to focus them on the humanity of Christ. Since Jesus the man is God, we reach God himself in some initial way by loving the man Jesus. Yet this love is still unstable and imprudent—it is not under the guidance of reason. The next step, therefore, is the *amor rationalis* (love guided and strengthened by reason in the light of faith). This rational love does not deviate into false teachings about Christ, and it avoids imprudent, blind emotionalism. Whoever is at this intermediate step pursues what is right and good but does not yet enjoy the virtuous life.

The goal of spiritual life is to attain the *amor spiritualis* (spiritual love), by which we are attracted not only to the Word in flesh but also to the "Word wisdom, the Word justice, the Word truth, the Word holiness, piety and virtue."[38] At this stage, Wisdom enters the soul, and her work is the source of great delight:

> Now Wisdom conquers Evil unceasingly in the minds it entered, expelling the taste of Evil, which the woman introduced, by a much better taste. When Wisdom enters the soul, it deprives the experience of the flesh of its taste,

[37] Bernard of Clairvaux, *Sermones in Cantica canticorum*, sermo 20, chap. 6, in *Sancti Bernardi Opera*, 1:118.
[38] Bernard of Clairvaux, *Sermones in Cantica canticorum*, sermo 20, chap. 8, in *Sancti Bernardi Opera*, 1:120.

purifies the intellect, heals and repairs the palate of the heart. Goodness is now tasty to the healthy palate, in fact, Wisdom itself tastes better than which nothing exists among good things.[39]

This Wisdom in the soul is Truth—it is Christ himself, who transforms first the heart and mind and then also the body, its every action, gesture, and word. The body mirrors the light of the soul, almost anticipating the body's eschatological beauty: "The Truth shines in the mind and the mind sees himself in the Truth."[40] Thus, the experience of God is mediated through the soul; the purified soul sees God in and through himself. At this point, the soul is ready for the spiritual marriage with the Word, of which nothing is more desirable or enjoyable:

> [Love] is sufficient to itself, it is pleasing in itself and because of itself. It is both the merit and its reward. Love does not seek any cause or fruit beside itself. Loving is its own fruit. I love because I love; I love so that I may love. Love is a great reality provided that, returned to its origin and poured back to its source, from there it will always flow without interruption.[41]

Origen, Augustine, and Bernard beautifully illustrate the mainstream of patristic and monastic spiritual experience. Affectivity is an essential ingredient at every point of the itinerary because the soul chooses to be where its affection draws it. Spiritual affection overrules the destructive

[39] Bernard of Clairvaux, *Sermones in Cantica canticorum*, sermo 85, chap. 8, in *Sancti Bernardi Opera*, 1:312-13.

[40] Bernard of Clairvaux, *Sermones in Cantica canticorum*, sermo 85, chap. 10, in *Sancti Bernardi Opera*, 1:314.

[41] Bernard of Clairvaux, *Sermones in Cantica canticorum*, sermo 83, chap. 4, in *Sancti Bernardi Opera*.

attachments, and then, by God's grace, the soul adheres to God's will. After some shorter or longer period of struggle, adhering to God's will transforms the soul and fills it with joy.

Many saints, however, testify that God takes away this spiritual joy at times in order to purify the soul. God remains in the soul but hides from it in the course of one's experience, and the feeling of the absence of the Beloved causes anguish and pain. The more the soul loves, the more excruciating is the suffering. In most cases, the joy returns and often redounds also upon the senses. Saint Teresa of Calcutta, however, endured this absence (with a short reprieve) for forty years. After a while, she told Jesus, "If you don't smile at me, I will smile at you." And the world saw only the perennial smile of Mother Teresa. Later, she understood that God deprived her of consolation in order to help her feel closer to the abandoned, dying destitute whom she served.

After these typical examples, here are some general conclusions. The religious experience of Christians is uniquely different for every individual, but its development shows certain common characteristics. What the Fathers called the *vita activa* or *bios praktikos* and later authors called the *via purgativa* is the period of fighting vices and sins by good deeds and mortifications. At this stage, discursive meditative prayers dominate. The *vita contemplativa* or *bios theoretikos* of patristic authors corresponds to the *vita illuminativa* and *vita unitiva* of later terminology, in which the soul becomes attracted to spiritual realities, truth, justice, goodness, beauty, and holiness. The mere rational, discursive prayer becomes affective; instead of a step-by-step meditation, the soul finds peace and nourishment in resting in words and images from the Bible.

At some point, the fully purified and virtuous (illuminated) soul is ready for the spiritual marriage and becomes one spirit with Christ.

Some scholars draw a sharp line between ordinary Christian prayer and mystical experience, the latter being characterized by God's overwhelming, transporting, rapturing activity and the soul's passive acceptance. God's grace, however, is at work at every step of spiritual development, and the soul's powers are intensely involved in the mystical rapture.[42] Perhaps the difference between mystical and ordinary Christian experience, then, lies in intensity rather than nature.[43]

Religious Experience outside Christianity

Our faith teaches us that God offers grace to all people, even if they have no knowledge of Christianity. These people do not possess the mutually deepening correlation of experience and explicit doctrine. The experience of incarnate grace cannot find full expression in any non-Christian religion or philosophy. But if non-Christians accept grace and cooperate with it, this implies the presence of the Holy Spirit and thus faith, hope, and charity. Charity, however, must ultimately manifest itself in outward acts, such as kindness, helpfulness, empathy, sacrifice, and forgiveness, so this distinctly Christian grace must bestow a distinctly Christian

---

[42] On the history of the Western Christian mysticism, see Bernard McGinn, *The Presence of God: A History of Western Christian Mysticism*, 7 vols. (New York: Crossroad, 1991–2021).

[43] For the teaching and experience of the Carmelite mystics, see Thomas Dubay, *Fire Within: St. Teresa of Avila, St. John of the Cross, and the Gospel— on Prayer* (San Francisco: Ignatius Press, 1989).

shape on the lives of non-Christians. Since true grace is always and everywhere of Christ, it conforms the souls of the people in whom it is active to Christ. Looking at the actions and lives of such people, a Christian could recognize close kin, even though they belong formally to a different religion. Perhaps in some ways Mahatma Gandhi was a Christ-like person outside of Christianity who loved and treated the pariahs, the lowest-caste Hindu Dalits, as the children of God. At the same time, the faith of such people does not fully bud, and they cannot give a full rational assent to the Gospel. They may suspect or intuit that giving their lives away for others out of love is noble and worthwhile, but they do not know why. They do not know that the one infinite Creator God *died* for each of them out of love and that he calls them to share in the eternal joy of the Trinity.

The prevailing and often unspoken fad in many theological circles, influenced by an idea of Karl Rahner, is that what matters is simply the transcendental experience of grace; its particular form—i.e., the divine-human person of Jesus Christ, as expressed in the Nicene Creed—is merely secondary. Transcendental experience, according to this view, is what touches and changes the entire person.

But the Creed—which, according to Rahner, would be formal—expresses the deepest objective truths of reality.[44] Faith, being an act of the intellect and will elevated by grace, appropriates this object of faith and thereby changes and transforms the believer himself in an experience that can strengthen him even to the point of martyrdom, to endure

---

[44] "Actus credentis non terminatur ad enuntiabile, sed ad rem." Thomas Aquinas, *Summa theologiae* II-II, q. 1, a. 2, ad. 2.

death rather than betray reality. Thus, the Church's distinctly Christian faith clarifies, deepens, and fulfills the religious experience.[45]

---

[45] Note that we do not deal here with the rich and fruitful theology of mysticism by Karl Rahner in toto but point out an ambiguity that can be concluded from statements like this: "The experience of being taken out of oneself makes what is normal and organized in the institutional Church seem provisional and questionable, incommensurate with the meaning it is supposed to signify. A man is thrown back upon his own subjectivity, which no longer seems to be manageable to him in terms of conceptual expressions and propositional criteria. He then has the courage to entrust himself to something within him which no longer has to be tested and sanctioned by categorical norms, but is experienced at least in a preliminary way, as not being subject to such control." "Religious Enthusiasm and the Experience of Grace," in *Theological Investigations*, vol. 16, trans. David Morland, O.S.B. (New York: Seabury Press, 1979).

9

The Unity and Diversity of Vocations

Faith in Christ is always a response to God's Word. However, not only does God address us through the general medium of the Scriptures and the preaching of the Church, but our outward hearing or reading of the Word is also always accompanied by the prompting of his inward grace. As the medieval theologians put it, our proclamation of the Word would not be effective if the inner voice of grace did not inspire the heart with the same message. Without the inward movement of grace, faith and personal vocation could not come into being.[1]

Since God addresses everyone in his inmost personal being, we must conclude that everyone has a calling, or a vocation. This is not fundamentally a question of one's ministry or job, which can change many times over the course of his life. Rather, it is a question of *state of life*: priesthood, consecration, or marriage—three distinct modes of love. God's Word not only asks for the assent of our intellects but also strives to shape our values, direct our decisions, and penetrate and transform every aspect of our lives. Because of this, the Christian with conviction turns to God in prayer before making decisions. Of course, he receives guidance and counsel from people he trusts regarding his vocation,

---

[1] See Vatican Council II, Dogmatic Constitution on the Church *Lumen gentium* (November 21, 1964), nos. 30–42 (hereafter cited as *LG*).

but in the end he is the only one who can see what must be done and make the final decision in obedience to God's grace. At the same time, this personal decision makes him into an adult Christian since it requires his acceptance of responsibility, commitment, and fidelity.

There is no limit to the variety of vocations. From a Christian perspective, every life is destined to embody obedience to the twofold commandment of loving God and loving one's neighbor. But, in their concrete forms, no two vocations are exactly the same. In addition to the great differences in personal abilities and individual gifts of grace that are needed for each vocation, every distinct calling serves a wide range of human needs. In his First Letter to the Corinthians, Saint Paul helps us understand the basic unity and multiplicity of vocations. He first lists the three main groups of church leaders: apostles (itinerant missionaries who proclaimed the Good News of Jesus Christ in many places), prophets (Christians living in a local community who were inspired by the Holy Spirit to warn, encourage, and deepen the faith of the local church), and teachers (who performed the continuing education of those who had converted upon hearing the Good News of Christ). However, after these "church functionaries," Paul extends the list with a number of other vocations only to assert that he does not consider the list complete.[2] He tells them, "Earnestly desire the higher gifts,"[3] but then he goes on to show them in detail a still more excellent way: the way of love that is the climax and source of all spiritual gifts. Thus, the multiplicity of vocations finds its unifying center in love. This love both unites

---

[2] See 1 Cor 12:28–30.
[3] 1 Cor 12:31.

all spiritual gifts and inspires its own diverse manifestations in a limitless multiplicity of individual vocations.[4]

Although there is an endless diversity of vocations, they have been categorized into several main groups in different ways throughout the history of the Church. During the theological renewal that followed World War II, ecclesiology had pride of place. The ecclesial community (priests, religious, and laypeople) developed an awareness that we all have a unique vocation to fulfill and that everyone must dedicate his life to the task assigned by his vocation. Following the Pauline metaphor of the many members in the one Body of Christ, theologians tried to divide vocations into the categories of parish priests, missionaries, contemplative monks, the various forms of religious institutes, and the lay life in the world. The theological truth that these are all true vocations is beyond doubt, but we should beware of a certain immobility in practice. That is, we should not consider our positions in the Church too statically as if the ideal would be always to stay in the same place and fulfill the same job with a rigid uniformity.

Of course, we've recently observed the opposite phenomenon in the Church: an exaggerated reaction to an overly rigid distribution of roles. Over the last fifty to sixty years, the Church has come to a new appreciation of the way life is full of movement and development. The individual is alive in the full sense of the word only to the extent that he reviews again and again his life situation and convictions. The living person develops. Consequently, he constantly changes both in his views and activities. However, going too far in this direction can lead to an attitude that

[4] See 1 Cor 13:1–13.

does not allow for perseverance and self-giving. Those who choose to remain completely and forever open choose also not to be committed to anyone or anything, and they do not develop the virtue of loyalty. The authenticity of love suffers if we cannot give ourselves to a person, community, or ideal irreversibly, without ulterior motive and calculation.

Within the Church, we are all able to find and faithfully live out our vocation while doing justice to this twofold requirement of openness and commitment. No matter whether one eventually chooses marriage, priesthood, or some form of consecrated life, the final decision is always preceded by a period of search and preparation, followed by some sort of trial period and, in the end, a definitive commitment.[5] The Church does not admit anyone to holy orders, religious vows, or the sacrament of marriage without adequate preparation and deliberation. The trial period (for example, novitiate, engagement, or seminary training) always serves the same purpose: the candidate must learn more about himself, the community, or the person to whom he plans to devote himself. After an adequate preparation, however, the pledged word is binding.[6]

[5] The trial period is different for religious life and marriage. Because of the very nature of sexual relations, cohabitation is harmful to marriage. Sexual relations affect the person too deeply to be tried out on an experimental basis. Engagement, on the other hand, is a much-needed conditional commitment to prepare for the unconditional commitment of marriage.

[6] This applies at least to normal circumstances. However, some extraordinary external or internal occurrence—with or without personal fault—may make our adherence to a given vocation practically impossible. But even in such cases we must live with the irreversible consequences of our commitments. For instance, someone who entered a valid sacramental marriage is called to remain faithful to his partner even if some compelling reasons make cohabitation harmful or impossible. A priest, even if he can no longer function as such, remains forever affected by his participation in the priesthood of Jesus Christ.

Continuous development and maturation are essential for any vocation. For instance, a priest should not get locked into the idea of the priesthood that he had formed as a twenty-five-year-old. If he does not develop his vocation, if he does not penetrate more deeply into the mystery of Christ's service, then his lack of development and openness to change is what will endanger his vocation. Similarly, someone with a religious vocation who wants to go through life clinging to a minimalistic understanding of his vows cannot avoid becoming stale and empty. As soon as growth or progress stops, the awareness of a vocation becomes clouded and may easily disappear altogether. The same holds true in the life of marriage partners: unless they progress in knowing, forgiving, and accepting each other, their relationship degenerates into a sour coexistence or mutual resentment.

As we will later see in more detail, the dynamics of a vocation are closely aligned with the stages of the natural life cycle. Youth is a time to search for ideals and learn to develop personal relationships. Growth toward maturity means a series of attempts, failures, and provisional victories. During this stage of life, we should not expect from ourselves or from others so much stability and certainty as to exclude the possibility of a fresh start. Maturity, however, requires the ability to make commitments and to create a stable framework wherein our lives may become fruitful in various ways, such as by giving life to children and bringing them up responsibly and by enabling our talents and knowledge to bear fruit. The fifteen-year-old who claims to have a fully developed worldview is as unnatural as the thirty-five-year-old man who has not yet decided what he wants to do with his life. Even more lamentable is the fifty-year-old who disowns his past and dreams about becoming young again.

From the perspective of spiritual life, old age should not

be identified with retirement just because one's potential for work is decreasing and he is less and less capable of learning in the secular sense of the word. According to ancient human experience, we acquire wisdom only in old age. This includes a deeper understanding, a unified vision, and a summation and digestion of accumulated experiences. The theology of death—a much-researched topic recently—points out that death invites us to summarize our lives.[7] But in order to surrender to God with one definitive gesture the totality of our existence, we first, as a rule, need to review our life and at least attempt to understand its meaning. Ordinarily, old age is the time to accomplish this task. Another responsibility of old age is to make sure that the insights we have gained from an evaluation of the accumulation of our life experiences may become a source of learning for a new generation. There is no more difficult and more necessary task for us in our old age than to remain open to the world of young people. Only then can we present the fruits of our experience in such a form and language that the upcoming generation will be inclined to take them to heart.

As we have seen, vocations necessarily vary not only among individuals but also by age groups. The greatest temptations of youth are rash judgment and reckless deeds. The hardest tasks for the adult are endurance, consistency, and concentration in service. The danger of old age is pessimism, that bitter and unfair judgment of the old man who questions or rejects the values of the present and future in order to exalt his past.

In what follows, we will consider three main kinds of vocations: marriage, consecrated life, and the priesthood.

[7] Karl Rahner, "On Christian Dying," in *Theological Investigations*, trans. David Bourke, vol. 7, *Further Theology of the Spiritual Life* (New York: Herder & Herder, 1971), 285–93.

Marriage

People are at once bodily and spiritual beings, called to integrate their body and soul into a harmonious unity. Like animals, they are endowed with biological instincts, yet they also are drawn to transcend and transform their instinctive activities of self-preservation and the preservation of the species into an expression of communion and love. In fact, God's revelation, as transmitted and explicated by the Church, confirms and expands these conclusions, reached as they were through a philosophical analysis of human experience. It tells us that men and women are a unity of body and soul created in God's image and likeness. Their sexual desires, relationships, and activities reflect both the material and spiritual aspects of their nature. God's original design, as inscribed at Creation in human nature, calls for man and woman—in and through sexual love and generation—to become gifts to each other. They are drawn to offer their entire selves to each other as gifts of faithful and enduring love: "They become one flesh."[8] From the beginning of Creation this union served as a great sacrament, a tangible sign that expressed and mediated mankind's final goal: man and woman are to find fulfillment and happiness in their union with each other, a union that participates in the divine communion of the Holy Trinity.

The Fall and the ensuing avalanche of personal sins, however, have dramatically wounded the original nuptial union of man and woman. Instead of becoming gifts for each other in their bodily union, instead of being the way to God for each other, men and women have wanted to find fulfillment in quasi-divine independence. Instead of love for each

---

[8] Gen 2:24.

other, each has tried to be a "god" for the other, ending up in a desperate struggle to possess each other in mutual lust. Even outside the Judeo-Christian tradition, the best representatives of mankind saw the need for a redemption in some sense of married love. God began this redemption as early as the Old Testament. First, he condemned any form of sacred prostitution in Israel that attempted to commune with the fertility gods and goddesses through intercourse with the divinities' representatives. Through this prohibition and throughout the continuing process of revelation to Israel, God made it very clear that he transcends sexuality and is in no need of a sexual counterpart. Once God's transcendence has been revealed, the prophets do not hesitate to show that God is not only Creator, Lord, and Father to Israel but also Israel's bridegroom.[9] He is a jealous lover who punishes his bride's every infidelity, and yet, in the Messianic times, he will espouse to himself the forgiven remnant of Israel forever.

God's unconditional faithfulness and love of Israel in spite of Israel's repeated adulteries with other gods began to transform sexual relationships within Israel. The surrounding pagan nations projected their sexual vices onto their gods, imagining their gods with one wife but with many lovers and scores of "illegitimate" children. Israel, on the contrary, evolved from the practice of polygamy, divorce, and concubinage toward monogamous, lasting marriage. Even though none of these vices were explicitly proscribed by the Torah, pious Israelites tried to avoid them. The prophet Malachi conveys God's word about marriage and divorce after the exile:

---

[9] Cf. Hos 1–3; Ezek 16; Song of Songs; Is 62.

The LORD was witness to the covenant between you and the wife of your youth, to whom you have been faithless, though she is your companion and your wife by covenant. Has not the one God made and sustained for us the spirit of life? And what does he desire? Godly offspring. So take heed to yourselves, and let none be faithless to the wife of his youth. For I hate divorce, says the LORD the God of Israel, and covering one's garment with violence.[10]

Through his Incarnation, Jesus inaugurates the Messianic times. He reveals to all those who know the prophecies of the Messianic wedding feast that he is the bridegroom of Israel and that in him God has come to celebrate the eschatological wedding feast with his people. As long as he is among them, the friends of the bridegroom should not fast.[11] However, the unfaithful bride, Israel, who represents all of sinful mankind, must first be rescued and purified. Jesus "gave himself up for her, that he might sanctify her, having cleansed her by the washing of water with the word, that he might present the Church to himself in splendor, without spot or wrinkle or any such thing, that she might be holy and without blemish."[12] In Jesus' redemptive work, the full depth of the nuptial union of man and woman—adumbrated first in Genesis—is revealed. Marriage becomes the image Saint Paul uses to express the self-sacrificing virginal love of the Son of God, who gives his life in order to bring about the new creation: his pure bride, the Church, consisting of the remnant of Israel and the converted nations.

As Saint Augustine remarks, no true Christian existence is possible without nuptials—or at least an earnest search

[10] Mal 2:14–16.
[11] See Mt 9:14–15; Mk 2:18–20; Lk 5:33–35.
[12] Eph 5:25–27.

for them. Some are called to share directly in the virginal union of love that unites Christ to his Church. We will speak about them when discussing celibacy for the sake of the kingdom. In this section, however, we intend to outline the spirituality that is appropriate for those who share in that same union through the sacramental mediation of Christian marriage.

The sacrament of marriage provides God's healing grace so that the man and woman may live up to the dignity of the marital relationship. This grace will help the couple find fulfillment in the ever-growing gift of their bodily and spiritual selves to each other. The spouses cannot give themselves to each other as a gift by selfishly forcing themselves upon the other. Rather, spousal love is a pledge of one's whole psychosomatic self to foster the flourishing of the partner. This means finding delight in the partner's existence as well as delighting in their union, not merely physically, but also spiritually, allowing each other freely to enter into the other's soul.

Most importantly, though, Christ's redemptive grace not only heals the natural marital relationship but also raises marriage to the dignity of sacrament, a real sharing in the virginal union of Christ and the Church. More precisely, through the virtue of being the sacrament of Christ's loving union with his Church, marriage offers the grace of preventing the relationship from sliding into lust, domination, or infidelity. Through the sacrament, the couple participates in the redemptive love of Christ himself—that love by which Christ offered himself on the Cross to create a pure and perfect bride for himself.[13] Affected as they are by original and personal sins, grace will help the spouses only if they

---

[13] See Eph 5:25–27.

learn to open themselves up to the very love of Christ, a love that always includes sharing his Cross. Just as Christ died on the Cross so that his bride, the Church, may be born holy and shining with splendor, husband and wife will accept the recurring pain of dying to themselves in order to exist for each other. By carrying each other's burdens (moral and physical weaknesses, idiosyncrasies, and neuroses) and by forgiving and accepting each other time and again with a renewed love, they will share in the Cross of Christ and grow closer to him. Thus, for all eternity they will remain grateful to each other since they have mediated Christ to each other through their marriage on earth. While at the beginning of their relationship their love for each other and their love for Christ may have seemed to be in tension or even in conflict, by purifying and deepening their love for each other, the two loves will come into complete harmony by the end of their lives. They will love Christ in the other and the other in Christ.

Christian spouses will plan their family reasonably but generously. By keeping their sexual union open to the gift of life, they may experience the great mystery of sharing in God's giving of a new life.[14] God is the Creator of the child, but husband and wife cooperate with him at their own level; they become true parents of the same child. As God creates a new human being out of love, the parents also accept their child out of love rather than merely tolerate him as a burden or liability. Moreover, if parents live the sacrament of marriage, their children will be profoundly influenced by it. These parents will not only want their children to unfold their natural potential but also offer them for baptism; they

---

[14] Practicing natural family planning is not contraception since it does not actively obstruct fertilization.

want to love them with the very love by which the Father loves them. Thus, they will cooperate not only in the natural development of their children but also in the growth of their life of faith.[15]

In a healthy marriage, giving life to children is part of the couple's hope from the beginning. Different motivations may be at work, depending upon each parent and the many situations of their lives. Some parents may be concerned about perpetuating the family name; others may want to ensure that they will be cared for in old age. If, however, an intense love joins the couple together, they will find their joy in the fruit of their love, the blessing of their gift to each other. As they look for the first time at their newborn baby, they are amazed at the miracle. Someone who has never existed before looks at them with worried and curious eyes that search for safety and comfort. Throughout gestation and birth, the mother has especially experienced the mystery of being intimately associated with God the Creator. She has felt more directly God's love for the child.

Although the gift of a child enriches the spouses' union, it comes with challenges. For example, the mother may find it difficult to be emotionally close to the baby without distancing herself from her husband. Yet there is no true conflict between these two relationships in a healthy marriage. In fact, the parents' harmonious, loving relationship is a cru-

---

[15] For a more detailed treatment of the scriptural doctrine, see Pierre Grelot, *Man and Wife in Scripture* (New York: Herder & Herder, 1964). For the phenomenology and theology of marriage, see John Paul II, *Man and Woman He Created Them: A Theology of the Body*, trans. Michael Waldstein (Boston: Pauline Books and Media, 2006). For the Church's view on marriage in the modern world, see Vatican Council II, Pastoral Constitution on the Church in the Modern World *Gaudium et spes* (December 7, 1965), nos. 47–52. For the Church's view on family life, see John Paul II, apostolic exhortation *Familiaris consortio*, (November 22, 1981).

cial factor for the baby's healthy development. It is like fresh air that invigorates the baby and like a safety net that makes the child feel secure. The husband may struggle with how busy his professional work keeps him, but he must remain faithful to the decision he made at the beginning of the marriage: family comes first. A devoted husband will relieve part of the burden from his wife, and his emotional support will diminish the dangers of postpartum depression.

Consecrated Life

Jesus treated people in different ways.[16] Though he preached to all who wanted to hear him and healed all who asked for healing, he did not let everyone become his disciple. The man from whom Jesus expelled many unclean spirits begged Christ to be allowed to join his company, but Jesus sent him home to proclaim how much God had done for him.[17] Jesus chose his disciples with sovereign freedom. He called them, and they left everything and followed him.[18]

Unlike other rabbis, Jesus also had women in his entourage. They followed him wherever he went and assisted him out of their means.[19] They stayed with him all the way to the Cross when all but one of his male disciples had abandoned him. They observed where and how he was buried.[20]

---

[16] See Vatican Council II, Decree on the Adaptation and Renewal of Religious Life *Perfectae caritatis* (October 28, 1965), nos. 1–25; John Paul II, apostolic exhortation *Vita consecrata* (March 25, 1996); Adrian van Kaam, *The Vowed Life* (Denville, N.J.: Dimension Books, 1968); Canon Jacques Leclercq, *The Religious Vocation* (New York: Kenedy, 1955).

[17] See Mk 5:18–20.
[18] See Mk 1:14–19; 2:13–17; 3:13–19; Lk 9:59.
[19] See Lk 8:1–3.
[20] See Lk 23:55.

At the earliest possible time after the Sabbath rest, they returned to the tomb. Thus, they became the first witnesses to the empty tomb and to the risen Christ.[21] They were commissioned by him to report the news of the Resurrection to the apostles and so, as some of the Church Fathers have said, they became "apostles of the apostles."

Religious communities of men and women originated from the desire to live this life as Jesus' disciples. While they cannot accompany him in the flesh, as his contemporaries did, they have a privilege the first disciples did not possess: through his Resurrection Jesus has become present in a new way. He no longer is walking *next to us* or speaking *to us*, but he is present *within us*, inspiring us *from within*; by nourishing us with his risen Body, he incorporates us into him. Thus, the intimacy of our relationship with the risen Lord in some sense surpasses that of the first disciples and the earthly Jesus. Yet our faith that embraces the Christ present in us remains anchored in the experience of the first disciples, who heard and touched and saw with their own eyes the Word made flesh dwelling among them.[22]

Not every community of consecrated life is enclosed in a convent, monastery, or habit. Some remain immersed in the world, heeding in a special way Christ's word to the Father at the Last Supper: "I do not pray that you should take them out of the world."[23] In the late 1940s, Pope Pius XII officially recognized and defined the "secular institute"—an organization of laypeople who live in ordinary society and yet, like religious, follow the traditional evangelical counsels of poverty, chastity (that is, celibacy), and

---

[21] See Mt 28:1–10; Jn 20:1–2, 11–18.
[22] See Jn 1:35–51.
[23] Jn 17:15.

obedience.[24] Perhaps the best known examples are the numeraries of Opus Dei and the Memores Domini of Communion and Liberation, though many smaller congregations exist across the globe, including the Community of Saint John (*Johannesgemeinschaft*), founded by theologians Hans Urs von Balthasar and Adrienne von Speyr. Some Christians, including Saint Giuseppe Moscati and Venerable Madeleine Delbrêl, have even lived their lay charism without any link to a formal institute. Consecrated laypeople typically have ordinary secular professions beyond the bounds of the hierarchical Church—doctors, teachers, mechanics, journalists, lawyers, accountants—and hope to serve as yeast in the world's thick dough, without any official ministry. Their total commitment to the counsels frees them for both prayer and merciful service to their neighbor, as well as for a dedication to work that is motivated by love rather than money or power. They bring to mankind, especially unbelievers, the fruits of their intimacy with the Lord. But this unique vocation—still somewhat rare in the Church—must be distinguished sharply from the state of a single Christian in search of a spouse, since lay consecration, by definition, requires a permanent vow or promise, at least once it reaches full maturity.

The sections that follow will discuss the elements of celibacy, community life, obedience, and poverty, which are each embraced in different ways by different consecrated vocations. For example, not all consecrated celibate people live in an organized visible community, and "poverty" has a wide range of expressions. However, these four aspects of the consecrated life are embraced in one way or another by all consecrated people.

---

[24] Pius XII, apostolic constitution *Provida Mater Ecclesia* (February 2, 1947).

a. Celibacy

Because of the intimate presence of the risen Christ in believers, consecrated life is more than a discipleship. We certainly learn from him and try to imitate his example, but we are also called to be one with him as the bride becomes one with the bridegroom. According to the New Testament and the Church Fathers, all of us in the Church—men and women, single and married—are called to become the bride of Christ[25] by uniting ourselves in pure love to him.

Some share in this union with Christ through marriage and others through celibacy.[26] The couples who receive the grace of the sacrament of marriage learn to love and serve Jesus Christ through loving and serving each other. Those who are called to celibacy freely renounce sexual relations "for the sake of the kingdom of heaven."[27] They do not despise marriage, but they want to reserve all their psychic and physical energies for God's reign. Consecrated celibates have become aware of the presence and value of God's reign as the great wedding feast between Christ and mankind. Rather than being bound to one man or woman, they want to unite themselves to Christ directly and help many others to become united with him. For these men and women who have received the call to celibacy, marriage would mean a division of heart[28] and a restriction. Were they married, they would have to honor their self-imposed limits; before

---

[25] See 2 Cor 11:2-3; Eph 5:22-33; Rev 21:1-4.
[26] See Lucien Legrand, *The Biblical Doctrine of Virginity* (London: Geoffrey Chapman, 1963); Raniero Cantalamessa, *Virginity: A Positive Approach to Celibacy for the Sake of the Kingdom of Heaven*, trans. Charles Serignat (Staten Island, N.Y.: St. Pauls, 1995); Roch A. Kereszty, *Rekindle the Gift of God: A Handbook for Priestly Life* (San Francisco: Ignatius Press, 2021), 83-89.
[27] Mt 19:12.
[28] See 1 Cor 7:33-34.

everyone else, they would have to love and serve their own families. As celibates, their vocation is to extend their love to many men and women and to present all of them "as a pure bride to her one husband."[29]

We may attempt to understand the mystery of Christian celibacy from another viewpoint: the central role of sexuality in personal communion and communication. Unless we have obscured its value by promiscuity, we are very much aware that sexual relations are meant to become an intimate way of communication. In marriage, where sexual relations can develop their full potential, giving one's body to the other may indeed express a radical way of giving one's whole self, both body and soul, to the other. This is indeed the most dramatic way of being in one another and for one another. The celibate senses, often instinctively, that his sexual powers hold the key to a radical way of giving himself. Through his celibacy, he longs to give God his whole self, both soul *and* body. In the words of Saint Paul, "The unmarried woman or virgin is anxious about the affairs of the Lord, how to be holy in body and spirit."[30]

The celibate is, of course, aware that God is not a sexual being who can be reached through the sexual powers of any man or woman. (The Bible condemned from the beginning any form of sacred prostitution, the perverse attempt of people to reach the sacred through sexual relations.) The celibate can do only what Mary did: renounce sexual relations in order not to give away the key to his own gift of self. Just as Mary did, the celibate wants to remain "unfulfilled," preserved in an attitude of prayer and expectation and awaiting God's initiative. He prays that God may look down on the

---

[29] 2 Cor 11:2.
[30] 1 Cor 7:34.

lowliness of his servant[31] and ignite his soul with the fire of his own love. As a result, the energy that would normally be used for loving one's spouse and children will be transformed into loving God and all those whom God entrusts to the celibate's care. For the celibate, then, his renunciation of sexual love becomes the form of his gift of self to God and to God's people.

However, the consecrated celibate runs a much greater risk than a married person. If his faith fades and his prayer dries up, he could close in on himself and become, in the end, incapable of loving either God or man. His humanness would wither away in a sterile isolation and egotism. Husband and wife, in contrast, must at least curtail their egotism and share their income, their time, and their bed if they want the marriage to survive. But if the celibate accepts the void of unmarried life and sustains his trust and prayer life, his hope will not be disappointed. Periods of consolation and aridity will follow each other, but he will be able to help those who come to him and ease the burden of those who suffer from loneliness and despair. His own suffering will let him understand and accept those who suffer. Still, his cross of celibacy should not be exaggerated. More often than not, it may not be greater than the hardships of those who have to raise a family.

If the celibate's love for Christ and for people is real, he will bear witness to the reality of Christ, who is the source of his love and peace. His presence among people will be a reminder that the "future age" is real, since his ability to become human and loving without the natural support of a marriage points to a power greater than his own: the power of God's coming kingdom. In the kingdom there is no need

---

[31] See Lk 1:48.

THE UNITY AND DIVERSITY OF VOCATIONS 227

for sexual relations because everyone will be united to the risen spiritual body of Christ and to one another in a virginal communion of body and spirit.

Looking at celibacy from this perspective, we should not be surprised that the Church clings to it in spite of great pressure even from within her ranks. In the Roman Rite of the Catholic Church, the only men ordained to the priesthood are those who believe they have received the gift of celibacy and have committed themselves to a celibate life. The Church, of course, could change this law. Saint Peter was married, and many bishops and priests were married in the first few centuries. Even today married men may be ordained in the Eastern Rite Catholic churches, and married deacons and priests of the Episcopal church who want to enter into full communion with the Roman Rite of the Catholic Church may be accepted for diaconal and priestly ordination and remain married. The charism of celibacy, as a prerequisite for priestly ordination in the Roman Rite and for episcopal ordination in the Eastern Rite churches, developed first as a spontaneous tradition before it became codified into Church law around the end of the fourth century. Presently, the Church considers the celibate state—freely chosen for the sake of Christ—so important that she accepts a lower number of candidates for the priesthood rather than change her law.[32]

Please note that although we have used the pronoun "he" throughout this discussion, everything we have said about

---

[32] Even if, at a later stage, the Church changed her requirement for the diocesan priesthood, priests in religious orders and brothers and sisters in religious orders would still continue to make a vow of celibacy. Remarkably, in the Eastern Rite churches, where most parish priests are married, people prefer celibate monks over married clergy for confession and spiritual guidance.

male celibacy also applies to women. In fact, spiritual motherhood is more perfectly expressed in the vocation of consecrated women than in that of men.

b. Community Life

While celibacy for the sake of the kingdom is the root and foundation of consecrated life, one way in which it may expand and flourish is in community. If God, Christ, and his kingdom are our most important goals, we naturally seek the company of those who share the same values with us. Even the first hermits in the history of the Church showed their love for Christ by welcoming guests and by sharing with others the fruits of their prayer and labor. The young, inexperienced hermits asked for the advice and guidance of those who had already learned how to fight the temptations of the world, the flesh, and Satan. A whole settlement of hermits grew up around the most famous hermit, Saint Anthony in the desert. Still, the individual hermits continued to live, pray, and work alone while coming together from time to time for instruction and for the celebration of the Eucharist. For many hermits, however, the solitary life proved to be a dangerous snare. They succumbed to depression or vices, or they engaged in a mindless ascetic competition to outdo one another with severe mortifications. For instance, if one slept on a stone slab, another decided not to lie down to sleep at all but to just rest in a sitting position. If one ate only bread for nourishment, another would top him by eating only every other day. Such extreme mortifications, combined with pride in one's achievement, could seriously damage both body and soul.

The practical need for training under an experienced superior who would curb exaggerated practices, pride, and self-will, as well as the realization that the law of Christ comprises two precepts—both love of God and love of neighbor—contributed to the emergence of monastic communities. As Saint Augustine wrote in his *Rule for the Servants of God*, "You were gathered into one community so that you might live in unanimity in the house and that you might have one soul and one heart in God."[33] Through the two millennia of Church history many different types of religious communities developed that proved helpful for their members, the Church, and the world at large. At one end of the spectrum, we see the large monastic "town" of Saint Pachomius, where all sorts of craft were practiced by the monks in silence and recollection, interspersed with periods of common prayer and meals. This was in many ways replicated in the twentieth century by Saint Maximilian Kolbe in Poland, who established the City of the Immaculate, where hundreds of Franciscan brothers worked. The major difference was that unlike the City of the Immaculate, the Pachomian community did not have an apostolic purpose but instead focused on the edification of its own members while serving outsiders by providing useful products. The City of the Immaculate, on the other hand, was a center of intense media apostolate. In Hippo, Saint Augustine gathered his presbyters into a family-like monastic community—a model for many future religious orders—that combined common prayer, community life, and apostolate. Even though the monasteries under the Rule of Saint Benedict had no apostolic purpose at the beginning, within a few centuries they became powerful centers for evangelization in the new Europe after the barbarian invasions. Their community life and prayer, stable lifestyle, and agricultural and cultural activities, combined

---

[33] Augustine, *Regula ad servos Dei*, no. 1.

with preaching and helping the poor, transformed the roaming pagan tribes into settled Christian societies.

The growing numbers of the urban poor and the wealth and secularization of the hierarchy called for a new form of religious life. Unlike the monastic orders, the mendicant orders of the Franciscans and Dominicans preferred smaller and more mobile communities, and they settled not in the countryside but within the cities among the poor. The practice of begging for food and the destitute lifestyle of the small Franciscan communities showed the solidarity of the Church with the poorest of the poor. In the sixteenth century Saint Ignatius of Loyola founded the Society of Jesus, with a unique kind of community structure. They even asked the Holy See for dispensation from reciting the Divine Office in common because their style of apostolic work required the greatest flexibility and mobility. Jesuits were ready to travel and work and live individually or in small groups without substantial common prayer, and yet the strong link of obedience and the vivid memory of a long and rigorous spiritual, intellectual, and community formation united them into a worldwide family.

Modern men and women are torn between two contradictory drives. At times, we would prefer to withdraw from the oppressing company of others and do our own thing, undisturbed by any outside pressure. But at other times, we might crave the appropriation of a group identity; we want to feel and think *with the group*. Sometimes the most gifted individuals end up brainwashed by a cult that offers them emotional shelter at the price of individual identity and responsibility. Today, we often see examples of these two extremes in certain religious communities. Some people, for instance, may enter a religious community because they think that within this group they can do their personal projects most expeditiously. The religious order exists, they believe, in order to develop their individual projects and talents. Superiors and the shared financial resources of the community should serve the projects of individual members. If this spirit prevails in an order, sooner or later that order must give up its institutions; as a community, it cannot take on any corporate commitment since the interests of its individual members are unpredictable and shifting. Predictably, communities that have devolved into such a collection of individuals have shown a rising average age and diminishing numbers.

In obvious reaction to these kinds of groups, we find religious orders and secular institutes that enforce strict identity of thought, rooted perhaps in the writings of one particular theologian. They believe that this narrow discipline is the only effective antidote to rampant individualism and dissent from Church teaching. Interestingly, this type of order can flourish for a while because it provides an insulated bubble for its members, and some do find such a safe haven comfortable. Yet for stronger, more independent persons, the intellectual and behavioral straitjacket becomes in the long run unbearable, if not destructive.

A healthy religious community avoids both extremes: individualism that destroys the community and group identity that suppresses individuality. Only a sufficiently mature person is strong enough to choose freely to become a constructive member of such a community. The members are asked to subject their own interests to those of the community and accept the community's tasks and commitments as their own. Obedience to the superior must be seen in this larger context: the superior assigns the tasks and responsibilities to each member and sees to it that everyone cooperates according to his own ability for the realization of the goals and ideals of the community. Of course, no religious community is a free-floating, independent group. They are all part of the Church and are dedicated to serving the Church.

In community life we experience again and again the truth of Jesus' words: "Whoever would save his life will lose it; and whoever loses his life for my sake and the gospel's"—we could add "and for the sake of his brothers and sisters"—"will save it."[34] If we work generously for the good of the community, our individual talents and personal potential will not be suppressed but rather will be stretched to the limit. We will be surprised to find out that we can achieve much more and can handle a greater variety of tasks and jobs than we had ever suspected.

Not only do our natural abilities blossom in a healthy community, but so also do our faith and love. Faith, on the one hand, is our most personal act. God invites me, individually, to accept his Word as true and entrust my destiny to his will. He calls me, sees me, and directs my steps as if I were his only concern. At the same time, my personal act of faith, if it is genuine, inserts me into the Body of Christ that stretches through the centuries and is perfected in the communion of heaven. I cannot believe in Jesus Christ unless I believe what the apostles have seen and heard and touched; they were eyewitnesses to the man Jesus during his earthly life and his Resurrection. By sharing in and being strengthened by their eyewitness experiences, we in the twenty-first century also "see" the Lord in our act of faith. The very genesis of our individual act of faith is communitarian because it includes the Church of the apostles. Its growth also requires a community of faith. Each one of us is only one member of the Body of Christ; therefore, we

---

[34] Mk 8:35.

each receive the infinite riches of God in a finite receptacle, while our experience of faith is limited by our own subjectivity. However, an individual's experience can be widened and enriched by the experience of the other members of the community. Even the great Saint Paul writes to the Romans that he expects to be encouraged by their common faith.[35] If we recognize how God is educating and leading other members of the community, our faith in his guidance of our lives is strengthened. By being grateful for the gifts of one another—for their faith, goodness, or wisdom—we can uproot jealousy and envy, potential cancers for religious life. Then, in a mysterious but very real way, the gifts of others for whom we thank God also become our joy and fulfillment.

Just as the virtue of supernatural faith is perfected in community, so, too, is the supernatural virtue of love. Christians receive the task and the ability from Christ to love all men and women. This means to will what is good for them and to help them to the extent that we can. By loving all, we approach, but never reach, the universal love of God, who wants them to live and to grow into the brothers and sisters of his Son and thus share in the Son's eternal life. Perhaps the greatest trials of community life are those situations where we are forced to admit our inability to love our brothers because our sins and their sins weigh so heavily on us that we begin to lose hope for the future. Then only prayer can help, but it will be a prayer that comes from faith the size of a mustard seed. He who prays this way knows in advance that if he asks for the ability to love his brothers, God will not, in the long run, resist him. Thus, a religious community never becomes a "finished product." It is both a gift and a task, a

---

[35] See Rom 1:12.

present reality and an object of hope. Sometimes, though, the community is a foretaste of our home in heaven, where fraternal love grows into friendship. This happens when we see members of the community love one another with God's forgiving and life-giving love. For friendship, a certain natural affinity is certainly needed, but the higher the values that join us together, the deeper and more lasting is the friendship that develops. As we help one another grow in the love of Christ and of our brothers or sisters in community, such friendship becomes one of the greatest blessings of religious life.

Blessed Aelred's book *Spiritual Friendship* should be read by everyone who is called to live in community. A short quote must here suffice:

> What happiness, what security, what joy to have someone with whom you dare to speak as if he were your own self; one of whom you are not afraid to confess your failings; one to whom you can unblushingly reveal what progress you made in spiritual life; one to whom you may commit all the secrets of your heart and entrust all your plans! What is more joyful than so to unite to yourself the soul of the other and to make one of the two so that no boasting may be feared, no suspicion dreaded, no correction of one by the other be resented; no praise on the part of one brings a charge of adulation from the other.[36]

A good friendship does not develop into an exclusive relationship. True friends remain an open circle, eager to share the joy of friendship with others in the community. Rather than forming a clique apart from the rest, they include oth-

---

[36] Aelred of Rievaulx, *Spiritual Friendship*, ed. Marsha L. Dutton, trans. Lawrence C. Braceland (Collegeville, Minn.: Liturgical Press, 2010), bk. 2, chap. 11, p. 72.

ers as much as possible and strengthen the community's cohesion.

c. Obedience

Our discussion of obedience will apply most directly to members of religious communities, although privately consecrated people also commit themselves to obedience in different ways. Since religious communities are ecclesial communities of the Church, their structure is analogous to that of other local church organizations, such as a parish or diocese. As Christ, the Church's head, is represented by the local pastor and by the bishop, so—analogously—the religious superior represents Christ for his community. Even on a purely practical level, the need for a superior in a community that intends to live, pray, and work together is quite obvious. Those religious communities that, in the aftermath of Vatican II, wanted to experiment with not having a superior (on the grounds that mature Christians outgrow a child's need for being told what to do and how to live) failed miserably. Either they disintegrated or the more aggressive members imposed themselves (and their own views) on the rest of the group.

Beyond the obvious need to assure harmony and order, religious obedience helps fulfill the desire of members who seek to find and carry out God's will in their lives. A religious community can flourish only if both the superior and the members of the community seek above all God's will and, consequently, the common good of the community. This attitude of faith and voluntary cooperation excludes both arbitrary orders by the superior and the spirit of individualism by the members according to which everyone tries to build himself up at the expense of the others. Since in today's world so many members of religious institutes have well-developed skills and knowledge, superiors should make important decisions only after listening to expert advice. Moreover, superiors will not, as a rule, determine all the details of the job assigned to a member but leave ample room for personal initiative and responsibility. The brothers or sisters in charge of a task will have to make their own decisions according to the intention of the superior and the goals and spirit of the religious institute. As the *Declaration of the General Chapter of the Cistercian Order* explains, "Superiors should listen willingly to the members of the community, yet their authority to discern and command what is to be done must remain firm. In giving counsel, the brothers should respect the person and judgment of others, and they should present their position with solid reasons and not follow the will of their own heart."[37] If a religious thinks that an order given by the superior is, for some reason, impractical or impossible, he should present his views to the superior openly and humbly. If the superior nevertheless insists on the order, the religious, trusting in God's help, should try to carry it out unless the order violates the law of God, Church law, or the constitution of the religious institute.[38]

While the practice of poverty or celibacy may be challenging only at certain times, obedience may be difficult from the beginning to the end. This is so because obedience lays claim to what is most noble and spiritual in us: our freedom. Religious, however, who desire to give themselves over to God without compromise actually wish to be under obedi-

---

[37] *Declaration of the General Chapter of the Cistercian Order (Rome, 1969–2000)* (Dallas: Cistercian Abbey, 2005), 49.

[38] *The Rule of Saint Benedict: Latin and English*, trans. Luke Dysinger (Trabuco Canyon, Calif.: Source Books, 1996), 161.

ence. They want to follow the example of the Lord, whose daily nourishment was to do the will of his Father. They know that the only way to be united with God, who is pure spirit, is to subject their own will in everything to the will of God and so to become "one spirit" (*unus spiritus*) with him. This perfect union of wills is possible by God's grace even in the case of utter spiritual aridity, when we do not experience any consolation or any feeling of love for God.

Of course, religious may compromise their obedience in several ways, while hiding the disobedience at all costs. For instance, when the superior discusses with them a possible new assignment, they may exaggerate their weaknesses so effectively that the superior finds it practically impossible to assign the job to them (unless, of course, the superior knows personally the real abilities of the religious). Another way to sabotage obedience is to accept the assigned responsibility but to fulfill it so half-heartedly and reluctantly, with so much moaning and groaning, that after a while, the superior has no other choice but to replace the complaining member. An openly hypocritical way would be to ask the superior's permission for something only after what he is asking for has already become a fait accompli—for instance, he has already accepted an invitation to give a lecture and bought the airfare ticket before he asks permission to go. But if we sincerely want to be united with God's will in everything, we will practice "active obedience": we will not simply fulfill explicit commands but actively seek ways to build up our community and carry out our tasks. The truly obedient religious has a peace that no person or natural disaster can take away from him. His will is anchored in God's will, where he finds his strength and his rest.

d. Poverty

The beatitude "Blessed are the poor in spirit"[39] is to be lived by all Christians. We should not be enslaved by the craving for material or spiritual possessions but rather become generous in sharing our material possessions with all those in need and using our talents and gifts of grace for the benefit of others. Moreover, if we strive for holiness, sooner or later in the process we will encounter a situation of conversion when we feel we have reached the end of the rope: our sinful habits and inordinate cravings resist the sincere efforts of our will to subject them to God's commandments. Then we are truly spiritually poor and ready to cry out for help since we feel as if we are drowning, just as Peter felt as he walked toward Jesus on the water. We are blessed in this extreme poverty because now we can more acutely perceive our need for God's grace and, consequently, receive his saving help. Without the attitude of this spiritual poverty, no one can enter the kingdom of God.

Jesus calls some people not just to generosity and spiritual poverty but to actual material poverty. He says to one, "You lack one thing; go, sell what you have, and give to the poor, and you will have treasure in heaven; come, follow me."[40] "Sell what you have": Jesus knows that clinging to possessions paralyzes the heart of this man and closes it off from God. Jesus knows the state of his soul. This might be one of the reasons he tells him to sell all he has. Another reason might be that Jesus wants him to become his disciple in the strict sense of the word, sharing Jesus' life and carrying out his mission. Ever since, some people have heeded this call of Jesus and others have not.

[39] Mt 5:3.
[40] Mk 10:21.

Throughout the history of the Church, many different forms of the practice of poverty have developed. In the Church of the apostles in Jerusalem, the first disciples "were together and had all things in common; and they sold their possessions and goods and distributed them to all, as any had need."[41] The hermits in the desert did not pool their material resources together, but they divested themselves of any significant possession before embracing the eremitical life. They lived separately in an extremely frugal and destitute form of material poverty. Saint Benedict's Rule, by contrast, does not consider destitution an ideal state for the monk but focuses instead on the relinquishment of private property:

> Above all, this vice [of private ownership] must be thoroughly uprooted from the Monastery. Without the Abbot's order, no one should presume to give or to receive anything or to possess anything whatsoever, not even his own book, writing tablets, tablets or stylus; in short, nothing at all, especially since monks may not have the free disposal even of their own bodies and wills.[42]

The abbot nevertheless should take into account the needs of each individual monk and should provide for each "all that is necessary, . . . taking into account the weaknesses of the needy, not the evil will of the envious."[43] In this way the monks learn to live in a family where "all things should be the common possession of all" and everyone should receive what he needs "from the father of the Monastery."

The mendicant orders of the Franciscans and Dominicans were founded in the High Middle Ages as the masses of the

[41] Acts 2:44–45.
[42] *Rule of Saint Benedict*, ch. 87.
[43] *Rule of Saint Benedict*, ch. 55.

urban poor felt abandoned by the Church. Saint Francis and his followers, especially, wanted to live as the poorest of the poor. And unlike the earlier monastic orders, they refused to have possessions, especially landed property, held in common. In our age the Little Brothers and Little Sisters of Jesus, founded on the spirituality of Blessed Charles de Foucauld, have chosen not only to live as poor among the poor but also to earn their living as the poorest of the poor do in their local area.[44]

None of these religious orders or communities that live out a certain form of voluntary poverty despise material goods. On the contrary, material things reveal their true value only to hearts freed from greed; material goods should be enjoyed as God's gifts—signs of his wisdom, goodness, and beauty. Saint Francis, who never owned an acre of land in his life, enjoyed the blooming meadows of Umbria more than those who actually owned the fields. We can appreciate the beauty of a flower much more if we refuse the urge to pluck it for ourselves.

Besides freeing the heart for God, renouncing wealth also has another purpose: helping those in need. Beginning with the first hermits and monks, religious have often produced more than they themselves could use, and they have shared their surplus with the poor. In the Middle Ages monasteries fed a huge number of poor people daily. Religious have also worked in hospitals, ransomed slaves, and taught in schools. Since they were never compensated monetarily, their schools and hospitals could more easily accept the poor and provide personal care and love for every student or patient.

The disciples who followed Jesus lived from a common

---

[44] Charles de Foucauld, *Oeuvres spirituelles de Charles de Jésus pere de Foucauld* (Paris: Editions du Seuil, 1958).

purse, and the first Christian community continued this practice. The members sold their property and gave the proceeds to the apostles, who distributed them to each according to his need. Thus, no one owned anything substantial as his own. By sharing material goods, they built up a close community. Similarly, members of a religious community do not earn money or accept donations for themselves, but rather for the community. The superior's job is to distribute to each member what is needed. In this way, material goods become both the expression of an existing unity and an effective means of fostering unity and a freely chosen dependence on one another. By accepting the sharing of material goods with our brothers or sisters, we find it easier to share ourselves with one another. And by accepting this material dependency on the community as a whole, the members come to trust in the community that supports them.

Priesthood

The identity crisis among priests is one of the major reasons for the sudden decline of priestly vocations after the Second Vatican Council. Priests must be convinced of the value of what they are doing in order to attract young people to share in that work.[45] Before the Council, the image of the priest

[45] See Vatican Council II, Decree on the Ministry and Life of Priests *Presbyterorum ordinis* (December 7, 1965), nos. 1-22 (hereafter cited as *PO*); Pope John Paul II, *Letters to My Brother Priests: Complete Collection of Holy Thursday Letters (1979-2005)* (Downers Grove, Ill.: Midwest Theological Forum, 2006); Joseph Ratzinger, *Teaching and Learning the Love of God: Being a Priest Today* (San Francisco: Ignatius Press, 2017); Yves Congar, *A Gospel Priesthood* (New York: Herder & Herder, 1967); Albert Cardinal Vanhoye, *Old Testament Priests and the New Priest: According to the New Testament* (Leominster, U.K.: Gracewing, 2009); Kereszty, *Rekindle the Gift of God*.

was clearly defined by the Church. Every Catholic knew that "Father" is the possessor of immense spiritual powers: he changes the bread and wine into the Body and Blood of Christ; he opens and shuts the gates of heaven by granting or refusing absolution; he facilitates the entry of the dying into heaven by giving them the last rites. He controls everything in the parish, both the Church and the school. If anyone has any problem of conscience, they go to Father.

After the Council, however, people began to rediscover the old Catholic truth that all members of the Church share in Christ's royal priesthood and that each member possesses a special charism by which he should contribute to the building up of the Church. Alongside what was coming to be called "the ministerial priesthood," a wide range of other ministries arose: from youth minister to marriage counselor to religious education director. And all these were open to lay men and women in the parish. The question then arose: What is the ministerial priest good for? Except for a few sacramental rites, everything, it seemed, could be accomplished by laypeople. In addition, lay ministries did not impose on the minister the often-misunderstood obligation of celibacy. Moreover, during the first two decades of the twenty-first century, the laity's confidence in the ordained ministry was severely shaken by the sexual abuse scandals of the clergy in the United States and a number of other countries, as well as the cover-ups perpetrated by a significant number of bishops. By now, effective measures of control have been implemented in the American Church, in cooperation with civil authorities, to ensure the safety of the young and the punishment of the offenders. More recently, the severe penalties imposed on some negligent or complicit bishops have generated hope that a chastened clergy and a more trusting laity will emerge.

In the aftermath of this tragic crisis of confidence, many people have begun to realize that a shameful minority of priests should not vitiate the immense sacrifice of the great majority of priests who expend their lives in service. Catholics are also yearning for the sacraments, and they have come to see that no matter how many dedicated lay men and women minister in a local church, the Christian community is paralyzed without priests—the laity cannot make present the sacrifice of Christ to which they can unite their lives; the sick cannot receive the strengthening of the sacrament of anointing; and repentant sinners are not absolved. The members of the community feel and act like sheep without a shepherd. In short, without priests Christ cannot be present among his people in a fully human, tangible, and sacramental way.

Thus, the rediscovery of the importance of the priesthood has inspired many recent efforts to investigate its roots in the New Testament, its history in the Church, and its latest articulation by the Second Vatican Council. Here we can provide only a short summary of these new theological developments.

Jesus accomplished what religious men and women have wanted to perform throughout history: that one perfect sacrifice. The Old Testament often insists that the value of a sacrifice depends upon the interior attitude of the person making the sacrifice—chiefly, the depth of the love and dedication of the sacrifice—as well as upon the value of the gift for the sacrificer. As the only Son of the Father, Jesus alone could fully understand the majesty, goodness, and holiness of God and how deserving of love God is. By the same token, only Jesus could completely see how unjustly the Father had been treated by sinful man. Thus, he alone, as the Son of God made man, could offer the Father the perfect love and dedication the Father deserves, a love and dedication that makes Jesus' atonement, thanksgiving, and praise truly worthy of God. Knowing that sinful man, left to his own resources, could never have accomplished such a sacrifice, the Son identified himself with mankind and accomplished it in our place and for our sake. The perfection of Jesus' sacrifice derives as well from the value of the offered gift. In freely accepting violent death, Jesus did not merely offer to God a material object from which he could walk away intact after the sacrifice had been made; he dedicated to God his entire life, including his death on the Cross. What could compare in value to the self-giving of the Son of God made man? By raising his Son from the dead, the Father demonstrated his acceptance of his Son's gift of self and drew him and mankind, for whom the Son offered his life, into intimate communion with himself.

All baptized Christians participate in the royal priesthood of Jesus Christ[46] and are called to offer their bodies—that is, their lives lived in the body—as a spiritual sacrifice in union with the one perfect sacrifice of the Son.[47] The apostle Paul explains his own priestly service as an offering up to God of all the Gentiles so that they might become an acceptable sacrifice, sanctified in the Holy Spirit.[48] Paul's vocation serves as a paradigm for the vocation of the ministerial priest, who represents Christ, the one Shepherd, Teacher, and Priest. His task is to guide (shepherd) and instruct (teacher) the faithful so that they may learn to unite their own self-offering to the perfect sacrifice of Christ. But they can do so in a tangible, visible way only if the ministerial priest, and he alone, makes present the sacrifice of Christ. *Thus, the ministerial*

---

[46] See 1 Pet 2:5–9.
[47] See Rom 12:1–2.
[48] See Rom 15:15–16.

priest is not Christ, but he represents both Christ and the Church by being Christ's servant for his people. Paul insists, "What we preach is not ourselves, but Jesus Christ as Lord, with ourselves as your servants for Jesus' sake."[49] To put it succinctly, as John Paul II did, the role of the ministerial priesthood is to actualize the priesthood of the laity. That is, the priesthood of the laity does not exist for the sake of the ministerial priesthood. On the contrary, the ministerial priesthood exists for the sake of the royal priesthood of all the faithful. Yet, the ministerial priest is indispensable, for he represents sacramentally the dependence of the Church on Christ, who is the head of the Church.

Priests now understand better that the sacraments transform the lives of the faithful only if they are received with living faith. Therefore, they spend more time and energy on preaching and teaching the Word of God in order to enkindle and deepen the faith of their people.[50] But the goal of their preaching and teaching is to prepare the faithful for a fruitful celebration of the sacraments, above all, the Eucharist. In addition, by preaching the Word and administering the sacraments, the priest builds up the Christian community. In other words, by reconnecting those who have fallen into grave sin with the Church through the sacrament of reconciliation and by feeding the people with the Word and the Body of Christ, the priest builds them into the Body of Christ that is the Church.

Building the Body of Christ is, of course, anything but an automatic process. A priest can feed the people with the Word only if he himself is fed by the Word and is striving to understand and live the Word in his own life. Good

---

[49] 2 Cor 4:5.
[50] Kereszty, *Rekindle the Gift of God*, 45–57.

preaching is, moreover, a result of the gift of prophecy: it discovers the vulnerable, sensitive spots in the life situations of the hearers and shows how Christ's grace can cut out tumors and heal the wounds in the soul. In their preaching, the bishop and priest must also address issues of social injustice and immoral laws or decisions of the government, but they should not become entangled in merely political matters where no evangelical or natural moral value is at stake. Mere politics should be left to competent politicians.[51] Bishops and priests should announce the Gospel not only to their own faithful but also to all people. Ministry in the Church is essentially missionary; the form of this missionary work will vary from place to place (for instance, through the media, publications, and different forms of dialogue).

Since the Church is the Body of Christ, Christ lives and acts in her. Each member is called to communicate Christ's love to one another and to the world. Just as Jesus gave his flesh for the life of the world, a Christian community exists not for its own sake but for the sake of the world. Christians cannot remain indifferent to the problems that plague mankind today—we must do our utmost to help eliminate poverty, injustice, oppression, and war. But we will succeed in improving society only if we do not limit the Gospel to social justice: our most important task is to give *Christ* to mankind. Without Christ, poor people made affluent would have a much emptier and more meaningless life than those still poor who retain their religion. The high suicide rate in the affluent but a-religious Scandinavian countries is convincing evidence for this point.

Faced with so many tasks, the post–Vatican II priest knows

---

[51] Naturally, the Church must teach publicly on basic moral issues, such as abortion, euthanasia, and same-sex marriage, even if her opponents accuse her of involvement in politics.

that he cannot do his job by himself. He must search for all the talented assistants he can find, not only financial experts and architects, but also people with special spiritual gifts. In a good parish, many different lay ministries flourish today. These might specialize in the care of the poor or the sick, the liturgy, or religious education. They counsel engaged and married couples and help the divorced. The number of these ministries is still increasing, and enlisting the active cooperation of members, coordinating their activities, and criticizing and encouraging their work is likely a much greater challenge than the one-man show of old. This new, more sophisticated leadership is badly needed in the Church today. We still see too many instances of the authoritarian pastor.

On the other end of the spectrum, some priests and bishops misunderstood the demands of the post-conciliar era: they abandoned the principle of one-man responsibility but allowed the parish staff to go their way without providing guidance and direction. If a pastor or bishop shifts responsibility for what is going on in his parish or diocese to others, the mistake is as grave as if he had tried to do everything himself. After all, he remains the shepherd, who will have to give an account to God for each of his sheep.

Besides the effects of the Second Vatican Council, the profound changes in the social position of American Catholics call us to rethink the tasks of the priestly ministry. In the nineteenth century and the first decades of the twentieth, the Catholic priest was the undisputed leader of a group of uprooted immigrants who lived on the margins of American society. German, Irish, Polish, and Italian Catholics faced the complex task of finding their place in a largely Protestant environment that fostered a deep-seated hostility toward all ethnic groups and toward Catholics in particular. Priests provided much-needed leadership in the Catholic ghetto. They built churches, schools, and hospitals; organized trade unions; and, to a large extent, managed to preserve the religious identity of their flock. Through the Catholic school system, they even promoted a slow but steady integration of immigrant Catholics into mainstream American life. Today, with some exceptions, much of the process of integration has been completed. According to a recent survey, the second-richest ethnic group in America is that of Irish Catholics. Little wonder that churches and parish halls serve less and less as rallying points for an insecure minority. Priests are no longer looked up to as fathers and protectors of uneducated immigrants.

As a result of this sociological change, a new challenge, barely perceived at this point, faces the Catholic priest today. More and more American Catholics are in desperate need of intellectual leadership that would help them preserve their Catholic faith in the midst of an increasingly secular culture. Just as a highly educated Protestant might disdain his fundamentalist origins, many educated Catholics do not find themselves at home in their neighborhood parish. Most priests cannot help them connect their faith with their education—God's revelation with the world of philosophy, science, literature, and the arts. To a large extent, we have forgotten that the Catholic Church, precisely because it is *catholic* and has as its mission to transform *all* men and *the whole life* of man, has inspired and shaped culture throughout her history. Who should prove convincingly to our laity that the Church is a promoter and inspirer of learning if not the Catholic priest? Some priests, then, should manifest through their lives that reason and faith, secular knowledge and theology, scholarship and Catholic identity are natural allies rather than irreconcilable enemies. Such priests would not be teachers and scholars *in addition* to their priesthood but priests who live and practice their priesthood *through* teaching and scholarly work. They would not punctuate a math class with religious exhortations or give first place in a literature competition to Christian authors. Instead, they would revere the truth wherever they found it. By fostering a knowledge of the truth, they would lead their students closer to God, the source of all truth. Only a commitment to all truths and to the truth *for truth's sake* is Catholic.

A sectarian approach is diametrically opposed to this vision of the priesthood. Whether non-Catholic or Catholic, the sectarian is interested in the truth only to the extent that it furthers his cause. Preoccupied with a narrow understanding of religion and morality, he is indifferent or even hostile to "merely" human values, such as science, literature, and the arts. If he is educated, his learning is a weapon to defeat the enemy, whether that means to him the Protestant, the atheist, modernity, or "the exploiting capitalist." This, then, is one of the greatest challenges the American Catholic priest faces today: to provide intellectual leadership in the formation of a Catholic intelligentsia that can understand and formulate its Catholic faith in such a way that it makes sense in today's world. He should inspire them to value, criticize, and deepen the intellectual life of the country.

We discuss extensively the need for intellectual leadership in the Church not because this is the only challenge facing the American Catholic clergy today but because it is the least recognized and most neglected challenge. Many other urgent tasks could be explored in a more detailed account, but we would like to mention a few here. More than half of all Americans do not belong to any Christian church. We need to devise ways to reach them and explain to them the Gospel of Jesus Christ. We should also educate rich and middle-class Catholics about their moral obligation to help the poor. Catholic lay men and women should cooperate with other Americans and find ways to eliminate poverty in our country and help economically developing countries raise themselves out of the quicksand of an ever-worsening poverty.

Paradoxically, the clergy will succeed at providing intellectual leadership and influencing the social consciousness of Americans only if it does not consider these its central tasks. The center of the Gospel is God's call to an eternal communion of life with him and one another by conforming ourselves to the life, death, and Resurrection of his Son. Transforming ourselves into Christ must extend to the whole of our lives and, in the process, reshape our culture and society. Our share in the love of Christ becomes real when we love not just by words but also by deeds. It can transform the world only to the extent that we allow the love of God to operate in it.

a. The Threefold Task of the Priestly Ministry

As explained above, the priestly ministry is essentially one, but we can speak of the priest's threefold roles as leader, prophet (or teacher), and sanctifier. This threefold mission participates in the royal, prophetic, and priestly mission of Christ himself and extends it through history.

I. MINISTRY OF GOVERNING THE CHURCH

This ministry should be understood only in its relationship to the tasks of preaching and sanctification. A Christian community should be so formed and governed that the most favorable conditions are assured for its sanctification by the Word and sacraments. Laws, duties, and rights in the community need to be spelled out in such a way that they serve the purpose of "building up the community in truth and holiness."[52] Neither the bishop in the diocese nor the priest in the parish should exercise his leadership in a dictatorial way by "domineering over" his flock.[53] He should apply the principle of subsidiarity so that he does not directly do things that someone else can do with more competence. His leadership will consist primarily in respecting, inspiring, supervising, and coordinating the various charisms for the good of the whole community.

In the Church the subject-superior relationship (such as parishioner-pastor, priest-bishop, or bishop-pope) is always embedded in and ordained to the more fundamental relationship of brotherly love and cooperation. This is expressed in many ways in the Council documents: the pope is head of the episcopal college but also brother to the other bishops; the bishop is father but also a friend and brother to his fellow priests; the pastor is father to his faithful but also brother to those who share the same Christian dignity and life. The distinction between subject and superior is temporary and valid only for the time of the Church's earthly pilgrimage; the communion of love, which this authority is called to build up, remains forever.[54]

2. MINISTRY OF TEACHING

Vatican II corrected many of the distortions of the offices of bishop and presbyter that had arisen throughout history,

---

[52] *LG*, no. 27.

[53] 1 Pet 5:3.

[54] Joseph Ratzinger, *The Open Circle: The Meaning of Christian Brotherhood*, trans. W. A. Glen-Doeple (New York: Sheed and Ward, 1966); *LG*, no. 27; Vatican Council II, Decree Concerning the Pastoral Office of Bishops in the Church *Christus Dominus* (October 28, 1965), nos. 16–20 (hereafter cited as *CD*); *PO*, no. 6.

including relegating the bishop's role to chiefly administrative functions and the presbyter's to merely liturgical and sacramental duties. Instead, Vatican II stressed that the primary duty and task of both bishop and presbyter (who also participates in the mission of the bishop) is to proclaim the Gospel. They should proclaim the entire integrity of the Gospel, not just those parts of it that are attractive to a contemporary audience.[55] While the valid administration of the sacraments requires only a minimum of personal involvement on the part of the priest,[56] preaching, in contrast, actualizes the Word of God through the faith of the minister who proclaims it. The Word of God becomes an actual living Word addressing the congregation here and now only through the minister's personal faith. First, the priest has to listen to the Word and be judged and changed by it; this experience will then enable him to translate and communicate the Word effectively so that it inspires a similar experience in the hearer: faith engenders faith.

But the priest has to preach even those truths of the Gospel that he has not yet personally experienced. His preaching must be coextensive with the faith of the Church, not merely with his own narrow personal experience. The purpose of preaching the Word is to engender or increase the faith of the hearers in order to prepare them to celebrate the Eucharistic mystery and to bear witness to the Gospel in both life and word. Thus, the teaching ministry of the priest serves to actualize and strengthen the universal priestly and prophetic function of the people of God.

---

[55] See *LG*, no. 25; *CD*, nos. 2, 7, 12–14; *PO*, no. 4.

[56] Of course, a priest should also enter personally into the sacramental act. He should live what he celebrates. The Church's prayers for the penitent, the sick, the bride and groom, and the newly baptized or confirmed, as well as the Eucharistic Prayer, should become the expression of his own personal prayer.

3. MINISTRY OF SANCTIFYING

Through the ministry of sanctification, to which preaching and pastoral government are also ordained, the service character of the ministerial priesthood becomes most evident. Sanctification serves to actualize the priesthood of all the people of God. By making the saving action of Christ present in the sacraments, in particular in the Eucharist, the minister enables the faithful to offer themselves to the Father in union with the incarnate Son. Thus, they are made one with each other, and they give themselves over to the Father in union with and through the Son. This is the very purpose of *thusia logike*, the perfect priestly worship of the New Testament. Saint Paul describes the purpose of his priestly ministry this way: "[God] has appointed me as a priest [*leitourgon*] of Jesus Christ, and I am to carry out my priestly duty by bringing the Good News from God to the pagans and so make them acceptable as an offering [*prosphora*], made holy by the Holy Spirit."[57]

The same goal for the priestly ministry is stressed by the Decree on the Ministry and Life of Priests of the Second Vatican Council: "As they fulfill within their own measure of responsibility the role of Christ the head and shepherd, priests gather the family of God in the name of the bishop into one fellowship inspired for one purpose, and lead them in the Spirit through Christ to God the Father."[58] So often today, one hears the question, Which is more important for the priest: the sacramental ministry or getting involved in "real life"? It now becomes clear that this question poses a false alternative. The authentic celebration of the sacraments leads one to live them in daily life; conversely, living

---
[57] Rom 15:16.
[58] *PO* 6.

the Gospel in daily life will awaken in us the need to deepen through the sacraments our union with Christ, without whom our efforts to serve in love remain an exercise in futility.

b. The Sacrament of Holy Orders

The essential sacramental sign, which goes back to the time of the apostles, consists of the prayer of the ordaining bishop and of his imposition of hands on the candidate.[59] The laying on of hands is the visible and historical sign that, through the chain of ordained and ordaining bishops, connects the ordinand to the apostles who were sent by Christ on earth. The prayer of the bishop calls down the Spirit of power and holiness from the risen Christ to enable the new priest to fulfill his mission. The twofold effect of holy orders is its sacramental character, which (1) conforms the ordinand irrevocably to Christ the priest, prophet, and king, and (2) enables him to represent Christ, the head of the Church. The effect of the sacrament's grace bestows Christ's help so that the priest may perform his mission worthily.

c. Sacramental Character of Holy Orders

Since today there is much controversy surrounding the nature of the priesthood and because of the far-reaching consequences of priestly spirituality, we should discuss the sacramental character of holy orders in greater detail. Some theologians are strongly opposed to what they call the "mystique and ontology of the priestly character." They claim that such "ontological enhancement" of the priest over the Christian layperson—that is, the belief that an ordained priest is elevated or distinct in his very being, rather than just in his role

---

[59] See 1 Tim 4:14; 2 Tim 1:6.

THE UNITY AND DIVERSITY OF VOCATIONS 255

—has created a theologically false justification of the higher social status of the clergy. These "progressive" theologians stress the functional nature of the sacrament's character, saying, for example, that it designates the recipient as a member of the college of office-bearers in the Church and that it does not necessarily demand a full-time and lifelong commitment to the ministry. They claim that this view is consistent with the best tradition of the Church and is compatible with the dogmatic definitions of the priestly character.

This view does not directly contradict the definitions of the councils of Florence and Trent,[60] whose definition of holy orders is that they confer "some spiritual and indelible mark" on the recipient that cannot be received repeatedly. It is also true that the Second Vatican Council declares that although the Church is made up of different functions, "there is true equality of all with regard to [their] dignity."[61] Likewise, it is true that although respect is indeed due to a representative of Christ, it is contrary to the spirit of the Gospel for bishops and priests to cling to social privileges: Christ came to serve, not to be served. The document on priestly life of the Second Vatican Council recommends that "to be fashioned more clearly to the image of Christ, and to be more available for their sacred ministry, [priests] are invited to embrace voluntary poverty."[62]

However, in response to theologians who reduce the meaning of the priestly character to merely the mark of an office-bearer in the Church, we should consider what logically follows from this minimalist position:

---

[60] Vatican Council II, Declaration on Religious Freedom *Dignitatis humanae* (December 7, 1965), nos. 1313, 1609.
[61] *LG*, no. 32.
[62] *PO*, no. 17.

- While exercising his ministry, the office-bearer in the Church acts not in his own name, and not even in the name of the ecclesial community alone, but in the person and name of Christ.

- This must be so since even an unholy minister can sanctify the recipient in a sacramental action. Christ sanctifies through him.[63]

- Carrying out the Father's work is daily food for Christ; to put it briefly, his mission is his very existence.[64] Acting in the person of Christ implies that the priest shares in Christ's mission. What exists in Christ in totality and in perfection exists in the ministerial priest through participation. By receiving the character of the sacrament, the priest's entire existence is expropriated—taken over by Christ in order to carry out his mission. This expropriation is a given reality (the character imprinted on his soul through ordination) but also a constant task and challenge. He is called to carry out his mission throughout his whole life.

Thus, it is clear that the priesthood is an ontological reality conferred upon the recipient by the character of the sacrament. No matter whether he is a teacher, worker, scientist, or physician, he is always the priest of Jesus Christ and he always carries out Christ's mission. Just as the very being of Christ the Son is determined by his being sent by the Father, *the priestly character determines the being of the priest*. This new reality is a new *relationship* to Christ and thereby a new relationship to the Christian community. Therefore,

[63] Yet, if the minister's personal life reflects Christ's love and goodness, then Christ acts through the minister more effectively, especially in the ministry of the Word (where the Word of Christ is not actualized without the personal faith of the minister).

[64] See Jn 4:34.

it cannot be expressed in terms of the priest being *more* fully a Christian than the layman. As Saint Augustine put it, "I am a Christian with you and I am a bishop for you."

d. Priestly Spirituality

Priestly spirituality should be based on the priestly reality that the priest is "set apart for the gospel of God"[65] so that he may act in accord with the charism that he received at ordination. "What we preach is not ourselves, but Jesus Christ as Lord, with ourselves as your servants for Jesus' sake."[66] The priest represents Christ for the Church and so serves Christ in the Church. He receives a permanent charism at ordination, but by his sins he may weaken or exclude the operation of grace in his life. This is why Paul asks Timothy to "rekindle the gift" that is in him through the laying on of Paul's hands.[67] This gift of the Holy Spirit makes the priest able to develop the virtues most important to fulfill the priestly ministry: *dynamis* (fortitude), *agape* (love), and *sophronismos* (self-control).

Fortitude derives from the almighty power of the Holy Spirit, who created the world; who shaped the new Adam, Christ, in the womb of the Virgin and raised him from the dead to new life; and who is the principle of the new creation operating in the Church and making all things new. The very power of God is at the priest's disposal, which will enable him to bear witness to the risen Christ and suffer for the sake of the Gospel. The power of God shows its full impact in and through the trials and weaknesses of his

[65] Rom 1:1.
[66] 2 Cor 4:5.
[67] 2 Tim 1:6.

ministers.⁶⁸ He prays in the name of the Church in union with Christ to the Father (in the Eucharist, sacrament of reconciliation, and Liturgy of the Hours), but he also acts in the person of Christ in pronouncing the words of consecration, absolution, and anointing of the sick. In the person of the priest, Christ's action and the Church's action meet and are joined together.

The priest should represent Christ by freely allowing himself to be expropriated by Christ. He is an unworthy slave of Christ.⁶⁹ *He is not Christ, but he represents Christ.* Following the example of John the Baptist, he should decrease so that Christ will increase in him. The priest who falsely identifies himself with Christ is a pitiful sight. He forces himself to play a role that compels him to become a hypocrite. He is like the proverbial horse who thinks all the honors are for him, not for the king who rides upon him. A priest's wise spiritual director once recommended, "Kneel down every day before your priesthood!" If he allows Christ to live and act in him, the priest can expand his heart and embrace with the very love of Christ (literally, "with the guts" of Christ⁷⁰) all his people and all the strangers who come to him for help. He is to become all to all so that he may save some of them.⁷¹

The priest should personally enter into the sacramental actions that he performs by making the prayers of the Church and Christ his own personal prayers. Just as Paul tells his faithful in all his letters that he constantly prays for them and thanks God for them, so, too, should the priest lift up his people to God in all his prayers. Also like Paul, the priest

---

⁶⁸ See 2 Cor 12:9–10.
⁶⁹ See Rom 1:1.
⁷⁰ Phil 1:7–8.
⁷¹ See 2 Cor 6:11–13; 7:2–4; 1 Cor 9:22–23.

should act as father and mother toward his people.[72] When necessary, he must be strong and uncompromising, using the authority (*exousia*) that he received from Christ.[73] His preaching and teaching will not be acts of Christian propaganda, but they will give birth to Christ and the formation of Christlike features in the souls of his people.[74] The priest will experience his inadequacy just as Paul did, but he should trust that the power of God will be perfected in weakness. He should strive to be effective but never dare to calculate how effective his ministry has been. Just as Paul did, he should accept giving away his life without tangible success.[75]

---

[72] See 1 Cor 4:15.
[73] See 2 Cor 12:19–21; 13:10.
[74] See Gal 4:19.
[75] See 2 Cor 12:7–10, 15.

10

Spiritual Growth through the Stages of Life

Beginning with the age of reason, the attainment of holiness is possible for every age group. While holiness means the perfection of the love of God and neighbor, love can be expressed in many different ways, and God offers his grace to everyone; little children are as capable of cooperating with it as are old people.

We will summarize here the most important challenges to obtaining true holiness for each age group. Understanding the challenges and opportunities presented by each of the stages of life is important for those who guide others through them, such as parents and spiritual guides. But it is also helpful for understanding our own spiritual growth and development through the seasons of life. Although we speak here of the chronological stages of life—childhood, adolescence, young adulthood, parenthood, and old age—we may find elements from every stage of development present in us spiritually at any time. For example, the child's struggle to learn unselfish love and the discipline to resist the desire for instant gratification is a challenge that recurs through life. Learning to handle freedom virtuously may be a special focus of the life of an adolescent or young adult, but it is also a lifelong task. And the perspective of old age, which can see more clearly the guidance of providence, can be cultivated even by a young person.

Children

Jesus the child gives us the image of the perfect citizen for the kingdom of God. The child is aware that he depends on others, and he trusts those who provide what he needs. For all his natural potential, the child's development is radically dependent on his parents. Although he cannot yet speak, the newborn baby already has an acute sense of his surroundings and of the sentiments of those who look after him, cuddle him, and feed him. If his mother and father love each other, the baby feels safe in the world. The first two years of a baby's life are decisive for the rest of his development. When true love penetrates his whole being, the child will be much more likely to believe that God is love. One adolescent said, "I experienced so much love in my family that it was easy for me to believe that Love exists." For children in loving families, believing in heaven is also easier. If God loves us, he wants us to live with him forever, and he does not allow us to be lost. These children do not experience death as a tragedy because they know the dead live with God. They are eager to know as much as possible about heaven.

The great challenge for little children, however, is to learn unselfish love. They think it is absolutely natural that they are the center of all attention, the sole object of the admiration of their parents and every visitor to the family. To share their toys and food with their siblings takes much persuasion, and relapses are frequent. Yet they can learn that causing joy for others brings them joy. They can be taught how to give joy to Jesus, who loves them so much. Francisco and Jacinta of Fátima, even when they were very young, were eager to offer their sufferings for the poor sinners and thus give joy to Jesus.

Children relate to the world in a very intense way. After

the first shock of being taken from the protective shelter of the womb, his lungs exposed to the harsh air and his eyes to the bright light, the baby develops a great interest and pleasure in his surroundings as long as he feels safe in the loving embrace of his parents. Toddlers feel a kinship with everything and want close contact with every object, so they put everything they can into their mouths. At the same time, however, babies are fallen human beings. Even if they have been reborn as children of God in baptism, at times their uncontrollable cravings, fears, rages, and despair wear out even the most patient parents. In a loving environment, however, they can learn to control their expectation of instant gratification.

A common mistake of parents is to fall for the notion that children should be trained and conditioned just like pets through a series of rewards and punishments to promote acceptable behavior and discourage infractions. This approach is easy to enforce and often quite successful at obtaining social conformity when children know that their actions are being watched, but it does not awaken moral sensitivity and personal growth. Rewards and punishments may serve as a supplementary reinforcement, but they should never become the only or the chief means of education. The baby, the toddler, and the child are persons, and as they grow, their innate sense of right and wrong should grow with them. Left alone, they remain in the state of wonder, experimentation, and confusion. A smart parent takes time to talk with the child and explain why certain ways of acting make sense and are good, and why their opposites are not. If after such talks the child still does what he knows to be wrong, he may need to be punished. But first, the parent must calm down so that the child senses that punishment is not the outburst of a bad mood but is for his own good. If the child sees and truly regrets the wrong he has done, punishment might not be necessary; the sorrow the child feels may be enough punishment. Punishment, if given, should serve only to reinforce the awareness that what the child has done was wrong. Once the child acknowledges and regrets his failing, the parent should forgive, sincerely and lovingly. The child should feel even more loved than before the infraction occurred. In this way, the parents imitate God and teach the child about God's attitude toward sin and the sinner. Children from such families will be well prepared, spiritually and emotionally, for their first confession.

A more pleasant task for parents is to nourish the child's interest in the world around him, educating and deepening his innate kinship with plants and animals. Children easily understand the song of the three young men in the furnace of Nebuchadnezzar,[1] and they know that the sun and moon, the stars of heaven, fire and water, seas and rivers, and all creatures praise the Lord, as mentioned in many psalms. They sense that God is hiding behind every leaf and flower. Everything they see and hear and smell speaks to them about a loving Father. The parents' task is to nurture this natural vision and turn their home into a small preview of paradise, where life is suffused with the light of the Creator and the love of God is reflected from the parents' faces. Children raised in such homes can indeed become saints by loving God and men, as well as all of God's creation, and they know how to enchant the Father's heart by their heartfelt sorrow.

Adolescence

In a happy environment, children reach a short period of equilibrium and harmony around the age of nine to eleven.

---

[1] See Dan 3.

They feel comfortable because they know their place in the family and school and they have developed some enjoyable friendships. They like to take on responsible chores that make them feel important, as well as tasks that earn them trust and praise. Under competent parents and teachers, they learn discipline and, even if prone to mischief, feel secure when law and order rule their world.

As children enter their teenage years and go through puberty, sexual feelings and powerful urges replace the playful daydreaming. Teenage boys especially feel intense pleasure accompanied by vague feelings of guilt if they manipulate their arousal. Sooner or later (mostly sooner), they will discover pornography. First, they watch pornographic videos out of curiosity, but soon some of them become addicted. For some teenagers, usually boys, this may become a daily event. The result is a weakening ambition, diminished zest for life, boredom in school, and estrangement from parents. In a loving, happy home, teenagers are less prone to such a hidden life of addiction. When teenagers trust their parents, find a good confessor, and develop healthy friendships, they can come out of the storm chastened, humbled, and stronger. The Church has several teenage saints who have shown us how best to meet the challenge of adolescence. They loved life and directed their burgeoning surplus energies to athletics, friendship, hiking, study, and prayer. They struggled with bouts of discouragement and depression like everybody else, but their growing friendship with Christ helped them gain mastery of themselves and increased their zest for life.[2]

---

[2] For example, Pier Giorgio Frassati, Carlo Acutis, Laura Vicuña, and Chiara Badano.

Young Men and Women

Beginning in their late teens, two major concerns preoccupy young minds. First, to what profession(s) are they attracted or, at least, in what direction do they want to go? To what colleges should they apply? Second, how can they develop satisfying personal relationships? The competitive and complex world can easily overwhelm some of them, so much so that they neglect friendships and focus only on relationships of mutual advantage or sexual satisfaction. Women, in general, focus sooner and more consciously on personal relationships because they realize they have a shorter span of time to find the right marriage partner.

There are, of course, many young people of both sexes for whom four or five years of college life is nothing more than carefree fun and experimentation with various majors. These young adults tend to find ways to postpone any serious decision. God, however, does not stop working with them. Some come to their senses only after serious blunders or falls, while others remain more or less tuned in to his invitations, take time for daily personal prayer, share as much as they can in the daily Eucharist, choose a reliable spiritual director, and try to discover God's plan for their lives. As we have seen, God has a life plan for every person. He asks him either to fully and directly give a gift of himself in the priesthood or consecrated life or to contribute to the good of society in some way through his work—most often serving God by giving himself to a spouse and raising children. Nobody is superfluous because everyone is assigned a part within God's plan. Whoever fulfills the task meant for him will have a peace that the world cannot give.

Besides finding a meaningful job, the other great challenge for young people who are not called to celibacy is to find not only good friends in general but also their future spouse—the woman or man with whom they want to spend the rest of their lives. True lovers discover in their spouse a special beauty and goodness that is so attractive that they want to devote their lives to that person. Their goal is to make their spouse happy. If they marry because they think this person is best suited to make *them* happy, the marriage is flawed from the beginning. In a good marriage, promoting the happiness of the one makes the other happy. Yet every marriage has a time of awakening, a moment of discovery that their love is flawed and selfish and far from satisfying. But if they realize that they received a sacrament at their wedding—in other words, that Christ himself pledged his presence to help them—they will not despair. Turning sincerely to Christ, they will receive a share in the very love of Christ, a love that envelops both of them, melting their hearts to forgive each and every day. Their human love will be transformed and will reach a new level of strength and purity.

Parenthood

We have discussed the sacrament of marriage and its relationship to raising children in the chapter on vocations. Here we add some considerations of the development of spirituality through family life.

The selfless love between the spouses must also be extended to the children. In many families, a hidden danger lurks, and its effects surface later in the life of the children. It is a poison that slowly but surely sours family relationships. Parents have a natural desire to see their children excel in as many areas as possible. They are proud of their achievements and like to brag about them. The problem, however, arises when some of the children are less talented academically or athletically than others, or when one is seriously disabled. If the children notice that the parents love their high-IQ children more, then every child in the family will feel that their parents' love is insincere. They will recognize that the parents love the credit the child is to them, not the child himself. The favorite child feels as cheated as the rest, since all feel unloved. The authenticity of parents' love is most evident in their relationship with a disabled child. If they love and cherish him, this shows that they truly love their children for their own sakes. Such a child becomes God's special blessing to educate a whole family concerning true love.

The selflessness of the parents' love for each other and for their children also manifests itself in the way they guide their children's lives. As children grow up, they begin to wonder about the direction their lives should take. They ponder what kind of jobs would fit their talents and spark their interest. This presents another delicate task for parents. Their input is obviously important, but pressuring or forcing children to choose a certain college or a job that the parents prefer may seriously damage their future. Wise parents realize that they do not own their offspring but should rather let them freely choose the direction of their lives. An understanding of their children's freedom is also essential regarding the grown children's choice of a spouse. The parents may see certain incompatibilities more clearly than the couple, in their enchanted state, does. But in the end, parents do not have the right to decide who their children will marry. The support of both sets of parents strengthens the marriage and reassures the couple.

A Christian family, especially if they are blessed with the financial means, will dedicate themselves in some way to serving the poor, asking themselves, "With what we have been given, how much should we give back to society by helping the poor, the homeless, or the deprived children in a poor school?" The words of Jesus at the last judgment are well known to every churchgoer: "I was hungry and you gave me food, . . . I was a stranger and you welcomed me."[3] Many contribute to charitable organizations, but few take seriously the words of Saint Ambrose, whom Pope Saint Paul VI quotes in his encyclical *Populorum Progressio*:

> He who has the goods of this world and sees his brother in need and closes his heart to him, how does the love of God abide in him? Everyone knows that the Fathers of the Church laid down the duty of the rich toward the poor in no uncertain terms. As St. Ambrose put it: "You are not making a gift of what is yours to the poor man, but you are giving him back what is his. You have been appropriating things that are meant to be for the common use of everyone. The earth belongs to everyone, not to the rich." These words indicate that the right to private property is not absolute and unconditional. No one may appropriate surplus goods solely for his own private use when others lack the bare necessities of life.[4]

This statement does not mean that we should give away all our surplus wealth in charitable donations. In most cases, there may be a need for direct charitable donations, but that is only one way to help. We should use our surplus wealth for the common good: providing work opportunities, building homes for the homeless, improving the standards of schools in poor areas, establishing nonprofit foundations for a variety of needs, becoming personally involved in the life of

[3] Mt 25:35.
[4] Pope Paul VI, encyclical letter *Populorum progressio* (March 26, 1967), no. 23.

abandoned children, and so on. Society would drastically change if Christian families took their social obligations seriously. "Give until it hurts," said Saint Teresa of Calcutta.

Old Age

We need not dread the coming of old age. Looking back on the past events of our lives, we discover more clearly the providential care of God. His mercy brought some good even out of our sins and deficiencies. In retrospect, his harsh treatment appears as a needed lesson, carefully adjusted to our character at every turn. When looking at our lives with the eyes of faith, our failures and successes, frustrated and fulfilled dreams, are seen from a new perspective. What seemed important now appears trivial; what we barely endured is now a source of peace and gratitude. At the end, we must admit that we have received much more than we ever deserved or expected. "All is grace," said the dying country priest in Bernanos' novel,[5] and it is true for every person who dies at peace with God.

As old people watch the younger generation, the urge to speak up may become irresistible: "Let me tell you how to do it right!" At the beginning, our grandchildren, the new teacher, the young doctor, the new boss—anyone who is just beginning a life we have already lived—listens politely and seems to take us seriously. But should we continue in this vein, the reaction might become less polite each time. Our very presence becomes an irritation. Happy are those old men and women who admit that the new generation might do certain things better than they themselves did! Happy

---

[5] Georges Bernanos, *The Diary of a Country Priest*, trans. Pamela Morris (Cambridge, Mass.: Da Capo Press, 1937).

are those old folks who rejoice in the achievements of the young as if they were their own! Where such things happen in a family or a workplace, old people will be a welcome presence, and, at times, their counsel may even be sought and heeded. To avoid negative results, old people should accept what some psychologists call "dethronement." On the graciousness of this acceptance depends their happiness and, to a great extent, their holiness.

People, however, give up one value only for another that is even more valuable. In fact, old age invites us to rediscover the forgotten joys of childhood—not the selfish greed of an inconsolable baby but the wonder and joy of the child as he looks at the world for the first time. As young or middle-aged professionals, we probably didn't even notice the trees and flowers in our neighborhood as we hurried by because we were always catching up with missed deadlines and appointments. We could not see anything beyond our own agenda. However, as older people, we can stop and smell the roses—and enjoy the lilies and petunias in the courtyard—as if we were seeing them for the first time. The hummingbird, zooming from flower to flower, becomes an extraordinary delight. In a loving family the child trusts in the goodness of things and people. The baby knows that he depends on others, but he trusts that he will be cared for. The challenge for old people is to entrust themselves —beyond good or bad caregivers—to the Father, without whose knowledge not a single hair drops from their heads.

The deepest joy in old age, however, comes from the realization that only one value is always worth pursuing because it is eternal, and that is love. Authority, wealth, and fame do not transfer to eternity. On the other hand, we can grow in true love until the last moment of our conscious lives because love is the only currency acceptable in heaven.

Our joy in eternity will be proportionate to the quality of our love at the end of our lives. If we know this, the darkness of our end will be transparent to the light. T. S. Eliot says it beautifully:

> Old men ought to be explorers
> Here and there does not matter
> We must be still and still moving
> Into another intensity
> For a further union, a deeper communion
> Through the dark cold and the empty desolation,
> The wave cry, the wind cry, the vast waters
> Of the petrel and the porpoise. In my end is my beginning.[6]

---

[6] T. S. Eliot, *Four Quartets*, "East Coker," pt. 5, in *The Complete Poems and Plays:*
1909–1950 (San Diego: Harcourt Brace, 1962), 129.

Conclusion

At the end of our journey, it will be helpful to provide a short review of what we intended to achieve and to draw some conclusions. Our fundamental conviction, which defined the structure and the content of this short work, can be summarized in these words of Jesus: "The words that I have spoken to you are Spirit and life."[1] The entire revelation of Christ aims at transforming and assuming mankind, and through it the entire cosmos, into God's Trinitarian life. Redeemed by the incarnate Son and united to him by the Holy Spirit, we become children of the Father. So closely united are we to Christ that we can be called his Mystical Body, not by the fusion of the divine and human natures, but as bride and groom united in love: the one bride, the Church (consisting of many brides), in the unity of the Spirit with the one bridegroom, Christ.

Everything we discussed—ongoing conversion and sanctification, the supernatural virtues, the many forms of vocation, the power and nourishment for this new life coming from the sacrifice of Christ present in the Eucharist and active also in the other sacraments of the Church—forms a process, the fruits of which begin to appear already in this life. "Spirit and life," or rather the new life in the Spirit, shines forth in those for whom the prayer of Jesus at the

---

[1] Jn 6:63.

Last Supper has already been fulfilled: "that the love with which you have loved me may be in them, and I in them."[2]

In this divine love, we already possess the eternal life of God and, at times, a foretaste of God's joy (though we can still lose it by mortal sin). As the Cistercian abbot Blessed Aelred of Igny and Saint Thomas Aquinas explain, in heaven we will love one another as ourselves, and therefore we will share in the experience and joy of all those we love as much as we rejoice in our own happiness. To the extent, then, that our love is perfected, already on earth we share in the experience and joy of all we love.

Jesus promised that those who win the battle against Satan will sit on his throne and that all in heaven will share in his kingship.[3] Those who fight on the side of the Lamb share in his kingly rule already on earth. To the extent that they share the Cross of Christ, they inspire justice, love, and forgiveness around them, and their professional work contributes to the improvement of society. If they sincerely believe the words of Paul—"in everything God works for good with those who love him"[4]—their inner peace cannot be destroyed and they can profit from defeat, hardship, and disaster. They look at the world with new eyes and see a new world emerging, as Father Zosima's brother, who was dying of tuberculosis, did: "Life is paradise, and we are all in paradise, but we do not want to know it, and if we did want to know it, tomorrow there would be paradise the world over."[5]

---

[2] Jn 17:26.
[3] See, for example, Rev 2:25–28; 3:21; 5:9–10.
[4] Rom 8:28.
[5] Fyodor Dostoevsky, *The Brothers Karamazov*, trans. Richard Pevear and Larissa Volokhonsky (New York: Farrar, Straus and Giroux, 2002), 288.